W9-AMZ-563

PRENTICE-HALL, INC., Englewood Cliffs, N.J.

INTERNATIONAL
MONETARY
ECONOMICS

H. ROBERT HELLER

Department of Economics
University of Hawaii
Honolulu, Hawaii

PRENTICE-HALL INTERNATIONAL SERIES IN MANAGEMENT

8217

Library of Congress Cataloging in Publication Data

HELLER, HEINZ ROBERT.
 International monetary economics.

 Includes bibliographies.
 1. International finance. 2. Balance of payments.
3. International economic relations. I. Title.
HG3881.H42 1974 332.4'5 73–8762
ISBN 0–13–473140–9

To LI and MI

© 1974 by PRENTICE-HALL, INC.,
Englewood Cliffs, New Jersey

All rights reserved.
No part of this book may be reproduced
in any form or by any means without
permission in writing from the publisher.

10 9 8 7 6 5 4 3 2 1

Printed in the United States of America

PRENTICE-HALL INTERNATIONAL, INC., *London*
PRENTICE-HALL OF AUSTRALIA, PTY. LTD., *Sydney*
PRENTICE-HALL OF CANADA, LTD., *Toronto*
PRENTICE-HALL OF INDIA PRIVATE LTD., *New Delhi*
PRENTICE-HALL OF JAPAN, INC., *Tokyo*

Contents

List of Symbols Used

A	Absorption
B	Balance of trade *or* balance of payments
C	Consumption
D	Demand
EX	Exports
G	Governmental Expenditures
H	Hoarding
I	Investment
IM	Imports
i	Interest Rate
L.F.	Loanable Funds
M	Money
P	Price
Q	Quantity
r	Exchange Rate (units of foreign currency/unit of domestic currency)
S	Supply *or* Saving
T	Taxes
TOT	Terms of Trade
UK	United Kingdom
US	United States
V	Value
Y	National Income *or* Product
ϵ	Elasticity *or* supply elasticity of currency
η	Demand elasticity of currency
δ	Demand elasticity of commodity
σ	Supply elasticity of commodity
σ^2	Variance
o	Autonomous

Preface

The field of international monetary economics means many different things to different people. In contrast to the pure theory of international trade where economists have succeeded in developing a coherent and unified body of basic theory, we find disarray and controversy among economists in the monetary area. Consequently, a large number of specialized monographs dealing with specific aspects or approaches to international monetary economics and an even larger number of conference volumes and symposia trying to represent the various viewpoints have been published. Only an *Encyclopedia of International Monetary Economics* would be able to satisfy every single adherent to a particular point of view.

In this volume we have attempted to (1) show the main problem which has to be solved by any international monetary system: the adjustment to disturbances in the international sector of the economy, (2) to present and analyze the way in which alternative systems bring about the desired adjustment, and (3) to compare the costs and benefits associated with each system and to show the rudiments of an optimal international monetary system. Throughout the volume a concerted effort has been made to present relevant data and empirical findings and to relate them to the theoretical models developed.

Many students and colleagues have caused me to rewrite one or the other portion of this book. Professors William Allen (UCLA) and Richard Sweeney (Texas A & M) and Mrs. Birgitta Swedenborg (Industriens Utrednings Institut, Stockholm) suffered through the frustrations of reading a half-finished manuscript. Mr. Won-Key Kwon (University of Hawaii) suggested several improvements. Ms. Emily Mitchell helped with the collection of the data. I am grateful to all of them.

H.R.H.

Honolulu, Hawaii

CHAPTER 1

The Gains from International Transactions

People engage in production and exchange because they expect to reap certain benefits in the form of satisfaction or utility from the goods and services that they are able to consume as a result of their production and trade activities. In this first chapter we will attempt to show in simple terms the benefits to be derived from these activities. In particular we will show how specialization in production and international exchange of goods and services will increase the welfare of the residents of the trading countries. Furthermore we will investigate the effects of international capital movements on economic welfare.

This first chapter will provide the background for the international monetary problems that will be discussed in the subsequent chapters. But in order to analyze international *monetary* relationships effectively, it will be necessary to start with an examination of the underlying *real* variables.

It is clear that we will not be able to give a complete exposition of the theory of international trade in just one chapter, and the reader is referred to many books that are available on the subject.[1]

PARTIAL AND GENERAL EQUILIBRIUM

Economic problems may be analyzed in a partial-equilibrium or a general-equilibrium framework. The fundamental difference between the two

---

[1] For example, H. R. Heller, *International Trade: Theory and Empirical Evidence*, 2nd ed. (Englewood Cliffs, N.J.: Prentice-Hall, Inc., 1973); or M. C. Kemp, *The Pure Theory of International Trade and Investment* (Englewood Cliffs, N.J.: Prentice-Hall, Inc., 1969).

approaches lies in the assumptions that are made about the interrelation-
ships between the variables studied and the rest of the economy. If we analyze
just a few variables in isolation and assume that all other variables remain
constant or have no significant effect on the problem at hand, we are using a
partial equilibrium approach. This approach may be compared to the
laboratory experiments of the natural scientist, who attempts to investigate
the relationship between a limited number of variables while holding all
others constant. Typically, it is not possible for the economist to duplicate
the laboratory approach of the natural scientist, but this should not deter us
from using the same partial equilibrium approach in situations where
feedback effects are either absent or of such small magnitude that they can
be neglected without invalidating the results. If these assumptions are not
fulfilled, a *general* equilibrium approach is called for. In general-equilibrium
analysis all variables are included, and their interactions are studied. As a
consequence, general-equilibrium models tend to be more complex than
partial-equilibrium models. In this chapter we will look at international
trade from a general-equilibrium viewpoint, leaving the partial-equilibrium
approach for Chapter 2.

INTERPERSONAL TRADE

In free market economies most economic decisions are made by private
economic units. Such units may produce the commodities they wish to consume themselves. Or, they may in their role as producers sell the commodities
that they produce and purchase their consumption commodities from other
units. In a free market system individual economic units are at liberty to
engage in any kind of market transactions that they find advantageous.

Specialization and exchange are at the heart of this free market mechanism. Individual economic units will find it advantageous to *specialize* in
production because they are in possession of unique resources that are
required for a certain production process, because they have superior
technical knowledge, possess managerial talent or labor skills that are better
suited for a certain production process, hope to reap certain benefits of large-
scale production, or a multitude of other reasons. Specialization increases
economic efficiency and provides an additional potential for profits. The
natural complement to specialization is found in the *exchange* of the commodities produced by specialized units. By engaging in exchange, preferred
commodity bundles may be obtained. The individual economic units will
attempt to modify their commodity bundles in such a way as to attain the
highest possible level of satisfaction.

Often, no conscious decision on behalf of the individual unit is involved
as far as the choice between domestic and international trade is concerned.

A person does not base his decision concerning which automobile to buy on the fact that the car is produced in Detroit, Michigan or Stuttgart, Germany. What he cares about is quality, performance, looks, and price of the automobile. If the foreign producer offers a more attractive package in terms of all variables entering into the decision, the consumer will buy the foreign product. Similarly, other things being equal, an automobile manufacturer will be willing to sell his products to domestic and foreign buyers.

For our purposes it is important that individual economic units make these consumption and production decisions, and that governments do not control or interfere with free international trade. That is not to say that the governments of these countries may not engage in international trade for their own purposes. But this situation should be contrasted to centrally planned economies, where all international trading is done by the state or state-controlled agencies.

The simple fact that individual economic units are responsible for all consumption, production, and exchange decisions explains the frequent observation that a certain commodity is both exported and imported by the same country. Although it is often convenient to treat all economic units located within a given country collectively and to talk about the country as engaging in production, consumption, and exchange, we should never forget that this is really only a shorthand expression for the cumulative effects of all the individual international exchange decisions taken. In that sense, then, we are able to talk about the aggregate production possibility curve for an entire country, indifference curves for the community as a whole, and about a country's trade patterns.[2]

INTERNATIONAL TRADE

The production possibility curve for a country is shown in Figure 1-1, where we measure quantities of commodity Y along the vertical axis and commodity X along the horizontal axis. The production possibility curve $EABF$ delineates the various commodity combinations that can be produced, given the country's resources and production functions. In the same diagram we show a set of community indifference curves—I_1, I_2, and I_3.

If a country does not engage in international trade, the choice set of the residents is limited $OEABF$. The community will produce that combination of commodities which will allow it to attain the highest possible level of welfare. By producing and consuming commodity combination A, the community attains the highest level of welfare possible under autarky. At that point

---

[2]We will not treat in detail the aggregation problems in this book. The interested reader is referred to Heller, *International Trade*, Chaps. 2, 3, and 5.

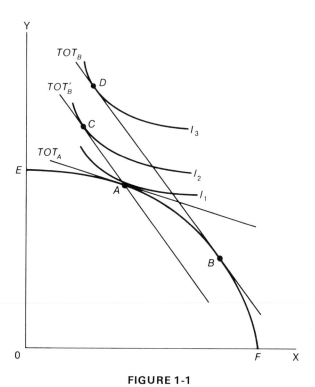

FIGURE 1-1

The Gains from Trade

the indifference curve I_1 is tangent to the production possibility curve, and the slope of the tangent TOT_A indicates the domestic exchange ratio between the two commodities Y and X. This price ratio, P_X/P_Y, is also referred to as the *terms of trade* (TOT). The slope of the production possibility curve shows the marginal rate of transformation (MRT), and indicates the rate at which units of Y may be transformed into units of X. Similarly the slope of the indifference curve denotes the marginal rate of substitution (MRS) in consumption between the two commodities. At point A the optimal production and consumption pattern is reached. We may summarize:

$$TOT_A = \Delta Y/\Delta X = P_X/P_Y = MRT = MRS \qquad (1.1)$$

Now let us assume that the country has the opportunity to engage in exchange with other countries at a given exchange ratio TOT_B. The country's residents will have to determine their new optimal production and consumption patterns. The amount of trade in which the country will engage is determined as the residual that makes the desired production and consumption patterns compatible. Production will be optimized at the point at which the country's production possibility curve is tangent to the terms-of-trade line TOT_B. In our example this occurs at point B. Here the highest possible terms-of-trade line with the slope TOT_B is reached. At point B we have:

$$TOT_B = \Delta Y/\Delta X = P_X/P_Y = MRT \qquad (1.2)$$

In an analogous way the consumption decision is made. We are able to attain the terms-of-trade line TOT_B by producing at point B on the production possibility curve. The commodity bundle B may then be modified by engaging in exchange. It is possible to attain any commodity combination along TOT_B. The optimal commodity combination is the one that allows the country to reach the highest possible indifference curve and therewith the highest possible level of welfare. In Figure 1-1 the optimal consumption point is labeled D, where the indifference curve I_3 is tangent to the terms-of-trade line TOT_B. At point D we have:

$$TOT_B = \Delta Y/\Delta X = P_X/P_Y = MRS \qquad (1.3)$$

Together equations 1.2 and 1.3 give us the optimality conditions for the country's production and consumption decisions if the country engages in international trade. By producing at B and consuming at D, the country attains the highest possible indifference curve and thereby optimizes its welfare, given its resources, technological knowledge, and exchange possibilities. All relevent marginal conditions are fulfilled:

$$MRT = \Delta Y/\Delta X = P_X/P_Y = MRS \qquad (1.4)$$

The total gains from specialization and exchange are shown by the movement from indifference curve I_1 to indifference curve I_3. We are able to subdivide the total gains into the gains from exchange and the gains from specialization. First let us look at the *gains from exchange*. Production and consumption takes place initially at point A. Now let us assume that the country is able to engage in exchange at the terms of trade TOT_B, while holding its production pattern fixed at A. The terms-of-trade line TOT'_B goes through point A, and the country can attain any commodity combination located on TOT'_B. The highest indifference curve that can be reached subject to the restriction that the terms-of-trade line pass through point A is indifference curve I_2. Point C describes our constrained consumption optimum. Hence the welfare gains realized by moving from I_1 to I_2 may be identified as the gains from exchange.

If we drop the assumption that the production pattern is fixed by point A, we may reap further *gains from specialization*. We notice that at the terms of trade TOT'_B, production at A is nonoptimal. The terms of trade TOT'_B are

not equal to the slope of the production possibility curve and therewith the
MRT. The marginal conditions are not fulfilled. By changing the production
pattern to B, we are able to restore the optimality conditions. At B we are
able to reach the terms-of-trade line TOT_B, which lies parallel to and above
TOT'_B. By producing at point B and moving along TOT_B to consumption
point D, we are able to reach indifference curve I_3. The movement from
indifference curve I_2 to I_3 denotes the gains from specialization. The total
gains from trade realized (I_1 to I_3) may therefore be subdivided into the gains
from exchange (I_1 to I_2) and the gains from specialization (I_2 to I_3).

The Gains from Trade and Country Size

International trade theory shows that the gains from trade to be reaped by
a relatively small country are larger than the gains that accrue to a relatively
large country.[3] The basic reason is that large countries already have the
opportunity to specialize within the country. Individual producers in a large
country are able to exploit most of the economies of scale that might exist,
locate in the region most advantageous for the production of a certain
commodity, and find the specialized resources and human skills most suitable
for the particular production process. Hence, in a large country with diversified regions it will be possible to reap most of the gains from specialization
within the country itself. The large size will also provide sufficiently large
markets to realize most of the gains from exchange.

Contrast this to the situation in a relatively small country. Because the
country is small, chances are that it does not have many diversified resources
at its disposal, that the opportunities for domestic exchange are restricted
by the limited size of the market, and that therefore the gains from purely
domestic specialization and exchange will be modest.

For a small country, international trade opens up the possibility of
specializing in the production of those commodities in which it enjoys a
comparative advantage and to exchange these goods in international markets.
The more world market prices differ from domestic prices, the greater the
benefits that the small country may reap. By way of contrast, the large
country may find that due to its own dominant role world market prices
differ only slightly or not at all from the domestic prices that prevail in the
absence of international trade.

The case can be easily illustrated with the help of Figure 1-2. In the
left part of the diagram we show the production possibility curve of a "large"
country, and in the right part the one of a small country. Both countries are
characterized by constant opportunity costs of production. Under autarky
the large country produces and consumes at point A, where one of its indif-

---

[3] See Heller, *International Trade*, Chap. 3.

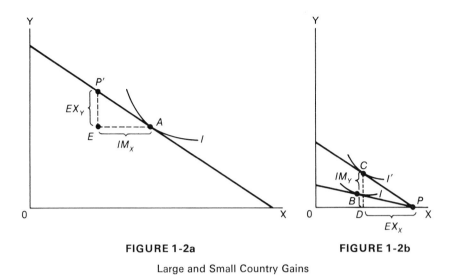

FIGURE 1-2a   **FIGURE 1-2b**

Large and Small Country Gains

ference curves, I, is tangent to the production possibility curve. The same is true for the small country at B.

Let us assume that after trade opens up the new international price ratio TOT coincides with the domestic price ratio prevailing in the large country. The small country is now faced with the possibility of exchanging the commodity bundle produced at the terms of trade TOT. It will find it advantageous to specialize completely in the production of commodity X and to produce at point P. Trading along the terms-of-trade line TOT, she will then be able to attain commodity bundle C and thereby reach indifference curve I'.

The large country in the left diagram is not able to reach any consumption bundle superior to A. But it will modify its production pattern to P' to conform with the small country's desire to engage in trade with the large country. The large country will export EP' of commodity Y to the small country (shown as DC of imports in the right diagram) and will import AE of commodity X from the small country, which shows exports equal to DP.

The crucial point is that the large country shows no gains from international trade—the small country reaps all the benefits. Of course, the case illustrated is a borderline case in that it relies upon (1) conditions of constant costs and (2) demand patterns that result in a change in the terms of trade for the small country only. Under conditions of increasing opportunity cost and different demand patterns, it is likely that the international terms of trade will find a new equilibrium somewhere between the domestic pretrade price ratios prevailing in the two countries. In that case, both countries share in the benefits from trade, with the proportion of the benefits accruing to each country depending on how much the international terms of trade change from the pretrade price ratios. Chances are that these price changes are more pronounced in the small country and that therefore most of the gains accrue to its residents.

The Size of the Gains from Trade

Estimates of the benefits to be realized by engaging in international trade rather than following a policy of autarky are virtually nonexistent in the literature. If we attempt to at least suggest the probable magnitude of the benefits involved, it should be borne in mind that not only the theoretical models underlying these estimates are highly simplified but also that the measures used are rather crude and may be more in the nature of "guesstimates" than of serious estimates. Nevertheless, something may be gained by having a rough idea whether the benefits of international transactions are to be measured in fractions of 1 percent of national income or represent a substantial increase in GNP over that attainable under autarky.

Two main parameters influence the size of the gains from trade that a country may realize: the size of the foreign trade sector and the ease with which foreign and domestic commodities can be substituted for each other. The first proposition may be stated simply: the larger the relative size of the foreign trade sector, the larger the relative gains to be realized by engaging in international trade. The common sense reason is simple: the more trade a country finds beneficial to engage in, the larger the benefits. In Figure 1-3a we assume that the country is characterized by the production possibility

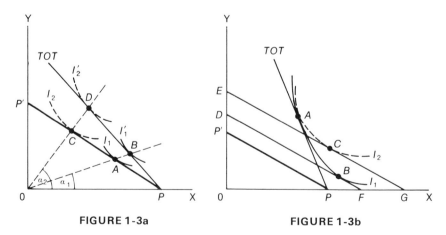

FIGURE 1-3a   FIGURE 1-3b

Effect of Trade Volume and Elasticity of Substitution on Gains from Trade curve PP'. After international trade starts the country is able to trade at the terms of trade TOT. The country will specialize in production of X. We now compare two different demand patterns: (1) A set of indifference curves I_1 (solid lines) that results in a relatively small trade volume and a modest gain from trade as indicated by the movement from I_1 to I'_1. (2) If the demand patterns are such that the country engages in a larger volume of trade, as depicted by the indifference curve set I_2, the gain from trade will be represented by the movement from I_2 to I'_2. If we can make direct utility comparisons between the movement from I_1 to I'_1 and I_2 to I'_2, we may conclude that the larger the relative trade volume, the larger the gains from trade.

The second important parameter that influences the gains is the elasticity of substitution between foreign and domestic goods. Again the common sense argument is obvious: if it is possible to substitute domestic commodities for foreign ones with great ease, the gains to be derived from being able to obtain the foreign goods will be modest. On the other hand, if it is not easy to substitute domestic for foreign goods, then the gains from trade will be larger. The *elasticity of substitution* is defined as the percentage change in relative quantities (foreign versus domestic) bought divided by the percentage change in relative prices:

$$\epsilon = \frac{\Delta(Q_f/Q_d)/(Q_f/Q_d)}{\Delta(P_f/P_d)/(P_f/P_d)} \tag{1.5}$$

Figure 3-1b illustrates the relationship between the elasticity of substitution and the gains from trade. Let us assume that the country is completely specialized in X, producing at point P. At the terms of trade TOT it reaches point A. Two alternative indifference curves, one with a high elasticity of substitution (solid line I_1) and one with a low elasticity of substitution, (dashed line I_2) are shown. Evaluated at the pretrade prices, the possibility of engaging in exchange results in a welfare gain equal to $P'D$ in the high elasticity of substitution case, while in the low elasticity of substitution case the welfare gain is equal to $P'E$. We conclude that lower elasticities of substitution are associated with higher welfare gains.

Professor Johnson has developed a formula that utilizes the size of the foreign trade sector and the elasticity of substitution to derive upper limits to the gains from trade to be expected.[4] This formula may be used to compute the approximate magnitude of the gains from trade for various countries.

In a pioneering study Professor Tinbergen[5] calculated elasticities of substitution between foreign and domestic commodities for a variety of

[4]Harry G. Johnson, "The Costs of Protection and Self-Sufficiency," *Quarterly Journal of Economics*, Vol. 79 (August 1965), Table VI, p. 370.

[5]Jan Tinbergen, "Some Measurements of Elasticities of Substitution," *Review of Economics and Statistics*, 1946, p. 109–116.

countries for the interwar period. His estimates fall in the range between 0.5 and 2.1, with the larger countries, like the United States, being at the top of the scale. This is to be expected, as a large economy like the United States may have close substitutes to foreign produced commodities available domestically.

Because recent estimates of the elasticity of substitution are not available for a variety of countries, we show in Table 1-1 a range of possible

TABLE 1-1

GAINS FROM MERCHANDISE TRADE

	(1)	(2)	(3)	(4)
	Assumed Elasticities of Substitution Between Foreign and Domestic Goods	*Welfare Gain as Percentage of GNP (Upper Limit)*	*1970 GNP (bill. of $)*	*Approximate Absolute Gain 1970 (Bill. of $)*
United States	.5	.33		3.2
	1.0	.25	974.1	2.4
apm ≈ .05	2.0	.17		1.7
United Kingdom	.5	5.18		6.3
	1.0	4.03	121.0	4.9
apm ≈ .20	2.0	2.77		3.4
Switzerland	.5	11.28		2.3
	1.0	9.19	20.4	1.9
apm ≈ .30	2.0	6.61		1.4
Netherlands	.5	19.26		6.1
	1.0	16.81	31.5	5.3
apm ≈ .40	2.0	13.07		4.1

Source: Columns (1) and (2), adapted from H. G. Johnson, "The Costs of Protection and Self-Sufficiency," *Quarterly Journal of Economics*, Vol. 79 (August 1965), Table VI, p. 370. Col (3), International Monetary Fund, *International Financial Statistics*, January 1972. Col. (4) = [(3) × (2)/100]. The average propensities to import (apm) were rounded off to the nearest convenient figure.

elasticities of substitution, from 0.5 to 2.0, for each country. But we should remember that large economies, like the United States, are likely to be characterized by a high elasticity of substitution, while small economies, like the Netherlands, are apt to be at the bottom end of the range given. The estimates for the United States range between one sixth and one third of 1 percent of GNP and between $1.7 and $3.2 billion (1970 data) in absolute terms. For the much smaller Netherlands, the gains are estimated to be between 13 and 19 percent of GNP, or $4.1 and $6.1 billion. This in spite of the fact that the trade volume of the United States of approximately $40 billion exceeds the entire GNP of the Netherlands, which amounted to $31.5 billion in 1970. Even when allowing for considerable margins of error we come to the conclusion that the gains from trade for a country like the United States are exceedingly small.

CAPITAL MOVEMENTS

The term *capital* is certainly one of the most overworked and ill-defined concepts in economics. For our purposes, the term *capital* will always refer to *financial* capital, that is, various forms of financial assets and liabilities.

Whenever we wish to talk about capital goods, such as machinery and equipment, we will explicitly refer to *real capital* or *capital goods*. International exchange of real capital goods is similar to an exchange of consumption goods in that tangible items are shipped between countries. The analysis of the gains from international commodity exchange also applies to the exchange of real capital goods. Before proceeding to an analysis of the welfare effects of international financial capital transactions, it will be useful to review some basic concepts of both real capital and financial capital and their interrelationship.

Real Capital Theory

The characteristic difference between real capital theory, or intertemporal economic theory, and the traditional single-period analysis lies in the explicit recognition of time as an important economic parameter. Conventional theory operates in a timeless framework, treating all economic actions as taking place simultaneously, or at least in the same time period. By explicitly recognizing the existence of time, capital theory adds a new dimension—and a new complexity—to economic problems.

Concepts of real capital theory can be defined analogously to concepts used in single-period analysis. We merely have to introduce the idea of a *vintage*, or age, of a commodity as a distinguishing characteristic. The conventional concepts of preferences, transactions, and transformations can be reinterpreted as intertemporal preferences, intertemporal transactions, and intertemporal transformations.

Intertemporal preferences take account of the varying degrees of satisfaction obtained by consuming an otherwise identical commodity in two different time periods. For instance, we may compare the relative utility of consuming a beer now and the prospect of consuming a beer a year from now.

Intertemporal transactions consist of the exchange of a commodity of one vintage against otherwise identical items of a different vintage.

Intertemporal transformations represent transformations of com-

modities of one vintage into commodities of a different vintage utilizing the
intertemporal productive opportunities of the economic unit. The standard
example is the planting and harvesting of agricultural commodities. One
ton of seed grains may yield 20 tons of grain a year from now.

The concept of economic maximization needs some further clarification
in the intertemporal setting. Economic values of different vintage have to be
rendered comparable to each other by *discounting* the value attached to all
future commodities. This process yields present-value equivalents to the
future values and may therefore be used for value comparisons of commodities of different vintages. Obviously, the present discounted value of a future
commodity depends on the discount rate used to convert the future value
into a present value. The appropriate formula is:

$$V_d = \frac{\text{value at time } t}{(1 + i)^t} \tag{1.6}$$

where V_d is the present discounted value, i the discount rate, and t the number
of years between the present and the future period under consideration.

A stream of future values that accrue in various time periods may be
converted into one present value by discounting the values accruing in each
time period to the present:

$$V_d = V_0 + \frac{V_1}{(1 + i)} + \frac{V_2}{(1 + i)^2} + \cdots + \frac{V_t}{(1 + i)^t} \tag{1.7}$$

A continuing controversy exists among economists over the question of the
appropriate discount rate to be used for the evaluation of future costs and
benefits. This is not the place to enter into the debate, and we will assume
that we are able to determine the appropriate discount rate without problems.
The interested reader is referred to the specialized literature on this subject.[6]

It may be helpful to give a geometric interpretation to some of the key
concepts of intertemporal economic theory in this simplified model. In Figure
1-4 we measure present (0) period commodities X_0 along the horizontal axis
and future (period 1) commodities X_1 along the vertical axis. The intertemporal transformation curve AD delineates the production possibilities
over time. If all resources are devoted to present production, the maximum
obtainable current output is $0A$ of commodity X_0. If all resources are used
for production of period 1 commodities, $0D$ is the maximum obtainable
output of the future commodity X_1. We note that there exists a net absolute
difference of CD between the maximum obtainable output of the present
commodity ($0A = 0C$) and of the future commodity ($0D$). This difference is

---

[6]A representative collection of papers is contained in: R. Haveman and J. Margolis,
Public Expenditures and Policy Analysis, (Chicago; Markham Publishing Co., 1970).

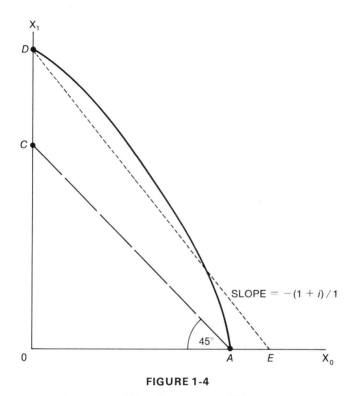

FIGURE 1-4

Intertemporal Transformations and Discounting

due to the fact that, in general, we are able to produce a greater quantity of the future commodity than of the present commodity. The future value $0D$ may now be rendered comparable by using an appropriate discount rate i. The slope of the intertemporal price line DE is equal to $-(1 + i)$, resulting in a present discounted value $0E$ of the future output $0D$. Hence, the gain from waiting in this example is AE. However, it is possible that AE is negative, in which case it would not be advantageous to engage in future production. Rather, present production (X_0) should be concentrated on instead. It is also possible that a combination of X_0 and X_1 represents the optimal output pattern.

Financial Capital in a Closed Economy

Based on the expectation of a future real return to be realized by investing, we may issue *financial* claims to these future commodities. The value of these financial claims is based on the expected intertemporal productivity. We may go one step further and allow for the exchange of these financial titles. If these financial claims change hands between residents of different countries, international financial transactions result.

The intertemporal transformation curve AD shown in Figure 1-4 is likely to be concave as viewed from the origin, indicating diminishing marginal returns from additional investments in real capital goods. Consequently, the expected marginal returns of the financial titles that are issued in anticipation of these real returns will tend to decline as well. That is, a transformation curve showing the opportunities to exchange current goods against dated financial titles representing claims to future goods will also be concave viewed from the origin. Such an intertemporal financial transformation curve is shown in Figure 1-5 by the curve DA. Current goods are measured along the horizontal axis, and the dated financial claims to future goods are measured along the vertical axis.

In a closed economy, where no financial titles may be exchanged with foreign economic units, equilibrium is determined by the familiar tangency condition of the (intertemporal) transformation curve DA and an (intertemporal) community indifference curve $_tCIC_0$. Such a situation is shown by point E in Figure 1-5. The common tangency to DA and $_tCIC_0$ determines the equilibrium interest rate in this closed economy. The tangent (dashed line) may be labeled the intertemporal terms of trade, $_tTOT_0$, and its slope is equal to $-(1 + i)$, where i is the interest rate. At point E, the equilibrium point, the marginal rate of time preference is equal to the intertemporal terms of trade and the yield of financial assets, which in turn is based on the intertemporal productivity of real assets.

If we now permit international exchange of financial assets, we may find—just as in the timeless barter case—that individuals in different countries may want to engage in international exchange. They will want to do this if their domestic interest rates are different. Poor societies may value present consumption much higher than future consumption, compared to affluent societies where there is no need to worry about immediate survival. Similarly, different economies may have different intertemporal productivity curves, and consequently the financial intemporal transformation curves will be shaped differently. Hence, it may be reasonable to expect that the equilibrium interest rates in various countries will be different. If this is the case, mutually advantageous exchange of current goods against financial claims to future goods—and vice versa—is possible.

Let us assume that the intertemporal equilibrium terms of trade, that is, the interest rate prevailing in international markets, is given by the line $_tTOT_1$. Under these circumstances it will be advantageous for the country depicted in Figure 1-5 to "produce" at point F on its intertemporal transformation curve and to "consume" at point C, where it reaches the highest possible intertemporal indifference curve $_tCIC_1$. The country will export KL of current goods in exchange for GH of financial claims to future goods.

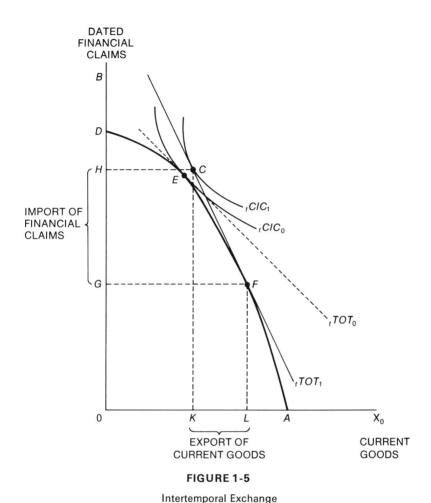

FIGURE 1-5

Intertemporal Exchange

Clearly, there are gains associated with this exchange of real against financial assets. The residents of the country will collectively reach the higher intertemporal community indifference curve $_tCIC_1$, instead of $_tCIC_0$, which could be attained under autarky. We may conclude that free international exchange of commodities as well as financial assets will increase the collective welfare of the residents of some or all countries involved in the international exchange. However, we should caution that this does not imply that every single resident will actually be better off as a result of international exchange. It may be that in a country there are some people who will be hurt by trade while others gain. But it can be shown that the gainers can compensate the losers and still leave some net gains.[7]

SUGGESTED FURTHER READINGS

CAVES, RICHARD E., *Trade and Economic Structure*, Cambridge: Harvard University Press, 1963.

HELLER, H. ROBERT, *International Trade: Theory and Empirical Evidence*, 2nd ed. Englewood Cliffs, N. J.: Prentice-Hall, Inc., 1973.

HIRSHLEIFER, JACK, *Investment, Interest, and Capital*, Englewood Cliffs, N.J.: Prentice-Hall, Inc., 1970.

KEMP, MURRAY C., *The Pure Theory of International Trade and Investment*, Englewood Cliffs, N.J.: Prentice-Hall, Inc., 1969.

LEONTIEF, WASSILY W., "The Use of Indifference Curves in the Analysis of Foreign Trade," *Quarterly Journal of Economics* (May 1933). Reprinted in H. S. Ellis and L. A. Metzler, eds., *Readings in the Theory of International Trade*, Philadelphia: The Blakiston Co., 1950.

MEADE, JAMES E., *A Geometry of International Trade*. London: George Allen & Unwin, 1952.

MILLER, NORMAN C., "A General Equilibrium Theory of International Capital Flows," *Economic Journal* (June 1968).

[7]See Egon Sohmen, *Flexible Exchange Rates*, 2nd ed. (Chicago: University of Chicago Press, 1969), Appendix; or Heller, *International Trade*, Chap. 11.

CHAPTER 2

Price Determination
In International Markets

In the first chapter we showed that countries that engage in international exchange of goods, services, and financial assets may reap certain gains from specialization and exchange. We established the existence of these gains in a general equilibrium framework and showed that the country as a whole is better off as a result of international exchange.

Clearly, many questions had to be left unanswered. Among other things we did not investigate to whom the gains will accrue, the effects of trade on product and factors prices, the determinants of international trade patterns, and the like. All these topics are traditionally treated in the pure theory of international trade and are covered in detail in a companion volume.[1]

In this chapter we will take a closer look at the determination of prices and trade volume in commodity markets. By this we are laying the groundwork for the analysis of international currency markets, which will be taken up in the following chapter.

COUNTRIES AND INDIVIDUALS

In the theory of international trade we often view countries as economic units. We say, for instance, that the United States exported $48.8 billion of merchandise to other countries in 1972 and imported $55.7 billion from

[1]H. R. Heller, *International Trade: Theory and Empirical Evidence*, 2nd ed. (Englewood Cliffs, N.J.: Prentice-Hall, Inc., 1973).

them. However, it was not the United States that did the exporting and importing, but individual firms, households, and government units located in the United States that traded with foreign economic units. To establish the microeconomic foundations of international trade and exchange, we will start our analysis by showing how we can aggregate the individual economic decisions taken by households and firms within a country. The aggregate manifestations of the individual decisions will then be presented as if they were the collective decision arrived at jointly by the residents of the country. This aggregation will save much time and energy by allowing us to avoid needless repetition.

Market Supply

We will assume that all industries are perfectly competitive. Under perfectly competitive conditions prices are determined in the market place, and the individual firms can sell all they want to sell at the going market price. All firms are price takers.

In Figure 2-1a we show a supply curve for one firm, let us say a wheat-producing farm, that is based on the firm's marginal cost curve. The supply curve shows the quantities of wheat that the individual firm is willing to supply at various market prices. If we assume that the number of firms in the industry remains constant—a short-run situation—we can aggregate the individual supply curves to obtain the aggregate supply curve for the wheat industry in the country. For instance, if the wheat industry consists of 100,000

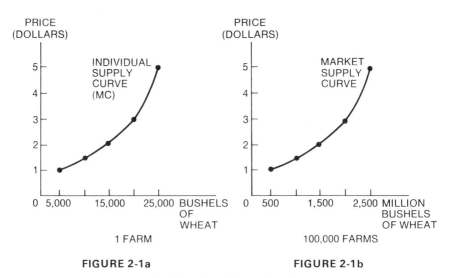

FIGURE 2-1a   **FIGURE 2-1b**

Individual and Market Supply

identical farms, then the market supply curve for wheat in the country will be as shown in Figure 2-1b.

Of course, the market supply curve of Figure 2-1b is only the short-run supply curve for wheat. If we selected a sufficiently long period of analysis so that new firms could enter or leave the industry, we would have to adjust the supply curve to take account of the changes in the number of firms in the industry. Typically, the long-run supply curve, which allows for the number of firms to vary, is more elastic than the short-run supply curve, which assumes that the number of firms is constant. In our subsequent analysis we will assume that we are dealing with a situation where the market supply curve can be obtained simply by aggregating the individual supply curves of all the firms in the industry.

Market Demand

In a similar way we are able to derive the market demand curve for wheat for all persons in a country. Let us assume that the country is composed of 100 million identical consumers, each one of which has a demand curve for wheat as shown in Figure 2-2a. The individual consumer's demand curve is based on his indifference map and shows the quantity of wheat that he is willing to purchase at various market prices. The demand curve slopes downward to the right, showing that the consumer is willing to purchase a larger quantity in response to a lower market price.

Again we are able to sum all the quantities demanded by the individual

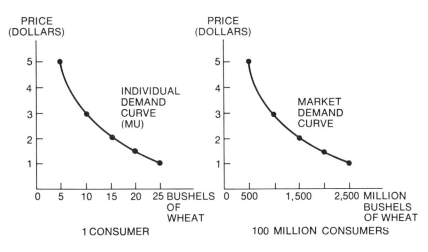

FIGURE 2-2a   FIGURE 2-2b

Individual and Market Demand

consumers at each and every price and derive the market demand curve for the 100 million residents of the country. Such a market demand curve is shown in Figure 2-2b.

Domestic Equilibrium

The intersection of the supply and demand curves in a competitive market determines the market price and the quantity that will be traded. Figure 2-3a shows the wheat market supply and demand curves previously developed. The market supply and demand curves intersect at a price of two dollars. Only at this price is the quantity of wheat that farmers are willing to sell equal to the quantity that consumers wish to purchase. At prices above two dollars, the quantity supplied exceeds the quantity demanded: there exists a surplus or an excess supply. Conversely, at prices below two dollars the quantity demanded exceeds the quantity supplied: there is a shortage or an excess demand for the product. If a surplus develops there is a tendency for the price to fall, just as there is a tendency for the price to rise in the face of a shortage. If there is no surplus or shortage the price will remain unchanged: the price has reached its equilibrium level—in our example, two dollars.

If the residents of the country of our hypothetical example do not

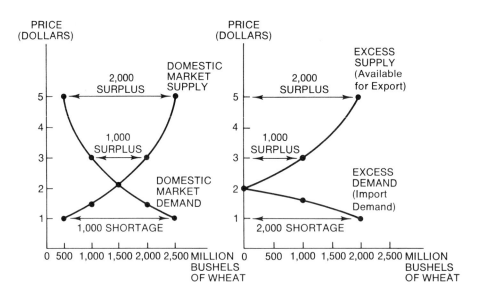

FIGURE 2-3a   FIGURE 2-3b

Excess Supply and Demand

trade with foreign economic units, the two-dollar price will be the price that prevails in the domestic wheat market. The surpluses and shortages that exist at other prices in the domestic market are shown by the excess supply and excess demand curves of Figure 2-3b. In Figure 2-3b we simply plot the horizontal difference between the domestic market supply and demand curves of Figure 2-3a.

Excess Supply and Demand and Foreign Trade

The excess supply curve shows the quantities that are available for export at various prices, and the excess demand curve depicts the amount that domestic economic units wish to import. At the domestic market equilibrium price of two dollars neither exports nor imports are likely to result because the country's domestic producers offer the same quantity for sale as is demanded by domestic consumers. Hence, there exists no incentive to engage in international trade.

The two-dollar domestic equilibrium price also represents the changeover price for the country from a wheat-exporting nation to a wheat-importing nation. Only at prices above two dollars will the country be a net exporter of wheat. At prices below two dollars it will become a net importer of wheat.

Next, we will have to determine the direction and volume of wheat trade in which the economic units of the country wish to engage. To answer this question we must say something about the potential trading partners with which the country might exchange wheat and the role of the country in the international wheat market.

We will assume that there are only two countries—the United States and the United Kingdom—and that both produce and consume wheat. Under these conditions, the collective actions of American producers and consumers of wheat will have an influence on the world market price of wheat, even though each individual unit takes the wheat price as given.

In Figure 2-4 we show the U.S. export supply and import demand curves for wheat. In addition, we show the hypothetical export supply and import demand curves for the United Kingdom. All prices are expressed in U.S. dollars by using the exchange rate to convert U.K. pounds. In later chapters we will pay considerable attention to the determination of the exchange rate. For now we will simply assume that the exchange rate is known. We note that at prices above three dollars the United Kingdom will be a net exporter of wheat and at prices below three dollars it will be a net importer of the commodity. Immediately we are able to delineate the feasible price range within which trade between the two countries is possible: at prices above three dollars both the United States and the United Kingdom want to export wheat. Clearly, if there are only those two countries, there will be nobody to sell the wheat to. There will be an excess supply of wheat on

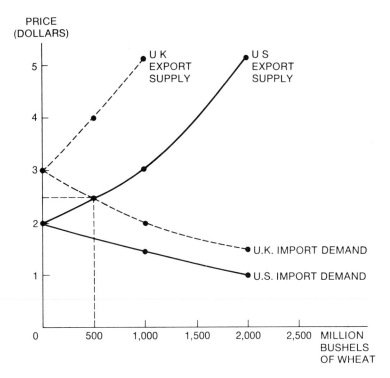

FIGURE 2-4

International Market Equilibrium

the world market, and prices will fall. The reverse is true at prices below two dollars. Now both countries wish to be net importers of wheat, and there are no suppliers who are willing to satisfy the existing excess demand.

Only in the range between the autarky prices in the two countries, that is $2.00 for the United States and $3.00 for the United Kingdom, is trade between the two countries possible. The exact price and volume of trade taking place is determined by the shape of the export supply and import demand curves of the two countries. In our example the U.S. export supply curve intersects the U.K. import demand curve at a price of $2.50 per bushel of wheat, resulting in an international trade volume of 500 million bushels between the two countries. Let us note that this quantity represents only the international wheat trade. In addition there are the trades between domestic producers and consumers of wheat that take place in the domestic sector of both economies. All these trades will take place at the new world market price of wheat of $2.50. At that price the total world wheat market is cleared, and no excess supplies or demands exist for the world as a whole.

Aggregate Export Supply and Import Demand

We may extend our analysis to cover all markets and derive *aggregate* export supply and import demand curves for entire countries. Naturally, individual prices and quantities have to be replaced by aggregate price and quantity indicators. These aggregate export supply and import demand curves are very useful in our subsequent analysis of international currency markets, the causes of international disequilibrium, and the alternative adjustment policies.

PROBLEMS OF EMPIRICAL ESTIMATION

Clearly, an important mission of economists is to provide empirical estimates of the supply and demand functions discussed. There are several problems of empirical estimation that should be called to our attention because many of the empirical estimates available may be criticized on these grounds. Because the problems of estimation are often severe, not too much confidence should be placed in some of the estimates. This is not a book on econometrics, and only some of the most rudimentary problems of empirical estimation can be discussed here. The reader is referred to the bibliography at the end of this chapter for sources that discuss the problem more thoroughly.

Length of Time Period

It is well known that the estimates of supply and demand elasticities depend on the time horizon under consideration. In the very short run, when no additional quantities can be produced or when consumers or users of inputs have no time to adjust their consumption and/or production patterns, supply and demand curves are highly inelastic. On the other hand in the very long run, when industries may expand their production by the addition of new firms and consumers and/or buyers of inputs can adjust fully to the price changes, both supply and demand curves are likely to be more elastic. *Ceteris paribus*, the longer the time horizon under consideration, the greater the elasticity of the respective supply and demand curves. Hence, estimates based on, let us say, ten monthly observations are likely to yield different values from those based on ten yearly observations.

Simultaneous Shifts of Supply and Demand Curves

Let us assume that we are trying to use time series data to estimate import demand or export supply functions. In a free market any observed price and quantity pair always refers to the intersection of a supply and a demand curve that exists at that moment in time. If the supply and demand functions stay constant over time, no time series data are generated that allow us to estimate supply or demand curves. Instead, we have only one price/quantity pair; that is, one point and not a curve. Therefore, a precondition for time series estimation is that some of the curves must have shifted over time. If we are trying to estimate a demand curve, our assumption must be that the demand curve remained unchanged over time, while the supply curve shifted about—thereby generating the various observed price/quantity pairs. The ideal case is illustrated in Figure 2-5a where we show a stationary demand

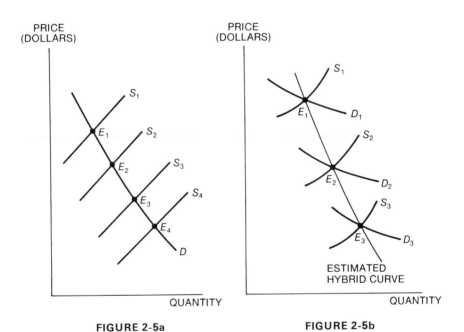

FIGURE 2-5a   FIGURE 2-5b

The Identification Problem

curve and a series of supply curves, S_1, S_2, S_3, S_4, that prevailed during four successive time periods. Under these circumstances, we can properly identify the true demand curve from the data at hand as the curve D.

However, in many instances both the supply and demand curves will shift about. Figure 2-5b illustrates this case. If the demand curve shifts from D_1 to D_2 to D_3 as the supply curve moves from S_1 to S_2 to S_3, the actually observed price/quantity pairs E_1, E_2, and E_3 are not points that are located on the same demand curve. If we were to try to estimate a demand curve from these observations, we would in fact estimate neither a pure demand nor a pure supply curve, but a cross between the two. Depending on the relative magnitude of the shifts of the two curves, the resulting hybrid may have a positive or negative slope.

Errors of Measurement

When using standard statistical techniques to estimate supply or demand curves, we typically assume that all errors of measurement and observation occur in either the price *or* the quantity variable. In fact, both variables are likely to contain errors. If this is true, the fundamental assumption is violated, and the estimated demand or supply curves will not conform to the true curves. Our results will be biased.

Aggregation Problems

Let us assume that we are trying to estimate the elasticity of demand for U.S. imports from the rest of the world. For simplicity we will assume that the rest of the world is composed of two countries: A and B. The import volume from both countries is assumed to be initially identical. If the *true* demand elasticity for U.S. imports from A is equal to -3 and from B equal to -1, a weighted average would yield an aggregate elasticity of -2. For instance, a price increase by 10 percent in the two countries would reduce U.S. imports from them by 20 percent.

Now let us assume that the price change was not uniform in both countries and that country A's prices increased by 5 percent while B's prices went up 15 percent—again an average of 10 percent. Due to the higher demand elasticity of U.S. imports from A, the quantity of imports from A will decrease by 15 percent, while the quantity of imports from B will go down by 15 percent, leading to an average drop in imports by 15 percent.

Conversely, if the price change in country A is 15 percent and amounts to only 5 percent in country B, then imports from A will decrease by 45 percent and from B by 5 percent. The average decrease in the quantity imported by the U.S. is now 25 percent.

We may conclude that aggregate estimates of demand elasticities are misleading if the demand elasticity is not identical for all items entering into the aggregate and individual components of the index experience different price changes.

What has been said about countries is also true for elasticity estimates covering several commodities.

Typically, commodities with an inelastic demand experience larger price fluctuations and will therefore bias empirical calculations of elasticities in a downward direction. If such estimates are used as a basis for policy recommendations regarding exchange rate changes or other policies influencing the relative price levels between the trading partners, appropriate allowances should be made.

Time Path of Adjustment

Adjustment to price changes is not instantaneous. It may take several months or even years before all economic units have fully adjusted to the price change. In the meantime, however, we may record several price/quantity pairs that do not lie on the true demand curve. For instance, let us assume that in Figure 2-6 the price drops from P_A to P_B. If we use the interim price/quantity pairs 1 through 6 as the basis for our statistical computations, the estimated demand curve will be more elastic than the true demand curve. Different time paths of adjustment will produce different biases in our estimates.

There are several other highly technical problems associated with empirical estimates of supply and demand elasticities, none of which can be discussed here. The interested reader is referred to the bibliography at the end of the chapter.

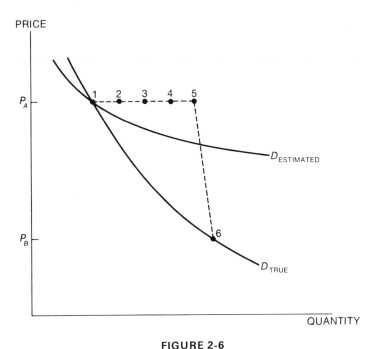

FIGURE 2-6

Timepaths and Demand Elasticities

THE ESTIMATES

We will not attempt to give a comprehensive survey of all the empirical estimates that have been made. Instead, we will limit ourselves to data from a study by Houthakker and Magee,[2] whose results are generally in agreement with previous studies by other authors. The Houthakker and Magee study yields comparable data for a wide variety of countries and commodity classes and represents one of the most recent contributions to a growing literature.

Houthakker and Magee provide us with three different sets of price elasticities for both imports and exports: (1) total imports and exports by country; (2) U. S. imports and exports to and from various countries; and (3) U. S. imports and exports by commodity group. The estimates are based on annual data from 1951 to 1966, except U. S. import demand by commodity group which is based on quarterly observations for the 1947 to 1966 period. The calculated elasticities are presented in Tables 2-1, 2-2, and 2-3.

A few observations regarding these price elasticity estimates are in order. Many of the price elasticities calculated were not significant at the 95 percent

TABLE 2-1

PRICE ELASTICITIES FOR TOTAL EXPORTS AND IMPORTS OF COUNTRIES
(annual data, 1951–66)

Import Price Elasticity	Country	Export Price Elasticity
.83*	Australia	− .21*
−1.02	Belgium–Luxembourg	.42*
−1.46	Canada	− .59
−1.66	Denmark	− .56*
.17*	France	−2.27
− .24*	Germany	−1.25
− .13*	Italy	−1.12
− .72	Japan	− .80
.23*	Netherlands	− .82*
− .78	Norway	.20*
− .52*	South Africa	−2.41
− .79*	Sweden	− .47*
− .84*	Switzerland	− .58
− .21*	United Kingdom	−1.24
−1.03	United States	−1.51

*These coefficients are not significant at the 95 percent level. Data corrected for autocorrelation have been used where provided.

Source: H. S. Houthakker and S. P. Magee, "Income and Price Elasticities in World Trade," *Review of Economics and Statistics*, 51, May 1969, pp. 111–25.

[2]H. S. Houthakker and S. P. Magee, "Income and Price Elasticities in World Trade," *Review of Economics and Statistics, 51*, May 1969, pp. 111–25.

level and are starred in the tables. The higher the elasticity, the larger the effect on export or import quantity brought about by relative price changes caused by inflation, exchange rate changes, and the like. A unitary price elasticity indicates that the value of exports or imports will not change due to price changes because quantity changes will compensate exactly for any price changes that may occur. The export price elasticities of several countries, notably the United States, France, and South Africa, are relatively high, indicating that price increases in these countries are likely to lead to a sharp deterioration of exports. Japan is characterized by a relatively low price elasticity for both her exports and imports.

Let us note again that these estimates are based on annual data covering 15 years. Hence, they should not be used to predict the short-run effects of exchange rate or price level changes. It will probably take several years until the full effects of a relative price change will be apparent in the international accounts.

It is interesting to note that the price elasticity for U.S. exports and imports to individual countries (Table 2-2) is markedly higher than the global price elasticity. This may be due to the possibility of substitution between

TABLE 2-2

PRICE ELASTICITIES FOR TOTAL UNITED STATES
TRADE WITH SELECTED COUNTRIES
(annual data, 1951–66)

U.S. Import Price Elasticity	Country	U.S. Export Price Elasticity
−4.69	Australia	−8.10
−2.08	Belgium–Luxembourg	−2.38
.49*	Canada	−1.45*
−6.05	Denmark	− .47*
−4.58	France	−3.14
−8.48	Germany	−2.39
−3.82	Italy	−2.04
−4.96	Japan	− .41*
−2.47	Netherlands	− .35*
−1.82	Norway	−2.26
−3.10*	South Africa	−2.68*
−2.49	Sweden	.73*
− .04*	Switzerland	−2.01
−4.25	United Kingdom	−1.69

*These coefficients are not significant at the 95 percent level. Data corrected for autocorrelation have been used where provided.

Source: H. S. Houthakker and S. P. Magee, "Income and Price Elasticities in World Trade," *Review of Economics and Statistics,* 51, May 1969, pp. 111–25.

various countries of origin, therefore making trade between individual countries more price sensitive.

In the commodity-group table (Table 2-3) the high price elasticity of the U.S. demand for imports of finished manufactured goods is significant. It shows a great willingness of American consumers to substitute foreign for domestic commodities in response to relative price changes. However, in view of the presence of tariffs, quotas, and other distorting barriers to trade, all these inferences should be taken with a great degree of caution.

Estimates of supply elasticities are much harder to come by. In general it is assumed that the supply elasticities in international trade are very high. This is confirmed in a study by Magee, who estimates the supply elasticity of U.S. exports to be 10.0, and for U.S. imports to be 8.5.[3]

All these elasticity estimates will be very important when we deal with the effects of exchange rate or price changes on the balance of payments. For example, without knowledge of these elasticities, it is not possible to estimate the quantitative effects of a currency devaluation or appreciation on the balance of payments. We will have occasion again and again to refer to these elasticity estimates.

TABLE 2-3

PRICE ELASTICITIES FOR UNITED STATES COMMODITY TRADE

U.S. Import Price Elasticity (quarterly data, 1947–66)	Commodity Group	U.S. Export Price Elasticity (annual data, 1951–66)
− .18	Crude materials	− .31
− .21	Crude foodstuffs	n.a.
−1.40	Manufactured foods	−1.91
−1.83	Semimanufactures	n.a.
−4.05	Finished manufactures	−1.22

n.a.—Information not available. Data corrected for autocorrelation have been used where provided.

Source: H. S. Houthakker and S. P. Magee, "Income and Price Elasticities in World Trade," *Review of Economics and Statistics,* 51, May 1969, pp. 111–25.

SUGGESTED FURTHER READINGS

CHENG, HANG SHENG, "Statistical Estimates of Elasticities and Propensities in International Trade," *IMF Staff Papers* (April 1959).

[3]Stephen P. Magee, "A Theoretical and Empirical Examination of Supply and Demand Relationships in U.S. International Trade," *mimeo,* Council of Economic Advisors, 1970.

HOUTHAKKER, HENDRIK S., and STEPHEN P. MAGEE, "Income and Price Elasticities in World Trade," *Review of Economics and Statistics* (May 1969).

LEAMER, EDWARD E., and ROBERT M. STERN, *Quantitative International Economics*, Chap. 2. Boston: Allyn and Bacon, Inc., 1970.

ORCUTT, GUY H., "Measurement of Price Elasticities in International Trade," *Review of Economics and Statistics* (May 1950). Reprinted in R. CAVES and H. G. JOHNSON, eds., *AEA Readings in International Economics*. Homewood, Ill.: Richard D. Irwin, Inc., 1968.

RHOMBERG, RUDOLF R., and LORETTE BOISSONNEAULT, "Effects of Income and Price Changes on the U.S. Balance of Payments," *IMF Staff Papers* (March 1964).

CHAPTER 3

International
Currency Markets

In modern economies money serves as an intermediary that facilitates the exchange of commodities. That is, most goods and services are not bartered directly against each other, but are bought and sold for money. Virtually all currencies of the world are issued by national monetary authorities, and hence the territory in which a particular currency is legal tender generally coincides with national boundaries.

CURRENCY MARKETS

All payments for international transactions between individuals are made by using a national currency. But because both parties in international transactions do not use the same national currency, the currency used has to be either bought or sold against the national currency of one of the trading partners. That is, either the recipient of foreign currency has to sell that currency to obtain his own national currency, or the person making the payment has to acquire first the national currency of his trading partner. The two following patterns are possible if an American sells wheat to an Englishman:

1. The U.S. wheat exporter accepts British pounds in return for his wheat shipment. He then sells the pounds in the international currency market for dollars, with his bank acting as his agent.
2. The U.S. wheat exporter asks to be paid in U.S. dollars. Now the British importer has to sell the pounds in the international currency market in exchange for the dollars he needs to make the payment.

In both instances there is a demand for U.S. dollars and a supply of British pounds. The demand for U.S. dollars is a *derived* demand. The ultimate demand is the demand for U.S. commodities, wheat in our example.

The foreign price of wheat $P_£^{UK}$ in terms of pounds is defined as the American dollar price of wheat $P_\$^{US}$ times the exchange rate between pounds and dollars (£/$). Formally:

$$P_£^{UK} \equiv \frac{£}{\$} \times P_\$^{US} \tag{3.1}$$

The ratio £/$ will be referred to as the *pound/dollar exchange rate*, or simply the exchange rate.

If either the U.S. wheat price $P_\$^{US}$ or the exchange rate £/$ falls, the U.K. price will fall as well. Assuming that the U.S. wheat price $P_\$^{US}$ stays constant, we can see that a larger quantity of U.S. wheat will be demanded by the U.K. if the exchange rate falls. As the dollar price of wheat $P_\$^{US}$ stays constant, a larger quantity of wheat purchases must also result in a larger quantity of dollars demanded. Hence, the demand curve for dollars will slope downward to the right as shown in the hypothetical example of Table 3-1 and Figure 3-1a.

TABLE 3-1

Point	Pound/ Dollar Exchange Rate £/$	Quantity of Dollars Demanded	Elasticity of Demand for Dollars	Quantity of Pounds Supplied	Dollar/ Pound Exchange Rate $/£
	(1)	*(2)*	*(3)*	*(4)*	*(5)*
A	5.00	1,000		5,000	.20
			3.00		
B	4.00	2,000		8,000	.25
			1.40		
C	3.00	3,000		9,000	.33
			.71		
D	2.00	4,000		8,000	.50
			1.40		
E	1.50	6,000		9,000	.67
			1.25		
F	1.00	10,000		10,000	1.00

But each time a dollar is purchased (demanded) in international currency markets, some other currency will be used to buy it. In our example British pounds are supplied in this fashion. The quantity of pounds supplied will depend on the quantity of dollars demanded and the number of pounds that have to be paid for each dollar, that is, the exchange rate:

$$Q_£^S = \frac{£}{\$} \cdot Q_\$^D \tag{3.2}$$

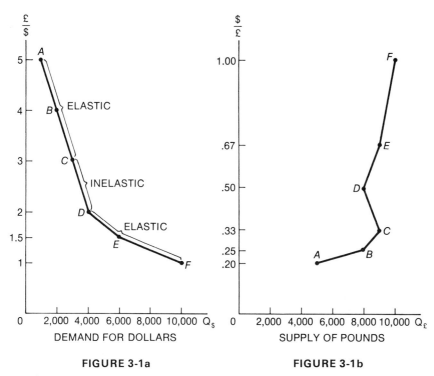

FIGURE 3-1a   **FIGURE 3-1b**

Interrelationship between Foreign Exchange Markets

In Table 3-1, column 4, we calculate the quantity of pounds supplied by multiplying the quantity of dollars demanded (column 2) by the exchange rate (£/$) (column 1).

The resulting supply curve for pounds is graphed in Figure 3-1b. Because we now show the quantity of pounds along the horizontal axis, we have to give the price of pounds along the vertical axis. The price of one pound is equal to the amount of dollars that has to be paid for it. Hence, we show the dollar/pound exchange rate as $/£ along the vertical axis of Figure 3-1a and in column 5 of Table 3-1. The dollar/pound exchange rate ($/£) of column 5 is nothing but the inverse of the pound/dollar exchange rate (£/$) of column 1.

The supply curve of pounds shown in Figure 3-1b has a backward bending portion between points C and D. To understand the reason for this backward bending part more fully, let us remind ourselves that from the viewpoint of British residents the supply curve of pounds is nothing but a *total expenditure curve*. It shows the total number of pounds that they will spend on the purchase of U.S. dollars and ultimately on U.S. commodities.

The British demand for dollars has an inelastic segment between points *C* and *D*, and a fall in the price of dollars from three pounds per dollar to two pounds per dollar (Figure 3-1a) will be associated with an increase in the quantity of dollars demanded from $3000 to $4000. But because the dollars are becoming cheaper, the fall in the dollar exchange rate means that instead of having to pay a total of £9000 (3£/1$ × $3000), U.K. residents now pay only £8000 (2£/1$ × $4000) for the increased quantity of dollars. Hence, the supply curve of pounds in Figure 3-1b slopes backwards between points *C* and *D*. In the corresponding segment, the demand curve for dollars is *inelastic*.

Whenever the demand for dollars is inelastic, the curve showing the supply of pounds will slope backwards. If the demand for dollars is elastic, the supply curve for pounds has its customary upward slope to the right.

THE DEMAND FOR AND SUPPLY OF DOLLARS

The demand for U.S. dollars in international currency markets is due to many factors, and only the most important of these can be mentioned here briefly. A full discussion of all the forces underlying the demand for U.S. dollars is postponed to the following chapter, where we deal with the balance-of-payments accounts in detail. The demand for U.S. dollars is due to (1) the desire by foreigners to purchase goods and services in the United States; (2) the desire by foreigners to make transfer payments (like gifts and pensions) to Americans in terms of U.S. dollars; (3) the desire by foreigners to purchase U.S. financial assets; (4) the desire by Americans to sell foreign financial assets and to bring the funds back to the United States; and (5) the desire by foreign individuals, banks, and official governmental agencies to increase their dollar balances.

In a similar way we can identify the sources of the supply of dollars for international purposes. Dollars will be offered for sale in international markets (1) when Americans purchase foreign goods and services; (2) when Americans make transfer payments to foreigners; (3) when Americans purchase foreign financial assets; (4) when foreigners sell financial assets that they hold in the United States; and (5) when foreigners reduce their dollar balances. The supply of dollars is directly linked to a demand for foreign currency, for example, British pounds.

It is important to see that supply and demand relationships in international currency markets can be expressed in *either* the domestic or the foreign currency. The choice between the two methods is necessarily arbitrary. In Figure 3-2a we show a set of hypothetical supply and demand curves for U.S. dollars and in Figure 3-2b the corresponding supply and demand curves for British pounds.

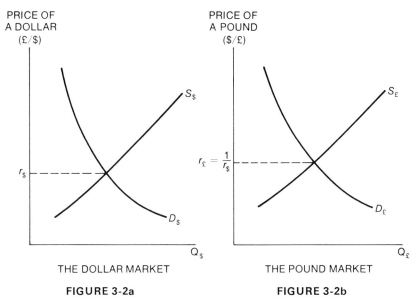

THE DOLLAR MARKET   THE POUND MARKET

FIGURE 3-2a   **FIGURE 3-2b**

Alternative Presentations of the Market for Dollars and Pounds

In Table 3-2 we show the exchange rates for many of the world's currencies. We should note that the exchange rates for most currencies are the result of market forces as well as official intervention on behalf of monetary authorities. The rates given are those which prevailed on February 21, 1973, a few days after the dollar devaluation of February 12, 1973. Most of the rates given are the official rates, around which the currency is allowed to fluctuate 2 1/4 percent up or down. The rates for Canada, Italy, Japan, Switzerland, and the United Kingdom are free market rates, as the currencies of these countries were allowed to find their own value in the foreign exchange market at that time.

In this book we will focus attention on the market for U.S. dollars whenever we deal with international currency markets. This practice runs counter to the convention adopted in some textbooks, but several reasons make the choice seem advantageous: For one, we follow the practice of many of the English-speaking countries in the world, which state the value of their currency unit in terms of foreign currency units. Second, the main focus of this book is on the United States, and the U.S. balance of payments is stated in terms of dollars. Excess supplies and demands for dollars will correspond to appropriate definitions of U.S. balance of payments deficits and surpluses. The traditional supply and demand apparatus is handled more easily and with less confusion if we deal with the market for U.S. dollars rather than with the market for some generalized concept of foreign exchange.

TABLE 3-2

SCHEDULE OF EXCHANGE RATES
(as of February 21, 1973)

Country	Currency	Values expressed in terms of units per U.S. dollar	Values expressed in terms of U.S. dollars per unit
Argentina	peso	5.000	0.0020
Australia	dollar	0.70586	1.4167
Austria	schilling	20.97	0.047687
Belgium	franc	40.33	0.024795
Canada*	dollar	0.99187*	1.0082*
Czechoslovakia	korona	5.97	0.167504
Denmark	krone	6.28205	0.159184
Finland	markka	3.90	0.2564
France	franc	4.60414	0.217196
Germany	mark	2.9003	0.34479
Ghana	cedi	1.15	0.869565
Greece	drachma	30.000	0.0333
Hong Kong	dollar	5.085	0.196657
Hungary	forint	24.90	0.04016
Indonesia	rupiah	415.00	0.002410
Iran	rial	68.60	0.014577
Iraq	dinar	0.29606	3.3777
Israel	pound	4.20	0.238095
Italy*	lira	571.43*	0.001750*
Japan*	yen	263.9916*	0.003788*
Malaysia	dollar	2.5376	0.394073
Mexico	peso	12.5	0.0800
Netherlands	guilder	2.910	0.34364
New Zealand	dollar	0.7401	1.3511
Nigeria	naira	0.6579	1.5200
Norway	krone	5.98086	0.1672
Pakistan	rupee	9.90	0.10101
Poland	zloty	19.92	0.05020
Portugal	escudo	25.50	0.039216
South Korea	wan	400.00	0.0025
South Africa	rand	0.70457	1.4193
Sweden	krona	4.56	0.219298
Switzerland*	franc	3.3445*	0.2990*
Taiwan	dollar	38.00	0.0263
Thailand	baht	20.80	0.048077
U.K.*	pound	0.4092*	2.4438*
U.S.S.R.	ruble	0.7461	1.3403
Yugoslavia	dinar	17.00	0.05882

*Currency currently floating.

Source: Federal Reserve Bank of Chicago, *International Letter*, No. 106, February 23, 1973.

Third, an appreciation of the dollar will correspond to an upward movement in the price of the dollar in currency-market diagrams. A dollar depreciation will show on the graphs as a fall in the dollar price. Fourth, the analysis of income and price adjustments is always carried out in terms of the domestic currency. Hence, it is logical to focus attention on the domestic currency when discussing exchange-rate adjustments and their effects on the national economy as well. Henceforth, the price of a U.S. dollar, defined as the number of foreign currency units required to purchase one dollar, is defined as the exchange rate, e.g.: $r \equiv £/\$$.

Stability of Equilibrium

In Figure 3-1 we showed that it is possible for the supply curve of a currency to have a backward bending portion. If the supply curve bends backward, it is conceivable that an unstable equilibrium results. This possibility is illustrated in Figure 3-3, where we show a set of hypothetical supply and demand curves for dollars. As the curves are drawn, three equilibrium points —labeled A, B, and C—exist. At each one of these points the quantity of dollars supplied equals the quantity of dollars demanded, and hence all three exchange rates, r_A, r_B, and r_C, are equilibrium rates.

Let us investigate the effects of a small displacement of the exchange rate from its equilibrium r_B to r'_B. The dollar appreciation to r'_B results in an excess demand for dollars (see Figure 3-3). An excess demand for an asset will generally result in a further price increase. Hence, if left free to respond to market forces, the exchange rate will continue to appreciate until the excess demand for dollars is eliminated at the exchange rate r_A. We see that a small displacement of the exchange rate from its equilibrium level r_B in the upward direction will result in a further move of the exchange rate away from r_B. The same is true for a small displacement of r_B in the downward direction. We therefore conclude that point B is an *unstable* equilibrium point.

On the other hand, both the equilibria at A and C are *stable* equilibria. We can show this by observing how a small displacement of the exchange rate will result in market forces that return the exchange rate to its stable equilibrium values of r_A or r_C.

From Figure 3-3 we can infer that the exchange rate will be stable if

$$\frac{dQ_\$^D}{dr} < \frac{dQ_\$^S}{dr} \tag{3.3}$$

That is, as long as an appreciation of the exchange rate results in a smaller fall in the quantity demanded than in the quantity of dollars supplied (if negative), the equilibrium is stable. Only if the supply curve is negatively sloping and flatter than the demand curve at the equilibrium point do we

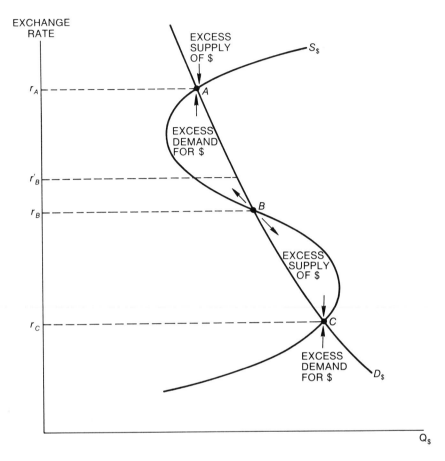

FIGURE 3-3

Stability of Exchange Market Equilibrium

find that the stability condition is not fulfilled and the equilibrium point is unstable.

It is convenient to restate the stability condition in terms of elasticities. The demand elasticity for currency is defined as

$$\eta_\$ = -\frac{dQ_\$^D}{Q_\$^D} \cdot \frac{r}{dr}$$

and the supply elasticity as

$$\epsilon = \frac{dQ_\$^S}{Q_\$^S} \cdot \frac{r}{dr}$$

We expand equation 3.3 and obtain:

$$\frac{dQ_\$^D}{dr} \cdot \frac{r}{Q_\$^D} \cdot \frac{Q_\$^S}{r} < \frac{dQ_\$^S}{dr} \cdot \frac{r}{Q_\$^S} \cdot \frac{Q_\$^S}{r} \tag{3.4}$$

Substituting elasticities and remembering that at equilibrium $Q_\$^S = Q_\$^D$ we arrive at

$$-\eta < \epsilon \tag{3.5}$$

as the new stability condition. We see that only if the supply elasticity of dollars is negative and numerically larger than the demand elasticity does an unstable equilibrium result.

Let us re-emphasize that the backward bending of the supply curve is a *necessary, but not a sufficient* condition for instability. Figure 3-4 illustrates this point further. In Figure 3-4a we show a backward bending supply curve,

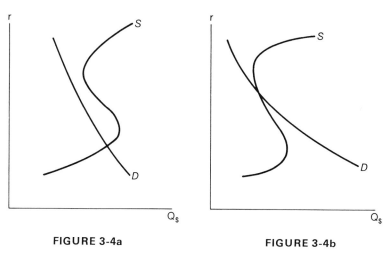

FIGURE 3-4a   **FIGURE 3-4b**

Examples of Stable Equilibrium Exchange Rates with Backward Bending
Supply Curves

but the demand curve intersects the supply in an upward sloping segment. In Figure 3-4b the supply curve has a negative slope at the equilibrium point, but its elasticity is not greater than that of the demand curve in absolute terms. In both cases the equilibrium point is stable.

ARBITRAGE

Foreign currencies are traded at various places around the world, but modern means of communication effectively link these various trading spots into one global marketplace. If, for instance, the dollar exchange rate in London is different from the exchange rate in New York, alert observers of international currency markets will seize the opportunity and make a profit by arbitraging between the two market places. For instance, let us assume that Figure 3-5 shows the supply and demand conditions in the markets for dollars in New York (3-5a) and London (3-5b). Initially, the price of

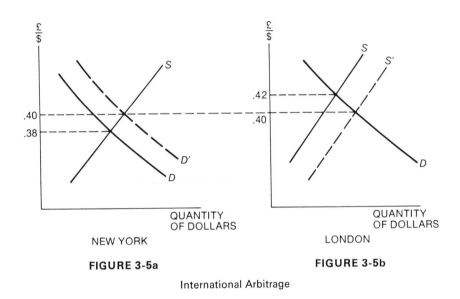

NEW YORK   LONDON

FIGURE 3-5a   **FIGURE 3-5b**

International Arbitrage

a dollar in New York is assumed to be £.38, while the exchange rate in London is £.42 per dollar. Alert arbitrageurs will purchase dollars in New York at £.38 and sell them in London for £.42. By buying in New York, the demand for dollars is increased at that marketplace, and hence the exchange rate will rise in New York. The simultaneous selling of the dollars in London will add to the available dollar supply in that market, and the exchange rate will fall. In our example, equilibrium is reached when an exchange rate of £.40 per dollar prevails in international markets.

The same principle may be used to make profits in *triangular arbitrage* transactions. Instead of dealings in two markets, as in our previous example, triangular arbitrage involves three markets. For instance, an arbitrageur may use pounds to buy dollars in New York, sell them in Zurich against Swiss francs, and trade the francs in London against pounds. By this triangular arbitrage the various cross-rates between different currencies will be made consistent.

Due to the existence of transaction costs, arbitrage may not perfectly equalize exchange rates in various markets. But due to the fact that transactions costs increase only slightly for larger transactions, very small exchange-rate differentials are sufficient to bring about arbitrage transactions. Let us emphasize that arbitrage is a riskless operation which results in consistent cross exchange rates.

KEY CURRENCIES

Of course, although in theory there exists a foreign exchange market for any currency against any other currency, many of these exchange markets are much too small to have any significance. Only very rarely will a transaction be carried out directly between Uruguay pesos and Icelandic kronas. Instead, foreign exchange dealers will utilize so-called *key currencies* or *vehicle currencies* to make the transactions. For example, the pesos may first be exchanged against U.S. dollars, and these dollars then be converted into kronas. By trading other currencies against U.S. dollars, or other key currencies, the myriad of exchange markets is reduced to a manageable number of markets between the individual currencies on the one hand and the key currencies on the other hand. Because the U.S. dollar occupies such a central rate in international currency markets, many transactions are conducted in terms of U.S. dollars. Consequently, foreigners—and especially Europeans—have found it desirable to hold increasingly large dollar balances. Because these dollars are traded directly between Europeans, the market for these overseas dollars is generally referred to as the *Eurodollar* market. In Chapter 10 we will discuss the Eurodollar market in greater detail.

FORWARD EXCHANGE RATES

So far we have dealt with the determination of exchange rates in international currency markets. In these markets currencies are traded for immediate or *spot* delivery. In addition to these spot markets there are markets in which contracts for future purchase or sale of currencies may be negotiated. These *forward* markets for currencies are the topic of this section.

A forward exchange contract specifies that the holder will buy (or sell) a specified amount of currency at some predetermined date for an agreed-upon price. The forward exchange rate is determined in free markets in the same manner in which the spot rate is determined: by the interaction of supply and demand.

Forward contracts are of particular importance to businessmen, who want to avoid any risks associated with exchange-rate fluctuations. Let us say that a foreign firm takes delivery of a computer that costs $100,000. The American manufacturer demands payment within three months. Thus, the foreign firm incurs an obligation to pay $100,000, ninety days from now.

Rather than taking the risk that the dollar might appreciate relative to their own currency, the foreign firm might want to purchase the $100,000 now for delivery three months hence. Such a currency purchase in the forward market made in order to eliminate the exchange rate risk associated with international transactions is called *hedging*.

Other businessmen might at the same time want to purchase foreign currency and sell dollars because they expect to have to make a payment in terms of foreign currency. Hence, they will sell dollars for forward delivery and purchase foreign currency. The forward supply and demand for a currency will determine its price in forward markets.

Let us note carefully that there is no requirement that some professional risk bearer has to sell the forward currency to our merchant. Instead, it may be an American importer, who is buying foreign automobiles and has to pay his bill three months from now in terms of foreign currency. He also may want to hedge his position and thus be willing to sell dollars and buy foreign currency forward.

In addition to merchants who are interested in hedging their positions we might find speculators active in the forward markets. But although these speculators may be present, there is no requirement that they actively participate in the foreign exchange market. Regular merchandise transactions will provide both a supply and a demand for forward exchange because merchants in both countries want to hedge against possible exchange-rate losses in the forward markets.

The Termstructure of Forward Exchange Rates

In Figure 3-6 (a) we show the spot exchange market for Swiss francs. The exchange rate of $0.25870 per franc indicated is the one that prevailed in the International Monetary Market in Chicago on May 17, 1972. In Figure 3-6

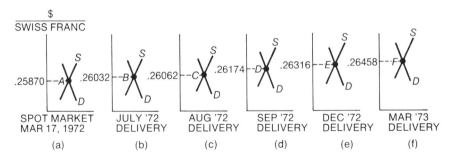

FIGURE 3-6

Spot and Forward Markets
Source: *Chicago Tribune,* March 18, 1972.

(b) we show the supply and demand curves for forward francs to be delivered in July 1972. The forward exchange rate in that market was $0.26032. Panels (c) through (f) show further forward rates for contracts with different maturities.

Rather than showing separate equilibrium diagrams for the various forward markets, we may combine the information contained in Figure 3-6 (a) through 3-6 (f) in one diagram. This is done in Figure 3-7 (a), where we graph

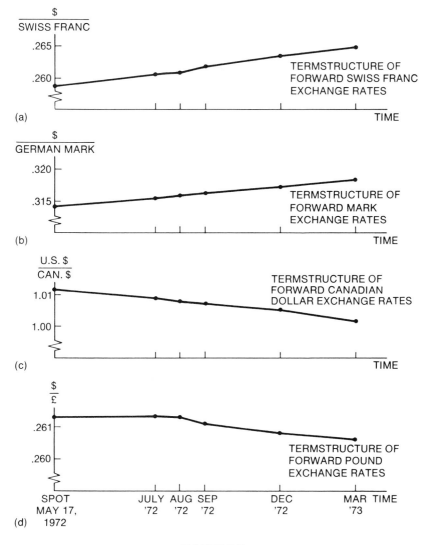

FIGURE 3-7

Source: Adapted from the *Chicago Tribune,* May 18, 1972.

the *termstructure of forward rates* for the Swiss franc as it existed on May 17, 1972. The vertical axis shows the exchange rate and the horizontal axis the time to maturity of the forward contract. Let us remember that we are dealing here with the market for Swiss francs and that we show therefore the exchange rate as $/franc: the dollar price of each franc.

We note that on that date, the forward franc—as well as the German mark shown in panel (b)—traded at a *premium* compared to the spot rate. At the same time, the Canadian dollar and the U.K. pound, whose forward termstructures are shown in panels (c) and (d), traded at a *discount* compared to the spot exchange rate.

Expectations

Two important factors determine the forward exchange rates: *expectations* and forward arbitrage. A person who expects that the foreign exchange rate will increase in the future will try to purchase that currency for future delivery. By doing so, he will drive up the forward exchange rate towards the value that he expects the currency to have at that point in the future, causing the forward currency contract to sell at a premium. Conversely, a person expecting the exchange rate to fall will attempt to sell the currency short, thereby driving down the forward exchange rate, which results in a discount.

Forward Arbitrage

Forward arbitrage or *interest arbitrage* is made possible due to the existence of forward markets for currency and regular capital markets in which funds may be lent or borrowed. The domestic capital markets provide an opportunity for investors to lend (or borrow) funds. Consider an American firm that has $10 million earmarked for the payment of taxes three months from now. The firm may invest these funds in 90 day U.S. Treasury bills and earn a return on its investment. But let us assume that the prevailing interest rates in the U.K. are higher. Under these circumstances, the firm might want to exchange its dollars for pounds in the spot market; invest them in U.K. Treasury bills; and in order to guard against any exchange-rate fluctuations that might eliminate its anticipated higher returns, it will enter into a contract to sell British pounds in the three-month forward market at a rate agreed upon now.

For instance, on January 7, 1972 (Table 3-3), the interest that could have been earned on 90 day U.K. Treasury bills was 4.32 percent (calculated on an annual basis). The rate on U.S. Treasury bills was only 3.45 percent; that is, the British Treasury bills offered an annual yield that was .87 percent above the yield obtainable in the United States. Whether the investment in

U.K. bills was attractive depended on the exchange rates that prevailed in spot and forward markets at that time. The firm, which had $10 million at its disposal for three months could have:

1. Exchanged the $10 million into British pounds;
2. invested the pounds in U.K. Treasury bills, earning more than they could have earned in the U.S.; and
3. sold British pounds in the forward market for delivery three months from now when the U.K. Treasury bills were to be paid off.

At the end of the three months, the firm would have received the principal and interest from the maturing U.K. Treasury bills and could have converted them at the previously agreed-upon exchange rate. Clearly, the profitability of these transactions depends on the forward exchange rate. If the forward pounds had sold at a discount of .87 percent, the interest rate advantage would have been just compensated for. But on January 7, 1972, forward pounds commanded a premium of .93 percent. Hence, there was a net incentive amounting to 1.80 percent per annum (see Table 3-3, column 5) to shift the funds to London.

TABLE 3-3

UNITED STATES AND UNITED KINGDOM ARBITRAGE ON TREASURY BILLS
(percent per annum)

| Date | 90 Day Treasury Bill Rates | | | Premium (+) or Discount (−) on Forward Pound (4) | Net Incentive (Favor of London) (5) |
	United Kingdom (1)	United States (2)	Spread (Favor of London) (3)		
1972					
Jan. 7	4.32	3.45	.87	.93	1.80
Feb. 4	4.29	3.24	1.05	− .13	.92
March 3	4.30	3.40	.90	− .40	.50
April 7	4.27	3.72	.55	.17	.72
May 5	4.19	3.44	.75	− .22	.53
June 2	4.34	3.77	.57	− .39	.18
July 7	5.41	3.96	1.45	−2.50	−1.05
Aug. 4	5.71	3.74	1.97	−3.59	−1.62
Sep. 1	5.81	4.48	1.33	−2.70	−1.37
Oct. 6	6.53	4.62	1.91	−2.30	− .39
Nov. 3	6.74	4.63	2.16	−2.72	− .56
Dec. 1	7.05	4.82	2.23	−2.93	− .70

Source: Board of Governors of the Federal Reserve System, *Federal Reserve Bulletin*, July 1972 and January 1973.

By investing the funds in London, the supply of loanable funds in the U.K. is increased, and the rate of interest there will tend to fall. The supply of loanable funds in the U.S. is lower than what it would be otherwise, and hence interest rates in the U.S. will tend to rise (*ceteris paribus*). Simultaneously, the selling of U.S. dollars in the spot market will drive the value of the dollar down in that market, and the buying of dollars forward will increase the value of dollars in the forward market. Hence, the incentive to engage in further international arbitrage will gradually be eliminated. In the second half of 1972 market conditions were such that there was an incentive to shift funds to the United States.

Whether an investor will find those arbitrage operations attractive will depend on his transaction costs, his aversion to investment in other countries, liquidity considerations, and similar factors. It has been estimated that the minimum profit (net of transaction cost) required to effect forward arbitrage is near 0.18 percent per annum.[1]

In the absence of transaction costs, equilibrium in international capital markets and exchange markets is reached when the interest rate differential and the spot-forward differential are equal to each other:

$$\frac{i_d - i_a}{1 + i_a} = \frac{r_f - r_s}{r_s} \tag{3.6}$$

Interest rates are denoted by i; foreign exchange rates by r; and subscript d = domestic, a = abroad, f = forward, and s = spot.

When the equilibrium condition (3.6) is fulfilled, no additional arbitrage transactions will occur. But let us note that this does not mean that arbitrage is nonexistent. The current amount of arbitrage is necessary to bring about the equality of interest rate and forward exchange-rate differentials. If arbitrage were to cease entirely, the differentials would be restored, and a disequilibrium situation would result.

Another point worth noting is that as soon as the termstructure of interest rates in the two countries is determined, we know something about the termstructure of exchange rates. That is, for any given pair of interest rates, we are able to calculate the forward premium or discount that will be consistent with the termstructure of interest rates in the sense that no further arbitrage transactions will be called for.

Figures 3-8 and 3-9 illustrate the interdependence between the termstructures of interest rates and forward exchange rates. In panel (a) we show the hypothetical termstructure of U.S. interest rates, in (b) the termstructure of U.K. interest rates, and in (c) the termstructure of the forward pound. In

---

[1] William Branson, "The Minimum Covered Interest Differential Needed for International Arbitrage Activity, *Journal of Political Economy*, November–December 1969, p. 1028–35.

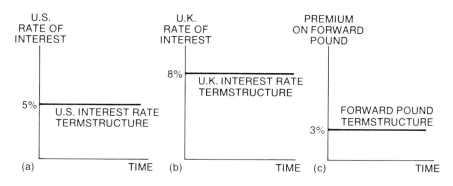

FIGURE 3-8

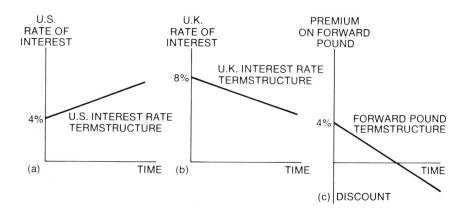

FIGURE 3-9

The Termstructure of Interest and Forward Exchange Rates

Figure 3-8 the U.S. has a uniform 5 percent interest rate, and the U.K. has a uniform 8 percent interest rate. Hence, there exists a 3 percent premium in favor of investment in London for all maturity dates. But if forward pounds trade also at a 3 percent premium at all maturities in the forward market for currency, there is no net incentive to shift additional funds between the two countries. In Figure 3-9 we show in (a) a rising interest rate termstructure in the U.S., in (b) a falling interest termstructure in the U.K., and in (c) the resulting falling equilibrium termstructure of forward rates for the pound.

We should note that our previous discussion implicitly assumed no risk differentials to be associated with foreign securities. However, if we assume that foreign governments or firms may default on their debts with a different probability as domestic debt issuers the substitution between foreign and domestic securities is not perfect. Also, governments may impose restrictions on the free transfer of funds into and out of their countries and therewith prevent the complete equalization of forward rates. The U.S. interest-equalization tax is a good example. Finally, even if the position of the international investor is covered in the forward market, he is certain to avoid exchange-rate losses only on the specific date at which the forward contract comes due. If he were forced for some reason to sell his foreign securities earlier to obtain cash for an emergency situation, he would still be exposed to the risk of having to convert at a less favorable exchange rate. Hence, there is a loss of liquidity involved as well.

Speculation

Speculators in international currency markets hope to make a profit by correctly predicting exchange rate changes that may take place. The most elementary type of speculation consists of buying a foreign currency and holding it in the hope that its value will appreciate. A hypothetical exchange-rate pattern that might have existed in the absence of speculation is shown

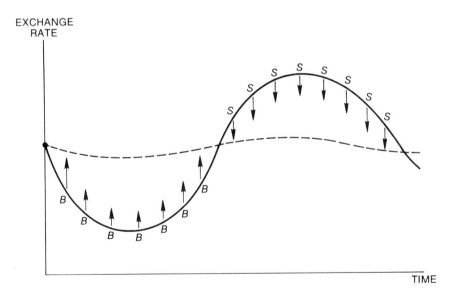

FIGURE 3-10

Effect of Speculation on Exchange Rates

in Figure 3-10 as a solid line. Speculators can make a profit by buying (*B*) the currency when the rate is below its normal level. By selling (*S*) the currency at a time of high exchange rates, the price is again moved closer to the equilibrium level. As a result of their actions, the exchange rate fluctuations will be dampened, as indicated by the dashed line.

Destabilizing behavior on behalf of speculators, which increases the amplitude of exchange-rate fluctuations, can be due only to persons who buy at higher-than-normal prices and sell at lower-than-normal prices. These speculators will not make any profits, and their losses will eventually force them to stop their activity. A speculator who purchases pounds for delivery three months from now will make a profit if the actual price of pounds at that date is higher, in which case he can sell the pounds that he bought for forward delivery at a profit. Table 3-4 shows the 90-day forward rates for U.K. pounds for the month in which delivery of the currency has to be taken. (That is, a person buying a forward contract for January 1972 delivery of pounds has to agree in October 1971 to a price of $2.4875 per pound.) In January 1972, when his forward contract comes due, a speculator who bought £100 for forward delivery will have to pay $248.75. But the speculator can immediately sell his pounds in the spot market in January for $2.5940 a pound. His £100 will bring him $259.40 Neglecting transaction costs, he has made a profit of $10.65. If the speculator would put up the entire amount of $248.75 when he bought the contract, he would have earned a rate of

TABLE 3-4

PROFIT RATES OF SUCCESSFUL 90-DAY FORWARD SPECULATION IN POUNDS

1972 End of:	Exchange Rate for Forward Delivery of Pounds in Month of —	Actual Spot Price of Pounds in Month of —	Profit (Percent per Annum)
January	$2.4875	$2.5940	17.1 if long
February	2.5031	2.6060	16.4 if long
March	2.5556	2.6145	9.2 if long
April	2.5927	2.6110	2.8 if long
May	2.6048	2.6130	1.2 if long
June	2.6137	2.4425	26.2 if short
July	2.6115	2.4500	24.8 if short
August	2.6078	2.4485	24.4 if short
September	2.4200	2.4200	0.0
October	2.4302	2.3420	14.5 if short
November	2.4308	2.3527	12.8 if short
December	2.4038	2.3481	9.3 if short

Source: IMF, *International Financial Statistics*, August 1972 and February 1973.

return of 4.28 percent on a quarterly basis or 17.1 percent calculated on an annual basis. In fact, however, forward contracts call only of a down payment of 5 or 10 percent of the value of the contract. If the down payment required was 10 percent, the speculator had to pay only $24.88, and he realized a return on an annual basis of 171.2 percent on his investment.

But let us note again that he could also have lost a sizeable amount. For instance, a speculator who bought 90 day pounds forward in March for June 1972 delivery had to pay $2.6137 per pound (see Table 3-4). In June the pound was worth only $2.4425, leaving the speculator with a loss of 26.2 percent on an annual basis. The loss would have been 262 percent for a speculator working on 10 percent margins.

Of course, rather than buying pounds for forward delivery in June 1972, the alert speculator could have sold forward pounds for delivery at that time. In that case, he would have sold each pound for $2.6137, while being able to buy the pounds at the low rate of $2.4425 when his contract called for delivery of the pounds. Such a person is said to engage in a *short sale*.

1972 was a year of much unrest in foreign exchange markets, and due to the wide fluctuations in spot and forward rates, it was easy to make or lose a lot of money.

Professor Jerome Stein[2] investigated the profitability of forward speculation during the years 1921–25, when a free market for British pounds existed. He came to the conclusion that in 62 percent of all cases speculators in forward markets made profits due to their ability to forecast exchange rate changes accurately.

Arbitrage, Speculation, and Hedging

It may be useful to briefly summarize the difference between arbitrage, speculation, and hedging operations in forward markets. Figures 3-11, 3-12, and 3-13 illustrate. In each case we show a spot and a forward market for both U.S. dollars and British pounds.

An *arbitrage* operation will make the rates in the spot and forward currency markets, as well as the interest rates in the capital markets, consistent. For instance in Figure 3-11 the interest rate A in the U.S. capital market has to be equal to the spot pound rate, times the interest rate on pounds, times the forward dollar rate ($B \times C \times D$). Arbitrage is riskless.

[2] Jerome L. Stein, "The Nature and Efficiency of the Foreign Exchange Market," *Essays in International Finance*, Princeton University, International Finance Section, October, 1962.

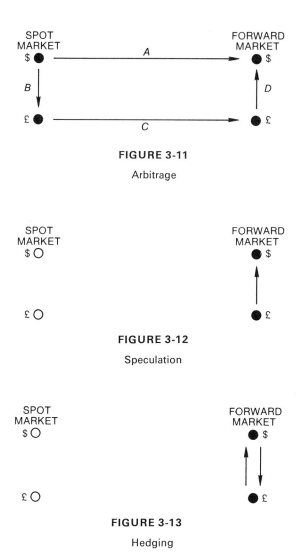

FIGURE 3-11

Arbitrage

FIGURE 3-12

Speculation

FIGURE 3-13

Hedging

A *speculator* in forward markets will either buy or sell pounds forward (Figure 3-12). He has an *open* position. The speculator will make a profit if he can sell his currency three months from now at a more advantageous price than he had to agree to in his forward contract. A speculator is a risk taker.

Hedging consists of covering a future obligation by engaging now in an opposite transaction in the forward market (Figure 3-13). A hedger avoids risk.

SUGGESTED FURTHER READINGS

AUTEN, JOHN, "Forward Exchange Rates and Interest Rate Differentials," *Journal of Finance* (March 1963).

HOLMES, ALAN, and FRANCIS SCHOTT, *The New York Foreign Exchange Market*. New York: Federal Reserve Bank of New York, 1965.

OFFICER, LAWRENCE, and THOMAS WILLETT, "*The Covered Arbitrage Schedule*," *Journal of Money, Credit and Banking* (May 1970).

PORTER, MICHAEL, "A Theoretical and Empirical Framework for Analyzing the Term Structure of Exchange Rate Expectations," *IMF Staff Papers* (November 1971).

SOHMEN, EGON, *Flexible Exchange Rates*, rev. ed., especially Chap. 4. Chicago: University of Chicago Press, 1969.

STEIN, JEROME L., "The Nature and Efficiency of the Foreign Exchange Market," *Essays in International Finance*, No. 40 (October 1962), International Finance Section, Princeton University.

CHAPTER 4

The Balance of Payments

Our purpose in this chapter is threefold: (1) to introduce the definitions and concepts used in balance-of-payments accounting; (2) to consider appropriate definitions of balance-of-payments equilibrium and disequilibrium; and (3) to relate the balance-of-payments accounts to the foreign exchange market.

All market transactions between individual economic units are recorded in the familiar national income accounts. Transactions between economic units located in different countries are summarized in the *balance-of-payments accounts*. Both the national income and the balance-of-payments accounts measure *flows* of commodities that take place over time.

A second set of accounts measures the accumulated *stocks* of assets and liabilities that exist at a given moment in time. On a national basis this is done in the country's wealth statistics, and the international counterpart is the *balance of international indebtedness*. Later in this chapter we will deal in greater detail with the balance of international indebtedness.

COVERAGE

A country's *balance of payments* is defined as the record of all economic transactions that take place during a specified time period between the country's residents and the rest of the world. For balance-of-payments purposes all individuals, institutions, and governmental units that are permanently domiciled in one country are considered 'residents' of that country. Members of consular or diplomatic establishments, foreign students, and members of the armed forces are assumed to be residents of their home country and not of the country in which they are temporarily living. Business enterprises are considered domiciled in the country in which they actually operate. Thus, foreign branches and subsidiaries are regarded as part of the country in which they are physically located. All governmental units are deemed part of the home country. International agencies are not considered part of any country, but rather an international area outside the national borders of all countries.

DEBITS AND CREDITS

The balance-of-payments accounts record in standard double-entry bookkeeping fashion all transactions between residents and foreigners as previously defined. That is, the two sides to every transaction are entered separately in the accounts. The simplest of all possible transactions is probably barter. If we exchange one American-made Oldsmobile against a German-made Mercedes in a barter exchange, we simply enter the values, say $5,000 each, of the two automobiles in the trade account. The export of the Oldsmobile will be booked as a credit entry in the U.S. balance of payments, and the import of the Mercedes will be booked as a debit entry.

	Credits	Debits	
Export of Oldsmobile	$5,000	$5,000	Import of Mercedes

In most cases, we will find that we do not engage in direct barter exchange, but instead purchase a commodity for money. If we buy a Mercedes and pay for it with a check, we still have the debit entry of $5,000 for the import of the Mercedes, but the corresponding credit entry now reads: increase in U.S. liquid dollar liabilities to foreigners by $5,000.

	Credits	Debits	
Increase in U.S. liquid liabilities	$5,000	$5,000	Import of Mercedes

There exists a third possibility, namely that somebody in Germany sends the Mercedes as a gift to an American. In this case neither a real asset (like the Oldsmobile) nor a financial asset (like the dollar check) will move to Germany. But in keeping with the principles of double-entry bookkeeping, we will book a credit entry of a private transfer. As it is an American who receives the transfer, it is a credit entry in the U.S. balance of payments.

	Credits	Debits	
Private transfer	$5,000	$5,000	Import of Mercedes

The treatment of financial capital flows is identical to that of real goods. But we must be careful to remember that when an American invests his money in foreign stocks or bonds, it is the American who *imports* a certificate of ownership, stock, bond, or other I.O.U. For balance-of-payments purposes a purchase of foreign bonds is similar to a purchase of foreign merchandise: both will be recorded as debit entries in the U.S. balance of payments. If we pay for the foreign stock or bond with a check drawn on an American bank, the appropriate counter booking is a credit entry showing the increase in U.S. liquid liabilities to foreigners.

	Credits	Debits	
Increase in U.S. liquid liabilities	$6,000	$6,000	Purchase of foreign securities

Another and perhaps more useful way of looking at the credit and debit entries is to focus on the relationship between the balance-of-payments entries and the international currency market. Every transaction that normally gives rise to a *demand* for dollars in international currency markets is booked as a *credit* entry. The export or sale of goods, services, or securities to foreigners gives rise to a demand for dollars because the dollars are needed to pay for these items. On the other hand, transactions that normally result in a *supply* of dollars in the international currency markets are booked as *debits*, such as imports of goods, services, and securities.

Exports of:	Imports of:
Goods	Goods
Services	Services
Securities	Securities
Result in:	Result in:
Dollar receipts	Dollar payments
Dollar demand	Dollar supply
Dollar inflow	Dollar outflow
Booked as:	Booked as:
Credit (+)	Debit (−)

It remains to be explained why we use the word *normally* when discussing the demand and supply of dollars. There are some transactions that are recorded in the international accounts but that are not accompanied by payments. Transfers are one such item. To preserve consistency, transfers are recorded as if they would give rise to a payment. That is, the making of a transfer is a debit entry that *normally* gives rise to a supply of dollars, and the receipt of a transfer is a credit item that *normally* results in a demand for dollars.

ACCOUNTS

Customarily, international transactions are grouped in four major accounts in the official balance-of-payments statistics: (1) the goods-and-services account, (2) the transfer account, (3) the capital account, and (4) the official-reserves account. We will discuss them in turn.

The Goods-and-Services Account

The goods-and-services account summarizes all transactions in goods and services between residents and nonresidents during the period under consideration. In Table 4-1 we show the U.S. goods-and-services account for

TABLE 4-1

THE GOODS-AND-SERVICES ACCOUNT, 1972
(in millions of dollars)

	Credits	Debits
Goods-and-services account, net		*4,219*
Merchandise, excluding military	48,840	55,656
Military	1,166	4,707
Travel	2,708	4,740
Passenger fares	694	1,555
Other transportation	3,732	3,422
Fees and royalties	670	138
Other private services	1,532	850
U.S. government miscellaneous services	413	808
Direct-investments income	10,293	692
Earnings on other private assets and liabilities	2,693	2,515
Earnings on U.S. government assets and liabilities	806	2,684

Source: *Survey of Current Business*, March 1973.

the year 1972, and in Figure 4-1 we graph its historical development. We distinguish three broad categories of entries in this account. The first group of entries records the commodity trade during the year. In 1972 merchandise exports (credits) amounted to $48,840 million; imports (debits) came to $55,656 million. We should note that these trade figures exclude military items, which are shown separately. Military credit items consist of $1,166 million of sales of military items to foreign countries and U.S. military expenditures abroad amounted to $4,707 million and are booked as debits. Military grants—as opposed to sales—are not included in these figures.

The second group of entries consists of service items, often referred to as invisible trade. Here we find entries for travel expenses, transportation of persons and goods, as well as fees and royalties received from or paid to foreigners on patents, copyrights, and trademarks.

The third category encompasses income derived from foreign investments. Americans earned a total of $13,792 million (credit) on their investments abroad, while we had to pay $5,891 (debit) to foreigners. Details are given in Table 4-1. Later in this chapter when discussing the balance of international indebtedness we will have occasion to discuss the total stocks of assets and liabilities that give rise to these payments.

The Transfer Account

The transfer account, shown in Table 4-2 and Figure 4-2, summarizes private and governmental international transfers. It shows the amounts of U.S. governmental non-military grants and financial-assistance payments and goods transferred under various aid programs. All these transfers are gifts

TABLE 4-2

THE TRANSFER ACCOUNT, 1972
(in millions of dollars)

	Credit	Debit
Unilateral transfers, net		3,764
U.S. government grants (excluding military)		2,208
U.S. government pensions and other transfers		572
Private remittances and other transfers, net		985

Source: *Survey of Current Business*, March 1973.

for which there is no obligation for repayment. U.S. government pensions, government grants for research abroad, and payments under the U.S. educational and cultural exchange programs are recorded next. The final item in the transfer account is private transfers of goods, services, and financial items between residents of the U.S. and other countries. Birthday gifts, donations to foreign charitable organizations, foreign inheritances, and the like are also reported in this account.

We should note that all items in the transfer account are customarily reported on a net basis. That is, debit entries are deducted from credit entries and only the differential is reported.

One very important item, governmental grants of military goods and services is reported in neither the goods and services account nor the transfer account. The total was $4,284 million in 1972 and to include it in U. S.

exports would unduly inflate that amount by items which we give away. Instead, the total is reported separately as a "memorandum" item.

The Capital Account

In the capital account shown in Table 4-3 and Figure 4-3 we summarize all transactions in financial assets. As pointed out previously, the capital account records the *flows* that result in the outstanding *stocks* reported in the balance of international indebtedness. That is, the U.S. international investment position is influenced by the annual financial flows recorded in the capital account.

TABLE 4-3

THE CAPITAL ACCOUNT, 1972
(in millions of dollars)

	Credits	Debits
Capital movements, net	*11,048*	
U.S. government		
Loans		3,815
Repayments	2,071	
Other	377	
U.S. private capital		
Direct investment		3,339
Foreign securities		619
Long-term		1,469
Short-term, nonliquid		1,773
Short-term, liquid		1,139
Foreign capital (other than official agencies)		
Direct investment	322	
U.S. securities	4,502	
Long-term	710	
Short-term, nonliquid	139	
Short-term, liquid	4,816	
Foreign official agencies	10,265	

Source: *Survey of Current Business*, March 1973.

The capital account is broken down into four major categories: U.S. government, U.S. private accounts, foreign capital, and foreign official agencies. The U.S. government capital account is self-explanatory. It records as debits the loans made by the U.S. government to foreign governments under various aid programs. Contrary to the grants recorded in the unilateral transfer account, there exists an obligation for repayment of the loans. Such repayments constitute a credit entry in the account.

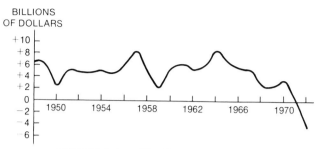

FIGURE 4-1   The Goods-and-Services Account

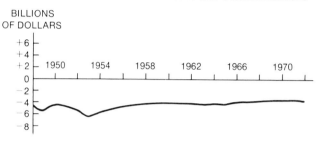

FIGURE 4-2   The Transfer Account

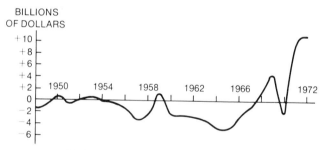

FIGURE 4-3   The Capital Account

FIGURE 4-4   The Reserve Account

NOTE: Reserves before 1949, gold only; since 1949, total reserves. Positive figures are reserve gains.

SOURCES: *Historical Statistics of the United States;* IMF, *International Financial Statistics;* and Dept. of Commerce, *Balance of Payments Statistics Supplement,* 1962; and *Survey of Current Business,* March 1973.

The U.S. private capital account records the effects of financial transactions by U.S. banks, corporations, and individuals. Any foreign investment in which American investors have more than 10 percent ownership is classified as a direct investment. Clearly, the 10 percent cutoff point is arbitrary, but it separates those investments in which Americans might have some control over the decisions taken by the enterprise from those in which they do not. Those foreign investments in which Americans own less than 10 percent are termed *portfolio* investments and are included in the securities entry. For foreign direct investments in the U.S. an arbitrary cutoff point of 25 percent is used instead of the 10 percent cutoff for U.S. investments. The next entries represent loans and bonds, broken down by maturity and liquidity classifications. The long-term versus short-term classification refers to assets with maturities of more versus less than one year. The further breakdown of short-term assets into liquid and nonliquid recognizes their immediate convertibility into cash at a predetermined value. For instance, a loan for nine months is short term, but not liquid, as it cannot be readily converted into cash. Demand and time deposits are examples of liquid short-term assets.

The foreign capital account is basically a recapitulation of the entries found in the U.S. capital accounts, with the obvious exception that the entries represent purchases and sales by foreigners. Transactions by foreign official agencies are shown separately, as they are often made for international monetary purposes only. *Foreign official agencies* include foreign central banks, government treasuries, and similar institutions. In 1972 foreign official agencies increased their dollar holdings by $10,265 million, which is a credit entry as it represents purchases of U.S. dollars by these agencies.

The U.S. Official-Reserves Account

The U.S. official-reserves account of Table 4-4 and Figure 4-4 records changes in the gold and convertible foreign currencies holdings by the Federal Reserve System and the U.S. Treasury as well as the transactions with the International Monetary Fund (IMF). In Chapter 11 we will have to say more about the role of official reserves. What is important for balance-of-payments purposes is that sales of gold and foreign currencies are treated just like other exports as far as the accounting procedures are concerned. A sale of gold or foreign currencies results in a demand for dollars and is therefore booked as a credit entry. A purchase of monetary gold or foreign currencies, which increases the U.S. reserve stock, is booked as a debit. For instance, in 1972 the U.S. sold $547 million of its gold stock for dollars, resulting in a credit entry of this amount.

Also the changes in the official U.S. position in the International Monetary Fund (see Chapter 11 for a more detailed treatment) are recorded here. Transactions in SDR's (*special drawing rights*) and the regular facilities of the

TABLE 4-4

THE U.S. OFFICIAL RESERVES ACCOUNT, 1972
(in millions of dollars)

	Credit	Debit
U.S. official reserves, net	742	
Transactions in U.S. official reserve assets:		
(decrease is credit)		
Gold	547	
Convertible currencies	35	
Reserve position in IMF	153	
SDR		703
Allocations of special drawing rights (SDR)	710	

Source: *Survey of Current Business*, March 1973.

IMF (the *reserve position*) are recorded separately. During 1972 United States SDR holdings increased by $703 million, while the U.S. used $153 million of its IMF reserve position (credit entry). Finally, there is a separate entry showing the periodic allocations of SDR's to member countries by the IMF. In 1972 the United States received $710 million of SDR's.

Errors and Omissions and the Accounting Balance

Because every economic transaction is supposed to be recorded twice in the balance-of-payments accounts in accordance with the principles of double-entry bookkeeping procedures, the credit and debit totals should be equal to each other. In that accounting sense the balance of payments will always be in balance. But due to the fact that in practice the data on credits and debits are reported through various channels, it is possible that certain errors and omissions occur. Therefore, a special errors-and-omissions entry (see Table 4-5) is made to insure that the accounts balance.

TABLE 4-5

THE ACCOUNTING BALANCE, 1972
(in millions of dollars)

	Credit	Debit
Goods-and-services account, net		4,219
Transfer account, net		3,764
Capital account, net	11,048	
U.S. official reserves, net	742	
Errors and omissions		3,807
Accounting Balance, net	11,790	11,790

Several reasons may be responsible for incorrect or incomplete accounting. First, there is the problem of the *timing* of the bookkeeping entries that can be handled according to three basic methods. We may record an international economic transaction as taking place at the time when the goods *physically* cross the border or when the service is rendered. An alternative manner of recording utilizes the *payments* date, while some people advocate the date when the *legal* obligation for delivery and payment is incurred.

For reasons of convenience it is customary to record real flows at the moment of the border crossing, while the accompanying financial flows are recorded at the moment the payment is made. If there are no time lags, this method of collecting the statistics on the two parts of a transaction separately does not give rise to any special problems. But if there are lags between the time the goods are shipped and the time payment is received, equality of credit and debit entries during any specified time period is not assured.

Second, many entries in the international accounts are only *estimates*, rather than precise figures. For instance, the travel data are arrived at by multiplying the total number of persons crossing the border as reported by the U.S. Immigration and Naturalization Service times the average amount spent by tourists as estimated from sample surveys taken.

Third, it is in the nature of *illegal* transactions to not be reported at all to the U.S. government. A person who engages in narcotics smuggling or is transferring funds from illicit gambling operations to a foreign country will hardly inform the U.S. government of his activities, and hence we do not find these data in the balance of payments.

SURPLUSES AND DEFICITS

We are now in a position to assemble the various accounts into a complete statement of the country's balance of payments. For analytical purposes it is convenient to present the various subaccounts of the balance of payments in a slightly different grouping. Table 4-6 shows the analytical presentation of the balance of payments. Various sub-balances are struck to aid in the analysis of the country's external position.

The goods-and-services account yields the first balance, referred to as the *balance of goods and services*. This balance shows the total trade in visibles and invisibles that takes place and is identical to the goods-and-services account of Table 4-1. The entries in this account also appear in the U.S. national product accounts, and the total shows the net export of goods and services by the United States. In 1972 the United States had a deficit of $4,219 million on the balance of goods and services.

If we add the transfer account, we obtain the *balance on current account*. The current account shows all transactions that do not give rise to a change

TABLE 4-6

THE U.S. BALANCE OF PAYMENTS, 1972
(in millions of dollars)

	(*Demand for $*) Credits	(*Supply of $*) Debits
Merchandise, adjusted, excluding military	48,840	55,656
Military	1,160	4,707
Travel	2,708	4,740
Passenger fares	694	1,555
Other transportation	3,732	3,422
Fees and royalties	670	138
Other private services	1,532	850
U.S. government miscellaneous services	413	808
Income on direct investments	10,293	692
Earnings on other private assets and liabilities	2,693	2,515
Earnings on U.S. government assets and liabilities	806	2,684
BALANCE ON GOODS AND SERVICES		*4,219*
U.S. government grants (excluding military)		2,208
U.S. government pensions and other transfers		572
Private remittances and other transfers, net		985
BALANCE ON CURRENT ACCOUNT		*7,983*
U.S. government loans		3,815
Repayments of U.S. government loans	2,071	
Other U.S. government loans	377	
Direct investment	322	3,339
Securities	4,502	619
Long-term capital	710	1,469
BASIC BALANCE		*9,243*
Short-term, nonliquid capital	139	1,773
Allocations of SDR	710	
Errors and omissions		3,807
NET LIQUIDITY BALANCE		*13,974*
Short-term, liquid capital	4,816	1,139
OFFICIAL SETTLEMENTS BALANCE		*10,297*
Foreign official agencies, net	10,265	
U.S. reserve assets:		
Gold	547	
Convertible currencies	35	
IMF: SDR		703
IMF: reserve position	153	
ACCOUNTING BALANCE		*0*

Source: *Survey of Current Business*, March 1973.

in the international investment position of the United States. The deficit on current account of $3,815 million means that the United States spent more than it earned on current expenditures in 1972.

If we add to the current account all long-term capital movements, we obtain the *basic balance*. This balance is often thought of as indicative of the long-term trends in the international accounts. Presumably, the items entering into the basic balance exhibit more stability than those that do not and may therefore constitute a fairly reliable guide for long-term policy planning. The U.S. basic balance showed a deficit of $ 9,243 million in 1972.

A few special items are used to transform the basic balance into the *net liquidity balance*. These items are not conveniently grouped elsewhere and include short-term nonliquid funds (like bank loans), special allocations of SDR's received, and the errors-and-omissions item discussed earlier. The net liquidity balance serves to measure the *potential* currency-market pressures that might arise against the U.S. dollar. It shows by how much the liquid asset position of the United States (the items below the line) has improved or deteriorated. We should note that U.S. and foreign short-term assets are treated symmetrically, an increase in the former improving the U.S. liquidity position and an increase in the latter leading to a deterioration of the U.S. liquidity position. The net liquidity balance is particularly important for countries like the United States, whose currency is widely held abroad. Such *key currency* countries have to worry about large amounts of liquid assets held abroad suddenly returning to the home country and thereby exercising strong pressures on the foreign exchange market. The net liquidity balance was in deficit by $ 13,974 million in 1972.

Finally we come to the *official settlements balance*. This measure shows more closely than any other figure the *current* pressure that exists in international currency markets. In terms of the supply-and-demand-for-dollars diagram, the official settlements balance is equal to the difference between the quantity of dollars supplied (debit entries in the accounts) and the quantity of dollars demanded (credits) at the exchange rate r_0. This is shown in the hypothetical example of Figure 4-5 by the distance AB.

If exchange rates were free to respond to market forces, the value of the dollar in international currency markets would fall to r_e. That is, the dollar would depreciate in value. If instead foreign and U.S. governmental agencies intervene in the international currency markets and purchase AB dollars in the currency market, they add their own demand to the market demand for dollars, shifting the demand curve from D to D' in Figure 4-5, and maintaining the exchange rate r_0.

Foreign official agencies bought $10,265 million in 1972, which they added to their international reserves. The U.S. monetary authorities purchased $32 million by selling an equivalent amount (net) of their own reserve

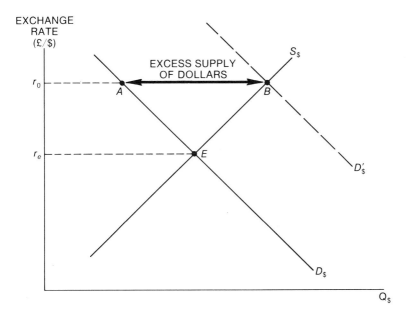

FIGURE 4-5

The Foreign Exchange Market with Government Intervention

assets. Total dollar purchases by foreign and U.S. monetary authorities amounted to $10,297 million. These interventions in the U.S. dollar market served to finance the deficit on the official settlements balance equal to that amount. On February 12, 1973 the U.S. government yielded to exchange market pressure and devalued the dollar by ten percent to bring its value closer to the free market equilibrium which would prevail in the absence of governmental intervention in the foreign exchange market. This was the second devaluation within fourteen months, following a devaluation by approximately 8.5 percent on December 18, 1971.

No single measure of the balance-of-payments deficit or surplus can give a complete answer to all questions about balance-of-payments equilibrium or disequilibrium. Which measure is the most appropriate depends on the particular analytical problem that has to be solved. The main balances discussed here give—in conjunction—an idea about the overall payments position of a country.

However, it is fair to say that the official-settlements balance is probably the most widely used concept in discussions of balance-of-payments equilibrium. We will focus on the official-settlements concept in the rest of the book. It should be noted, too, that for all those countries that do not have any short-term capital movements, the official-settlements balance and the net-liquidity balance are identical.

THE BALANCE OF INTERNATIONAL INDEBTEDNESS

We pointed out previously that the balance of payments is a flow statement of the transactions taking place during a given time period, usually a year. The total value of all international assets and liabilities of a country is reported in the *balance of international indebtedness*. The balance of international indebtedness is taken at a specific date, usually December 31 of a given year. Table 4-7 presents the balance of international indebtedness of the United States as of December 31, 1972, and Figure 4-6 shows the historical development of total U.S. assets and liabilities.

TABLE 4-7

THE INTERNATIONAL INVESTMENT POSITION OF THE UNITED STATES
DECEMBER 31, 1972
(in millions of dollars)

Assets			*Liabilities*
U.S. assets abroad	*199,285*	*148,650*	*U.S. liabilities to foreigners*
Nonliquid assets	**180,932**	**65,719**	**Nonliquid liabilities**
U.S. Government	36,146	1,796	U.S. Government
Direct investments abroad	94,031	14,363	Direct investments in U.S.
Foreign securities	24,893	38,558	U.S. securities
Other nonliquid assets	25,862	11,030	Other nonliquid liabilities
Liquid assets	**18,353**	**82,931**	**Liquid liabilities**
Private	5,202	21,389	To private foreigners
U.S. monetary reserves	13,151	61,542	To foreign official agencies
Gold	10,487		
SDR	1,958		
Currencies	241		
IMF gold tranche	465		
U.S. net investment position		*50,635*	

Source: *Survey of Current Business.*

There are three main sources of changes in the stock of foreign assets and liabilities: (1) capital flows reported in the balance of payments, (2) the reinvestment of foreign earnings, and (3) valuation adjustments due to price or exchange-rate changes. Let us briefly look at these changes.

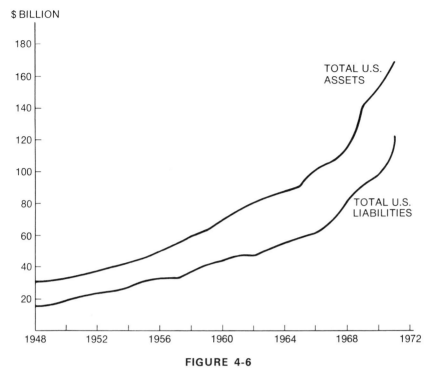

$ BILLION

FIGURE 4-6

The International Investment Position of the United States

NOTE: U.S. assets exclude international monetary reserve assets.
SOURCE: *Historical Statistics of the United States* and *Statistical Abstract of the United States* (various issues).

International capital movements have been discussed in the previous section. The debit entries in the balance of payments represent imports of foreign securities, "import" of ownership rights in foreign direct investments, and the like. Hence, debit entries in the capital account of the balance of payments result in increases in United States assets abroad (or a decrease in U.S. liabilities). The reverse applies to credit entries in the balance of payments, which result in increased liabilities to foreigners or decreased U.S. foreign assets in the balance of international indebtedness. In 1971, net recorded balance of payments outflows amounted to $11,048 million. If this change would represent the only factor influencing the U.S. international investment position, things would be relatively easy. Unfortunately, this is not the only change to be considered.

A second source of changes in the international investment position is due to the *reinvestment of foreign earnings*. Earnings accruing to foreign direct investments, stocks, and bonds are not necessarily transferred back to the home country immediately. Instead they may be reinvested in foreign assets and therefore not be recorded in the balance of payments, which measures only the flows that cross international borders. These amounts are not reported in the balance of payments, but they do change the balance of international indebtedness.

The third factor responsible for changes in the value of foreign assets and liabilities are *price and exchange-rate valuation* adjustments. If foreign exchange rates change, the value of all foreign assets in terms of U.S. dollars changes. Similarly, when prices of foreign stocks or bonds change, the value of these foreign assets in terms of dollars changes.

Comparing total U.S. international assets to liabilities at the end of 1972, we find that U.S. assets amounted to $199.3 billion, while liabilities to foreigners came to $148.7 billion. The result was a net international investment position or net international worth of $50.6 billion.

If we were to compare this balance sheet to that of a firm or bank, we would probably come to the conclusion that the firm is solvent. But the liquidity position of the United States is more precarious. In Table 4-8 we summarize the liquid and nonliquid assets and liabilities of the United States.

TABLE 4-8

THE LIQUIDITY POSITION OF THE UNITED STATES
AS OF DECEMBER 31, 1972
(in millions of dollars)

	Assets	Liabilities
Nonliquid	180,932	65,719
Liquid	18,353	82,931
Totals	199,285	148,650

Source: *Survey of Current Business.*

Although most U.S. assets abroad are in a nonliquid form, we find that U.S. liabilities tend to be liquid. Hence, if—and this is an unlikely event—foreigners would demand repayment of all liquid liabilities, the United States would be in a precarious position. To continue the previous analogy a bit further: the United States is somewhat like a bank, which has many liquid liabilities in the form of demand or savings deposits by its customers but does not have enough liquid assets at hand to satisfy every customer during a rush on the bank. But the bank has its funds invested in long-term assets, and the net worth position of the bank is considerable. Hence, the bank is solvent. It has also been argued that the U.S. performs international financial intermediation services for other countries by borrowing short-term funds abroad and relending these funds on a long-term basis to other countries.

SUGGESTED FURTHER READINGS

DEVLIN, DAVID, "The U.S. Balance of Payments: Revised Presentation," *Survey of Current Business* (June 1971).

HOST-MADSEN, POUL, "Asymmetries between Balance of Payments Surpluses and Deficits," *IMF Staff Papers* (July 1962).

KINDLEBERGER, CHARLES, "Equilibrium in the Balance of Payments," *Journal of Political Economy* (December 1969).

LEDERER, WALTER, "Measuring the U.S. Balance of Payments," in *Factors Affecting the U.S. Balance of Payments*, U.S. Congress, Joint Economic Committee, 1962.

MEADE, WALTER, *The Balance of Payments*, Chaps. 1 and 2. London: Oxford University Press, 1951.

MACHLUP, FRITZ, *International Payments, Debts, and Gold*, Part I. New York: Charles Scribner's Sons, 1964.

SCHOLL, RUSSELL, "The International Investment Position of the United States: Developments in 1971," *Survey of Current Business*, October 1972 (or any other October issue).

CHAPTER 5

Balance
and Instability

The purpose of this chapter is twofold: first, we will investigate in greater detail the meaning of external and internal balance, and second, we will attempt to say something about the disturbances to equilibrium that may arise.

In previous chapters we defined the *equilibrium exchange rate* as the exchange rate that prevails in international currency markets in the absence of governmental intervention. At that juncture we referred to absence of governmental intervention as noninterference in the currency market. But it is obvious that other governmental actions may also have an impact on the supply and demand for a country's currency. Rather obvious examples are the country's policy with regard to tariffs and quotas in international commodity markets, regulations imposed on international capital movements, and the like. In addition the country's fiscal and monetary policy actions will have an impact on the external sector. Often it is difficult indeed to determine whether a particular policy measure is adopted with domestic or foreign sector goals in mind. For instance, a more restrictive monetary policy may be intended to reduce domestic inflationary pressures, while it will at the same time make the country's goods more competitive in world markets and via a higher interest rate induce foreign capital to flow into the country. We are forced to conclude that the supply and demand curves for currency introduced in Chapter 3 are not independent of the fiscal and monetary policy actions taken by the country. External and internal balance are closely intertwined.

EXTERNAL-INTERNAL BALANCE MODELS

Let us start our discussion of the interrelationship between external and internal balance by analyzing some very simple models. The number of possible models that may be constructed is large, and we will be able to deal only with some of the most simple models.[1] The logical culmination of the discussion of external-internal balance models would be a full-blown econometric model that could explain the interrelationship between the domestic economy and the foreign sector, taking account of the linkages between the foreign sector and the foreign economies as well. Such a comprehensive econometric model does not yet exist, though first attempts have been made to hook up the various econometric models of the world's largest trading nations in project LINK.[2]

Figure 5-1 shows a simple *price-level* model. In the left part of the diagram we depict a country's aggregate supply and demand curves, showing the relationship between the domestic price level and the aggregate quantity

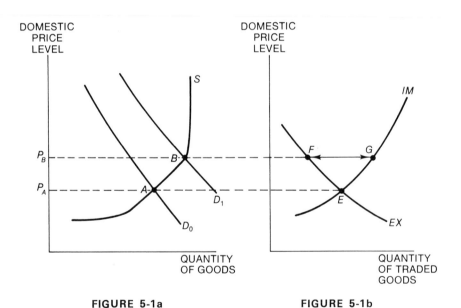

FIGURE 5-1a   FIGURE 5-1b

Internal and External Balance: A Price Model

[1]The reader unfamiliar with the basic concepts of the theory of economic policy is urged to refer to the Appendix.

[2]The results of Project LINK are being published in a series of working papers by the Economic Research Unit of the University of Pennsylvania.

of commodities supplied and demanded. The right diagram shows export and import quantities as a function of the domestic price level, assuming that the foreign price level and the exchange rate will remain constant. If the aggregate demand curve for goods and services is given by D_0, the domestic price level will be P_A. At that price level the volume of exports will be equal to the volume of imports as indicated by point E.

If we now assume that aggregate domestic demand increases to D_1—let us say, due to increased government spending—the domestic equilibrium will move to point B and the new domestic price level will be P_B. At that higher price level, the volume of imports will exceed that of exports by FG due to the decreased competitiveness of domestically produced goods. If the policy makers consider point B the desirable full-employment equilibrium, they have to accept a balance-of-payments deficit in the magnitude FG if we ignore induced shifts in the export and import curves. This simple model shows the interrelationship between domestic economic conditions and the foreign sector.

A model focusing attention on *national income* is shown in Figure 5-2. In the diagram we show national income Y along the horizontal axis and exports, imports, governmental spending and taxation, saving, and investment along the vertical axis. The export and import functions intersect

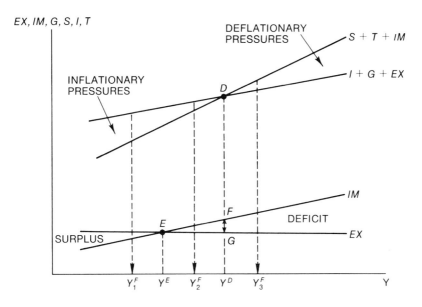

FIGURE 5-2

Internal and External Balance: An Income Model

at point E, indicating that the foreign sector will be in balance at the income level Y^E. At income levels higher than Y^E, the trade balance will show a deficit; at income levels lower than Y^E it will be in surplus.

The equilibrium level of national income is determined by the intersection of the two curves showing aggregate injections $(I + G + EX)$ into the income stream and the leakages $(S + T + IM)$ from it. At Y^D the economy as a whole is in equilibrium. Yet, at that income level, we find an external deficit equal to FG. Overall equilibrium and external balance do not coincide.

Problems will be compounded if we introduce the full-employment level of income as a desirable policy target. If the full-employment income target is Y_1^F, there will be inflationary pressures and a balance-of-trade surplus. One possible solution in this case is a currency appreciation that will eliminate the external surplus and reduce the domestic pressures of aggregate demand. Similarly, if the full-employment target is given by Y_3^F, a depreciation of the currency will help to restore both overall and external balance. Full-employment targets such as Y_2^F pose a policy problem in that a currency depreciation is called for to eliminate the external deficit, while an appreciation will ease the inflationary pressures. Clearly, one policy instrument alone is not sufficient to accomplish both conflicting objectives. To bring about both external and overall equilibrium at the full-employment level Y_2^F, we need two policy instruments. For instance, we might use a currency depreciation to eliminate the external deficit while at the same time lowering governmental spending (or increasing taxes) to reduce the inflationary pressures.

It may be instructive to show the two policy instruments and the external-balance–overall-balance conditions in a diagram. Sticking with our previous example, we show the exchange rate (£/$) along the vertical axis in Figure 5-3 and the size of the governmental budget deficit along the horizontal axis. *External balance* is defined as equality of exports and imports; *overall balance*, as equality of total injections $(G + I + EX)$ and total leakages $(S + T + IM)$. The various exchange-rate and budget-deficit situations under which external balance prevails are shown by the line EE. For instance, if we are initially in external balance at point B and run a budget deficit larger by BA, we will be in an external deficit situation because imports will increase along with the expansion of national income. We may restore external balance by devaluating the currency by AD, reaching point D on the line EE. All points to the right of EE are associated with balance-of-payments deficit; all points to the left of EE show situations of external surplus. Similarly, we may establish the line of overall balance OO. Starting at a point of balance, such as C, a decrease in the size of the budget deficit will lead to unemployment, denoted by point G. An exchange-rate devaluation of GH will serve as a stimulus to aggregate demand and return us to overall balance at H. All points to the left of the external balance line OO are points of underemployment (or deflationary pressures); all points to the right of it denote inflationary pressures.

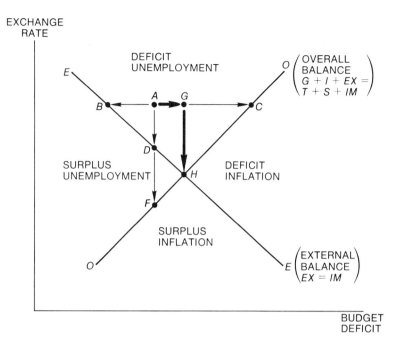

FIGURE 5-3

Two Targets—Two Instruments Model

Starting at a randomly selected point, such as A, it is possible to bring the economy either to external or overall balance by using just one policy instrument. For instance lowering the exchange rate by AD would restore external balance, but leave us in an overall situation of unemployment. A further depreciation by DF would bring about overall balance, and a balance-of-payments surplus. Similarly, a reduction of the budget deficit by AB would restore external balance, while an increase of AC would be called for to assure overall balance. Only a joint use of both policy tools will bring us from A to a point of both external and overall balance. Such a possibility is indicated by an increase in the budget deficit of AG and a lowering of the exchange rate by GH. The Appendix to the book discusses the use of various policy tools to attain multiple targets in greater detail.

STABILITY, BALANCE, AND EQUILIBRIUM

We will now turn to the second topic of this chapter: an analysis of the sources of international disturbances. For this analysis it is necessary to distinguish among stability, balance, and equilibrium. This distinction may apply to the individual subaccounts as well as the balance of payments as a whole. *Stability* refers to the absence of any fluctuations over time in an account. It implies that the overall value of the parameters under consideration remains constant over time. But even if the value of exports and imports remains constant, this does not imply that the trade account is also in equilibrium or balance. It is entirely possible that imports exceed exports consistently by a fixed margin, and that therefore the account is not in balance. All the while, stability is maintained in the sense that neither exports nor imports fluctuate. Such a situation is shown in Figure 5-4a, where imports exceed exports by a constant margin. No fluctuations are recorded, hence stability prevails.

On the other hand, an account may be in *balance* even if exports and imports fluctuate widely. For this to hold true, both exports and imports must fluctuate by the same absolute amount, thus completely offsetting the instability of one item against the other. Such a situation is shown in Figure 5-4b where balance is maintained in the presence of strong fluctuations.

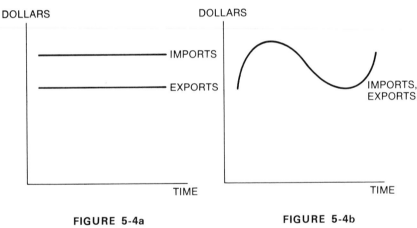

FIGURE 5-4a

Trade Account Stability
with Imbalance

FIGURE 5-4b

Trade Account Instability
with Balance

Furthermore, external balance does not require balance in each and every subaccount. All that is required is that the sum of the surpluses in the subaccounts is equal to the sum of the deficits. Thus it is entirely possible to attain and maintain external balance without achieving balance in a single subaccount.

The third concept, *equilibrium*, is generally associated with a free-market situation. For instance, the monetary authorities may interfere in the free market for currency by issuing quotas to exporters and importers. Balance may be attained in this fashion, but free-market forces would tend to restore equilibrium at a different exchange rate. Here we will be mainly concerned with the sources of instability in the external accounts.

Many policy makers aim for the target of overall external balance. *How* the balance is achieved is generally considered of secondary importance. Thus, policy makers may try to attain an even greater surplus in an account that can be influenced with relative ease in order to counterbalance a deficit in another account. However, by doing this, they create a new instability. It is apparent that the policy of trying to achieve external balance by the introduction of additional imbalances in selected subaccounts may magnify the instability problem on a global scale. This is so because the creation of a surplus in a subaccount in one country may lead to a corresponding deficit in the same account of this country's trading partners. If the latter country responds by using a similar policy, the first country will soon experience a deficit in some other subaccount, and the process may continue. Ever larger imbalances are likely to be generated by this process, and balance-of-payments problems may be aggravated.

A policy designed to achieve external balance has a greater probability of eventual success if it aims at stabilizing individual subaccounts. By eliminating the instability in a subaccount, the same subaccount will also become more stable in the partner countries, and thereby reduce the magnitude of their problems. But there is no reason why each and every subaccount should be in balance at all times. Instead for each subaccount a "normal" state of imbalance can be established, and the policy maker can try to influence each subaccount in order to minimize the fluctuations of each subaccount around the established level. For example, a country may run a consistent surplus on current account and a deficit on capital account while always maintaining *overall* balance in the external accounts.

THE COST OF INSTABILITY

We stated earlier that the ultimate goal of economic policy is to maximize the welfare of the residents of the nation. Let us assume that a country has attained a position such that welfare is being maximized. An instability that is introduced into the system through the international accounts may inflict certain costs on the country. These costs include adjustment costs to the disturbance, as well as costs of information, communication, decision making, and resource reallocation.

Welfare maximization may also require an imbalance in some individual subaccounts of the balance of payments. For instance, for underdeveloped countries it may be optimal to run a deficit on current account and to rely on external borrowing to bring about overall balance in the external accounts. Once an optimal state of the balance of payments is achieved, an instability introduced in the international accounts may represent a costly disturbance. In terms of the external balance it is immaterial whether a disturbance is introduced in the current, capital, or transfer accounts. Each one of these disturbances can have the same effect on the external accounts. For instance under a system of flexible exchange rates the reaction of the exchange rate to a $1 million disturbance originating in the current or capital account will be identical.

It follows that if one subaccount is characterized by greater instability and thereby imposes greater adjustment costs on the economy, benefits accruing from that particular subaccount should also be commensurately larger.

Sources of Instability

We will deal here with aggregate instability in the currency market and the effects on the balance of payments. We will be concerned with changes in the supply and demand for dollars that call either for adjustment in the external accounts or for financing the imbalance by the use of reserves. It will be convenient to deal separately with the causes of disturbances on the supply and demand side of the currency market. For simplicity we will refer only to the trade account, although the analysis applies to the other accounts as well.

1. *Demand for Currency*   The demand for dollars is a result of the export of U.S. commodities. Foreigners have to pay dollars to acquire these goods. In Figure 5-5 we show the market for U.S. export commodities. The

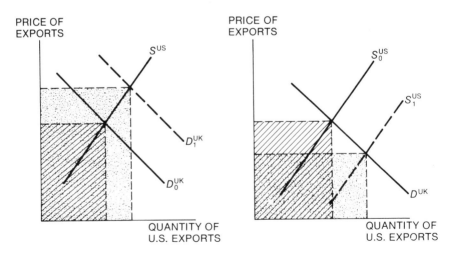

FIGURE 5-5a

Shift in Foreign Demand
for U.S. Exports

FIGURE 5-5b

Shift in U.S. Supply
of Exports

analysis of a shift in the demand for U.S. export goods is straightforward and may best be illustrated by the customary two-country example. Figure 5-5a shows an increase in the foreign excess demand for U.S. commodities D_0^{UK} to D_1^{UK} and given an unchanged U.S. export supply function, S^{US}, the volume of dollars demanded will increase. Assuming no other changes, the demand curve in the market for foreign currency (Figure 5-6) will shift to the right as well. If we start with initial equilibrium in the dollar market, as indicated by point E in Figure 5-6, a U.S. balance-of-payments surplus equal to AB will result at the old exchange rate.

The demand for U.S. dollars may also be affected by changes in the supply of U.S. export goods S^{US} shown in Figure 5-5b. The change in the total quantity of dollars demanded depends on the elasticity of the foreign demand curve for U.S. exports. If the demand curve D^{UK} (Figure 5-5b) is of unitary elasticity throughout, no shifts in supply will change the total dollar value of U.S. exports, and will therefore leave the demand curve for U.S. dollars in Figure 5-6 unchanged. The greater the departure of the elasticity of demand for U.S. exports from unity, the larger the expected effects on the dollar demand due to changes in the supply curve of U.S. exports.

A country that supplies only a small share of the total world market of a certain commodity will find that the demand curve for its products is highly elastic. Hence, shifts in its own export supply curve will result in large changes in the demand for its own currency. Curiously, the same result holds true for a country that is the sole supplier of a commodity which is in inelastic demand in world markets. It will also experience strong fluctuations

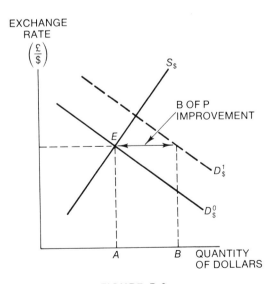

FIGURE 5-6

Effect of Change in U.S. Exports on Dollar Demand

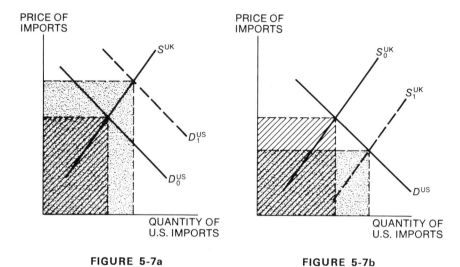

FIGURE 5-7a

Shift in U.S. Demand for Imports

FIGURE 5-7b

Shift in Foreign Supply of U.S. Imports

in export earnings as a result of changes in supply conditions. In Chapter 2 we estimated the demand elasticity for total U.S. exports to be about 1.5. Hence, we might expect that rightward shifts in the U.S. export supply curve will result in some increase in dollar earnings from exports.

2. *Supply of Currency* The analysis of the effect of supply and demand shifts in the underlying commodities markets on the supply curve for dollars is similar. Increases in the demand for imports by the U.S., as shown in Figure 5-7a will lead to an increase in the supply of dollars. *Ceteris paribus* the supply curve for dollars in Figure 5-8 will shift to the right, resulting in a deterioration of the U.S. balance of payments by MN.

The effects of shifts in the foreign supply curve S^{UK} of U.S. imports goods are again more complicated. Figure 5-7b shows an increase in the foreign supply function from S_0^{UK} to S_1^{UK}. The effect on the volume of dollars sold by U.S. importers in the currency market depends on the elasticity of U.S. demand for import goods. If the elasticity is equal to unity, no changes in the dollar volume will result. The greater the divergence from unity, the larger the shift of the dollar supply function shown in Figure 5-8. The empirical estimates cited in Chapter 2 give an elasticity of U.S. demand for imports equal to 1.03, and if this estimate is reliable, little if any balance-of-payments changes are to be expected as a result of shifts in foreign supply curves.

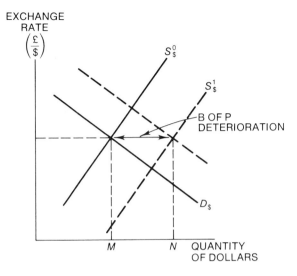

FIGURE 5-8

Effect of Change in U.S. Imports on Dollar Supply

Subaccount Instability

We will now turn to an investigation of the relative size of the imbalances introduced in the various accounts of the balance of payments.

There have been several studies[3] that investigated the instability of the foreign trade sector. These studies were mainly concerned with the causes of instability in the export sector alone. Here we will concentrate on identifying the individual accounts where the instabilities occurred.

One of the crucial decisions to be made is the level of aggregation of subaccounts to be utilized. The operationally useful categories are those over which the policy maker has some degree of control. As a general rule, the policy tools available to the national authorities can affect only the larger subgroupings employed in the balance of payments in a predictable fashion. A classification scheme that tends to approximate this condition is the one employed by the International Monetary Fund in its summary statement of the balance of payments. Table 5-1 lists the various IMF subaccounts employed. In addition, the unweighted world averages of individual countries' instability indices for each of the subaccounts are shown. Although the

[3]See especially Joseph Coppock, *International Economic Instability*, (New York: McGraw-Hill Book Company, 1962), and Benton Massell, "Export Concentration and Export Earnings," *American Economic Review*, March 1964.

TABLE 5-1

INSTABILITY INDICES
(unweighted world averages of individual countries' ratios of trend corrected
standard errors of estimate to mean, 1956–64)

Exports	.11
Imports	.25
Freight, insurance	.45
Investment income	1.24
Private transfers and other services	.99
Government transfers	1.04
Private long-term capital	1.85
Government long-term capital	2.24
Private short-term capital	8.66
Government short-term capital	5.37
Errors and omissions	4.51

Source: H. Robert Heller, "Instability in the International Accounts," *Weltwirtschaftliches Archiv*, Band 104, Heft 1, 1970, p. 120–26.

absolute levels of the instability indices are not too meaningful, their relative magnitudes identify those accounts that show the relatively greatest instability. Current-account items exhibit by far the greatest stability, showing an average country instability index of .11 for exports, .25 for imports, and .45 for freight and insurance. The indices for investment income and transfer payments are slightly larger. Next in line are the long-term capital movements. The most unstable accounts are the short-term capital accounts. Private short-term capital transactions contributed a relatively large degree of international instability as evidenced by an instability index of 8.66.

The index for governmental short-term capital movements was 5.37. However, we are not justified in concluding that the monetary authorities actually contributed to international instability to the extent implied by the high value of the instability index. For the most part, the actions of the monetary authorities are market interventions designed to equate the aggregate supply and demand of the country's currency at the agreed-upon par value. Hence, the instability index of the governmental monetary transactions is more a reflection of the overall imbalance that existed and had to be financed by the monetary authorities.

These findings indicate that the capital accounts are subject to a considerably greater degree of instability than the transfer account, which in turn is less stable than the current account. This shows that most of the instability in the overall balance of payments is due to capital movements and especially to short-term capital. To the extent that total external balance is the target, we can conclude that capital account disturbances contributed more to balance-of-payments problems than the relatively more stable transfer and current accounts.

SUGGESTED FURTHER READINGS

COPPOCK, JOSEPH, *International Economic Instability*, New York: McGraw-Hill Book Company, 1962.

HELLER, H. ROBERT, "Sources of Instability in the International Accounts, "*Weltwirtschaftliches Archiv* (1970).

MACBEAN, ALASDAIR, *Export Instability and Economic Development*, Chaps. 1–3. Cambridge, Mass.: Harvard University Press, 1966.

MASSELL, BENTON, "Export Concentration and Export Earnings," *American Economic Review* (March 1964).

MASSELL, BENTON, "Export Instability and Economic Structure," *American Economic Review* (September 1970).

SCITOVSKY, TIBOR, *Money and the Balance of Payments*, Chaps. 9–11. Chicago: Rand McNally & Company, 1969.

CHAPTER 6

Exchange-Rate Adjustment

In the previous chapter we discussed the sources of international disequilibrium. In this and the following chapters we will analyze various adjustments that may help the country to return to international equilibrium. In this chapter we are concerned with exchange-rate adjustments. The following chapter deals with price-level adjustments, Chapter 8 with income adjustments, and Chapter 10 with adjustment via international capital movements. Chapter 11 presents an alternative to adjustment, namely the financing of an existing disequilibrium by the use of international reserves. Before we launch our discussion of exchange-rate changes as a means of bringing about balance-of-payments equilibrium, we must draw an important distinction between adjustment *mechanisms* and adjustment *policies*—a distinction that is important to the various methods of balance-of-payments adjustment to be discussed in the subsequent chapters.

ADJUSTMENT MECHANISMS AND POLICIES

Most economic variables, such as prices, incomes, quantities traded, and the like may either be determined by free market forces or be set by administrative fiat. That is, prices may either respond to fluctuations in supply and demand or be determined by administrative action. The same applies to exchange rates, interest rates, incomes, trade volume, and a host of other variables.

Consequently, we find two different types of adjustment: adjustment via free-market forces, which constitutes an *automatic mechanism* of adjustment; or adjustment as a result of administrative *policy* decisions.

Exchange rates may be determined by market forces, in which case we speak of *flexible, floating,* or *fluctuating* exchange rates. In this case, only the forces of free market supply and demand will determine the exchange rate. No official governmental transactions for the purpose of influencing the exchange rate take place. The government will, however, still conduct its usual international transactions at the going market exchange rate. Flexible exchange rates have been utilized during various periods: the United States had freely fluctuating rates between the Civil War and 1879; most European countries had them between the end of World War I and the mid-twenties; Canada used them from 1950 until 1962 and has had them since June 1, 1970; 48 countries, including the United States, Japan, and a large number of European countries abandoned fixed exchange rates between August 15, 1971, and the Smithsonian Agreement of December 18, 1971. At the beginning of March 1973 (following the dollar devaluation of February 12, 1973) Canada, India, Italy, Japan, Switzerland, the United Kingdom, as well as several smaller countries had flexible exchange rates. In most of these countries, however, the monetary authorities still intervened occasionally in the foreign exchange market: it was a "dirty" float.

If exchange rates are freely fluctuating in response to market conditions, an excess supply of a currency will result in a downward pressure on the value of that currency in foreign exchange markets. The resulting depreciation of the exchange rate will tend to restore equilibrium in the exchange market. These market forces are set into motion automatically, without action on behalf of any governmental authorities. Hence we speak of freely flexible exchange rates as an *automatic adjustment mechanism.*

In contrast to exchange-rate adjustment via automatic market forces, we may have administratively *fixed* or *pegged* exchange rates. In that case, all exchange transactions have to take place at an exchange rate that is determined by the monetary authorities. The governmental authorities can fix the exchange rate either by appropriate legislation that makes all exchange transactions at other exchange rates illegal within the territory subject to its jurisdiction, or it may intervene in the free market by standing ready to buy or sell its own currency against gold, Special Drawing Rights, or some *intervention currency* at a fixed rate. A monetary authority that intervenes in international currency markets in order to maintain fixed exchange rates vis-à-vis the rest of the world generally does so by operating in the market of its own currency and some specified intervention currency. Intervention is carried out by buying and selling intervention currencies, such as the U.S. dollar, the British pound, or the French franc. It is also possible to stabilize the value of a currency in terms of other commodities, such as gold, by intervening in the gold market.[1] A country that maintains a fixed exchange rate

---

[1]We will deal in detail with the international reserve assets used for intervention purposes in Chapter 11.

by legislation or intervention in currency markets may change its exchange rate by *administrative policy* decision. In that case any currency appreciation or depreciation takes an explicit policy decision.

Most countries of the world employ a hybrid system, where the value of their own currency is allowed to fluctuate freely within a narrow band around a *central exchange rate*, or par value, which is established in terms of the intervention currency. The band within which exchange rates are free to fluctuate is generally 1 percent above or below the central rate, according to the rules of the International Monetary Fund. However, several nations use a wider band of 2.25 percent since December 1971. Small exchange-rate changes within the band are typically the result of free-market forces. However, for exchange-rate changes exceeding the band, administrative action is required. Hence, the present international monetary system employs exchange-rate changes both in its automatic and its policy-directed form. In this chapter we will generally ignore whether a particular exchange-rate change is due to free-market forces or administrative policies. We will concentrate on the *effects* of any exchange-rate change on the balance of payments and the terms of trade.

EXCHANGE-RATE CHANGES
AND THE CURRENCY MARKET

We will start with an investigation of the effect of exchange-rate changes on the international currency market. This will be followed by an analysis of the effect of exchange-rate changes on the market for import and export commodities.

International currency markets were introduced in Chapter 3, where we dealt with the determination of foreign exchange rates. In this chapter we will analyze the effect of a change in the exchange rate on the quantity of currency supplied and demanded in international currency markets. We will also establish the relationship between the exchange rate and the size of the balance-of-payments disequilibrium.

We define the *balance of payments* as the difference between the quantity of dollars demanded and supplied in international currency markets. If the quantity of dollars demanded exceeds the quantity of dollars supplied, we have a balance-of-payments *surplus*. If the reverse is true, we have a balance-of-payments deficit. This definition is analogous to the official-settlements concept introduced in Chapter 4.

$$B = Q_\$^D - Q_\$^S \tag{6.1}$$

Changes in the balance of payments can be decomposed into changes in the quantity of dollars demanded and supplied. Writing *d* for small changes we get:

$$dB = dQ_\$^D - dQ_\$^S \qquad (6.2)$$

Relating the changes in the balance of payments to changes in the exchange rate r, we obtain:

$$\frac{dB}{dr} = \frac{dQ_\$^D}{dr} - \frac{dQ_\$^S}{dr} \qquad (6.3)$$

We have to show now how the balance of payments dB changes in response to exchange-rate changes dr. Looking at Figure 6-1 we see that an increase in the dollar exchange rate from r_0 to r_1 will be accompanied by an increase in the quantity of dollars supplied and a decrease in the quantity of dollars demanded. Hence, $dQ_\$^S/dr$ will be positive and $dQ_\$^D/dr$ will be negative. Consequently, according to equation 6.3 an increase in the exchange rate (appreciation of the dollar) will result in a deterioration of the balance of payments reckoned in terms of U.S. dollars. Conversely, a dollar depreciation will improve the U.S. balance of payments.

Clearly, these conclusions depend on the precise shape of the supply

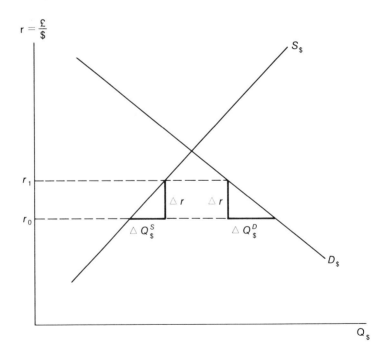

FIGURE 6-1

Effect of an Exchange Rate Change on Currency Supply and Demand

and demand curves for dollars shown in Figure 6-1. We established in Chapter 3 that the demand curve for dollars will always slope downward to the right, but the supply curve may be characterized by backward bending segments as illustrated in Figure 6-2.

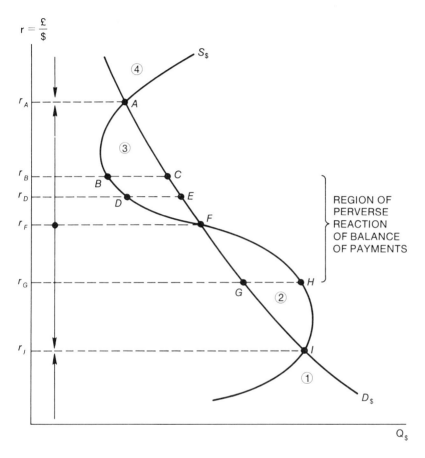

FIGURE 6-2

Normal and Perverse Reaction of the
Balance of Payments to Exchange Rate Changes

Consider the exchange rate r_D in Figure 6-2. At this exchange rate the quantity of dollars demanded exceeds the quantity supplied, and hence the U.S. balance of payments is in surplus by *DE*. A normal reaction to this excess demand for dollars is an increase in its relative price (£/$↑), that is, an appreciation of the dollar or a depreciation of the pound. But we see from the diagram that the dollar appreciation will *widen* the gap between quantity demanded and supplied and therefore increase the U.S. balance-of-payments surplus. This perverse reaction of the balance of payments in the neighborhood of the *unstable* equilibrium point F prevails until the exchange rate r_B is reached. After that the surplus will tend to decrease, until it is finally eliminated at the exchange rate r_A. Further appreciation of the dollar beyond r_A leads to an excess supply of dollars, with a natural tendency for the exchange rate to move to the equilibrium at A. A is a stable equilibrium point, characterized by the condition that a small disturbance of the exchange rate will set market forces into motion that will return the exchange rate to its equilibrium point A. Similarly, point I is a stable equilibrium point.

To sum up: in regions (1) and (3) of Figure 6-2 the U.S. balance of payments is in surplus and in regions (2) and (4) it is in deficit. The balance of payments will react normally to exchange-rate changes in the region above r_B and below r_G. In the region between the exchange rates r_B and r_G the balance of payments will react perversely.

The size of the balance-of-payments improvement or deterioration may also be stated in terms of elasticities. For this purpose we expand equation 6.3 as follows:

$$\frac{dB}{dr} = \frac{dQ_\$^D}{dr} \cdot \frac{r}{Q_\$^D} \cdot \frac{Q_\$^D}{r} - \frac{dQ_\$^S}{dr} \cdot \frac{r}{Q_\$^S} \cdot \frac{Q_\$^S}{r} \tag{6.4}$$

Substituting the expressions for the elasticities

$$\eta_\$ = -\frac{dQ_\$^D}{dr} \cdot \frac{r}{Q_\$^D} \tag{6.5}$$

and

$$\epsilon_\$ = \frac{dQ_\$^S}{dr} \cdot \frac{r}{Q_\$^S} \tag{6.6}$$

we obtain

$$\frac{dB}{dr} = \frac{-\eta_\$ Q_\$^D - \epsilon_\$ Q_\$^S}{r} \tag{6.7}$$

That is, the balance of payments will react normally if the numerator is negative:

$$-\eta_\$ Q_\$^D - \epsilon_\$ Q_\$^S < 0 \tag{6.8}$$

or

$$-\eta_\$ \frac{Q_\$^D}{Q_\$^S} < \epsilon_\$ \tag{6.9}$$

The likelihood of a normal reaction increases: (1) the more the supply elasticity $\epsilon_\$$ exceeds the demand elasticity $\eta_\$$; and (2) the more the quantity of dollars supplied $Q_\$^S$ exceeds the quantity of dollars demanded $Q_\$^D$. At points of balance-of-payments equilibrium where $Q_\$^S = Q_\$^S$, the simplified condition

$$-\eta_\$ < \epsilon_\$ \qquad (6.10)$$

holds.

This condition for a normal reaction of the balance of payments corresponds to inequality 3.5, which stated the condition for a stable equilibrium. We may conclude that in the neighborhood of a *stable* equilibrium point the balance of payments will react *normally* to exchange-rate changes, and in the vicinity of an *unstable* equilibrium point the balance of payments will react *perversely*.

Let us note that this is a sufficient but not a necessary condition. The balance of payments may also react perversely to exchange-rate changes if there is no unstable equilibrium point present. Figure 6-3 illustrates this case. In the region between the exchange rates r_A and r_B the balance of payments will react perversely. That is, an exchange-rate depreciation of the dollar from r_A and r_B will result in an increase in the size of the deficit. But the equilibrium point E is a stable equilibrium point.

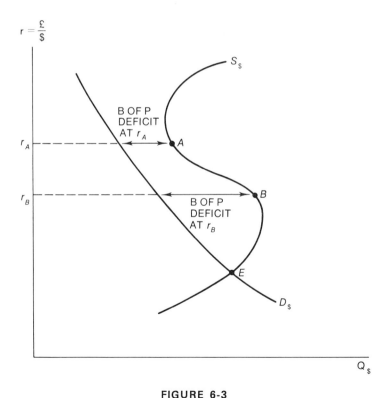

FIGURE 6-3

Perverse Reaction of the Balance of Payments
in the Absence of an Unstable Equilibrium

Let us add a final note of caution. As pointed out previously, we use the ratio £/$ as the exchange rate in our calculations. In other writings we frequently encounter the exchange rate $/£ instead. Naturally, this implies that inequalities and/or signs will be reversed. Let us mention again that all our calculations are in terms of the home currency ($).

EXCHANGE-RATE CHANGES
AND THE COMMODITY MARKETS

In the previous section we analyzed the effects of exchange-rate changes on international currency markets. But currencies are—for our present purposes—used solely to buy or sell commodities. To understand the effects of currency devaluation or appreciation on these commodity markets, it is necessary to establish in detail the link between commodity and currency markets. In Chapter 2 we introduced the supply and demand curves for commodities, and in Chapter 3 we analyzed the international markets for currencies. Here we will investigate primarily the linkage between the two.

In Chapter 2 we derived the excess supply and demand curves for a commodity from the domestic supply and demand curves for that good. Let us assume that the United States exports commodity X and that the United Kingdom exports commodity Y. Figure 6-4a shows the international market for commodity X, and Figure 6-5a the international market for

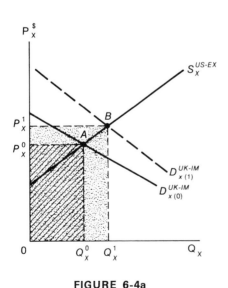

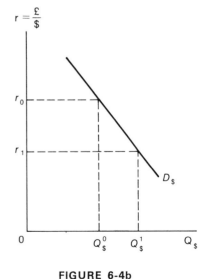

FIGURE 6-4a

The U.S. Export Market

FIGURE 6-4b

The Demand for Dollars

commodity Y. Initial equilibrium prices are labelled P^0 and equilibrium quantities traded between the two countries Q^0.

Our next step is the derivation of the supply and demand curves for currency from the excess supply and demand curves for the commodities. The supply and demand curves for currency show how the quantity of currency supplied and demanded in international currency markets varies with the exchange rate. Hence we have to investigate how total revenues from exports and imports are influenced by changes in the exchange rate. Let us assume that the U.K. curves are arrived at by using the exchange rate r_0 to convert pounds into dollars. Naturally, the U.S. curves are already stated in dollars.

The total number of dollars demanded by U.K. residents to pay for their imports of good X is equal to the price of the imports P_X^0 times the quantity purchased Q_X^0. The crosshatched area $0P_X^0AQ_X^0$ in Figure 6-4a shows the total demand for dollars at the exchange rate r_0. This information is now transferred to Figure 6-4b, where we show the quantity of dollars demanded $Q_\$^0$ at the exchange rate r_0. One point on the demand curve for dollars is thereby defined. Let us note that the crosshatched area $0P_X^0AQ_X^0$ in Figure 6-4a corresponds to the distance $0Q_\$^0$ in Figure 6-4b.

Now let us assume that the dollar depreciates in relation to the pound. That is, it now takes fewer pounds to buy each dollar. The exchange rate falls to r_1.

The dollar devaluation means that U.S. export goods will now have a lower price in the United Kingdom. We recall that the price in pounds is the product of the exchange rate and the dollar price: $P_£ = r \cdot P_\$$. As there is no reason to assume that the U.K. excess demand curve for good X *in terms of pounds* has shifted, a fall in the exchange rate means that U.K. residents are now willing to pay a higher dollar price for each quantity of X demanded: the excess demand curve for X has shifted upwards by the same percentage as the exchange-rate change. The increase in effective dollar demand for X at the exchange rate r_1 is shown by the new dashed demand curve $D_{X(1)}^{UK-IM}$. The dollar price of commodity X increases to P_X^1, the quantity traded to Q_X^1, and the quantity of dollars demanded to $0P_X^1BQ_X^1$. This new quantity of dollars demanded at the exchange rate r_1 is shown in Figure 6-4b by $0Q_\$^1$. A second point of the demand curve for dollars $D_\$$ is thereby defined. By letting the exchange rate vary further, the entire dollar demand curve $D_\$$ may be derived.

The U.S. excess supply curve for X will not shift.[2] Americans are still willing to sell the same quantity of X at the same dollar prices.

---

[2]This statement does not hold true if we permit international trade in inputs as well. Under these circumstances it is possible that the dollar devaluation will result in higher prices for inputs imported from the U.K., and therefore an upward shift of the supply curve is possible. We will neglect this possibility in our two-commodity model.

In a similar fashion we may obtain the supply curve of dollars for the U.S. import commodity Y. Again we let the dollar depreciate from r_0 to r_1. The U.K. excess supply curve in Figure 6-5a will shift upward from $S_{Y(0)}^{UK\text{-}EX}$ to $S_{Y(1)}^{UK\text{-}EX}$ due to the dollar devaluation. As the dollar is worth less in terms of pounds, only a smaller quantity of good Y will be supplied by the U.K. at the same dollar price. Or, to get the U.K. suppliers to deliver the same quantity, a higher dollar price has to be paid. The U.K. supply curve shifts upward after the dollar devaluation from r_0 to r_1. The dollar supply changes from $0P_Y^0 C Q_Y^0$ to $0P_Y^1 D Q_Y^1$.

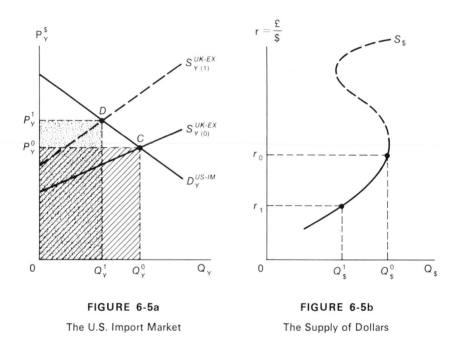

FIGURE 6-5a   FIGURE 6-5b

The U.S. Import Market   The Supply of Dollars

From Figures 6-4 and 6-5 it is obvious that the effect of an exchange-rate change on the balance of payments[3] depends on four important elasticities: the elasticities of demand for imports, δ_{IM}, and exports, δ_{EX}, and the elasticities of supply of imports, σ_{IM}, and exports, σ_{EX}. In addition, the volume of exports and imports are of significance. Equation 6.11 shows the precise relationship between exchange rate changes, dr, and the balance of payments. The equation itself is derived in the appendix to this chapter.

$$\frac{dB}{dr} = -\left[EX_0 \frac{\delta_{EX}(\sigma_{EX} + 1)}{\delta_{EX} + \sigma_{EX}} + IM_0 \frac{\sigma_{IM}(\delta_{IM} - 1)}{\delta_{IM} + \sigma_{IM}} \right] \qquad (6.11)$$

[3]Strictly speaking, we deal here only with the balance of trade. When we use the term balance of payments, we implicitly assume that all the other subaccounts are in balance.

Let us note that the right-hand term is prefaced by a minus sign. Consequently, a devaluation, which will result in a negative change in the exchange rate, will result in a positive change in the balance of payments, B, if the term in brackets is positive. We will investigate the reaction of the balance of payments in four extreme cases, each time assuming that we start with an initial situation where trade is balanced, that is, where $EX_0 = IM_0$.

All Supply Elasticities Are Infinite $(\sigma_{EX}\sigma_{IM} = \infty)$

This popular assumption states that all buyers face given prices in international markets. Output can be expanded at constant cost. Under these conditions equation 6.11 simplifies to

$$\frac{dB}{dr} = -EX_0(\delta_{EX} + \delta_{IM} - 1) \qquad (6.12)$$

This equation shows that the reaction of the balance of payments is influenced only by the trade volume and the two countries' demand elasticities for our export and import commodities.

The precondition for a normal reaction of the balance of payments subsequent to an exchange-rate change is that the term in brackets is positive. That is, a devaluation will improve the balance of payments if $\delta_{EX} + \delta_{IM} > 1$. This condition is generally referred to as the *Marshall-Lerner Condition* and states that the demand elasticities have to sum to more than one for a normal reaction of the balance of payments to exchange-rate changes.

Figure 6-6 illustrates this case. In Figure 6-6a we show the U.S. export market and the effects of a dollar devaluation on the U.K. demand for U.S. goods. The dashed demand curve D^1_{EX} shows the U.K. demand for U.S. exports after the dollar devaluation. The export volume will increase at constant prices and hence improve the balance of payments. In Figure 6-6b the import market is depicted. Devaluation shifts the supply curve of foreign imports S_{IM} upwards to S^1_{IM}. The higher price paid for imports after devaluation worsens the balance of payments; the lower import volume contributes to an improvement. The net effect depends on the elasticity of demand. As equation 6.12 shows, the balance of payments will improve if the sum of the export and import demand elasticities is larger than one.

All Supply Elasticities Are Zero $(\sigma_{EX} = \sigma_{IM} = 0)$

In this "pure rent" case, equation 6.11 reduces to

$$\frac{dB}{dr} = -EX_0(+1) = -EX_0 \qquad (6.13)$$

The balance of payments will always improve after a devaluation— a normal reaction. As can be seen from Figure 6-7, the entire improvement is due to an increase in export prices received. The improvement is proportional to the amount of devaluation. There is no change in import prices or quantities.

All Demand Elasticities Are Infinite ($\delta_{EX} = \delta_{IM} = \infty$)

If both countries are willing to purchase any quantity offered for sale at the going price, equation 6.11 reduces to

$$\frac{dB}{dr} = -EX_0(\sigma_{EX} + \sigma_{IM} + 1) \tag{6.14}$$

As long as the commodity supply curves have their familiar upward to the right slope, this condition is always fulfilled. Figure 6-8 illustrates the case graphically for a devaluation, showing that exports as well as imports contribute to the balance-of-payments improvement.

All Demand Elasticities Are Zero ($\delta_{EX} = \delta_{IM} = 0$)

This is the case if the goods are extreme necessities that cannot be done without. For demand elasticities that approach zero, equation 6.11 becomes

$$\frac{dB}{dr} = -EX_0(-1) = +EX_0 \tag{6.15}$$

and consequently we will find that a devaluation will lead to a deterioration in the balance of payments in proportion to the size of the devaluation. We have a perverse reaction due to the fact that import prices (Figure 6-9b) increase while the import volume stays constant. In the export market there is no change at all. Hence, the balance of payments will deteriorate after a devaluation.

So far, we have assumed that initially exports are equal to imports. However, in most practical discussions of the effects of exchange-rate changes we start out with a situation of *initial imbalance*. In case of a balance-of-payments deficit, $IM > EX$, and for a balance of payments surplus, $IM < EX$. Focusing attention on the deficit case, we see that in equation 6.11 EX_0 is smaller than IM_0. As the export term will always work in the proper direction (provided demand curves for commodities slope downward to the right and supply curves upward to the right), the chances for a normal reaction are smaller than in the case of initial surplus.

The previous discussion clearly establishes the need for empirical estimates of the relevant elasticities. If the two demand elasticities add to at least unity, a normal reaction of the balance of payments is assured regardless of the size of the supply elasticities. Hence we will concentrate our discussion of empirical magnitudes on demand elasticities.

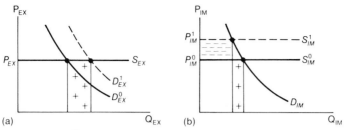

FIGURE 6-6 Infinite Supply Elasticities

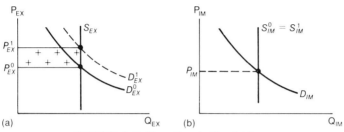

FIGURE 6-7 Zero Supply Elasticities

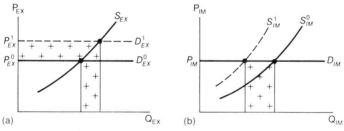

FIGURE 6-8 Infinite Demand Elasticities

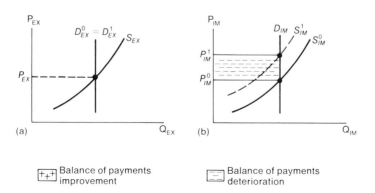

| | Balance of payments improvement | | Balance of payments deterioration |

FIGURE 6-9 Zero Demand Elasticities

ELASTICITY OPTIMISM AND PESSIMISM

Already in Chapter 2 we presented relevant empirical data on the size of the elasticities. Here we may note a few additional theoretical points:

1. It is a familiar proposition that the elasticity of the supply and demand curves increases with the time period that is allowed for adjustment to the new prices. That is, the longer the time horizon over which the elasticities are measured, the higher the elasticities are likely to be. The main reason for this phenomenon is that it takes time for the new information to be disseminated throughout the economy and for economic units to adjust their behavior accordingly.

Thus it is quite likely that in the very short run—say a period of less than two or three months—the elasticities are quite low and that a devaluation will *initially* lead to a deterioration of the balance of payments. But as time passes, the elasticities are likely to increase and the balance of payments will consequently improve.

2. We must recognize that the elasticities of the excess demand and supply curves that are relevant for our analysis are larger than the elasticities for the domestic supply and demand curves upon which they are based. This is due to the fact that the excess demand curve shows not only the demand response to the price change but incorporates also the supply response. A similar argument holds for the excess supply curves. In Figure 6-10a we show the domestic supply and demand curves and in Figure 6-10b the excess demand curve calculated as the horizontal difference between the domestic supply and demand curves. If, for instance, prices drop from $3 to $2, the domestic quantity demanded increases from 10 to 12 units. The domestic

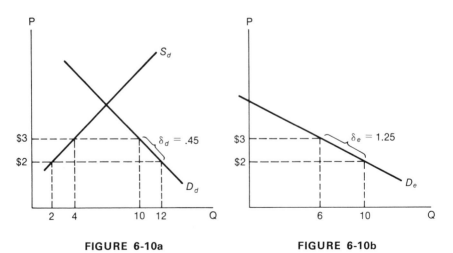

FIGURE 6-10a   FIGURE 6-10b

price elasticity of demand δ_d in that range if therewith

$$\delta_d = \frac{\Delta Q/Q}{\Delta P/P} = \frac{2/11}{1/2.5} = 0.45 \qquad (6.16)$$

The price elasticity of the excess demand curve δ_e of Figure 6-10b in the same price range is more than twice as large.

$$\delta_e = \frac{\Delta Q/Q}{\Delta P/P} = \frac{4/8}{1/2.5} = 1.25 \qquad (6.17)$$

As long as the supply curve is not negatively sloped it is always true that $\delta_e > \delta_d$.

Problems of empirical estimation of the relevant elasticities were already discussed in detail in Chapter 2. There is no reason to repeat this discussion here. Let us note, however, that in all cases (Tables 2-1, 2-2, and 2-3) where the elasticity coefficients were significant at the 95 percent level, the sum of the demand elasticities for exports and imports was greater than one—thereby fulfilling the basic condition for a normal reaction of the balance of payments. The elasticity pessimism that characterized the early post-World War II literature seems therefore not to be of quite as much relevance in recent years.

Estimates

We may combine some of the empirical information presented in Chapter 2 with the theoretical analysis establishing the link between exchange-rate changes and the balance of payments to estimate the effects of the December 1971 change in the U.S. exchange rates vis-à-vis other countries by 8.57 percent.

Equation 6.11 shows the effects of an exchange-rate change dr on the balance of payments:

$$dB = -\left[EX_0 \frac{\delta_{EX}(\sigma_{EX} + 1)}{\delta_{EX} + \sigma_{EX}} + IM_0 \frac{\sigma_{IM}(\delta_{IM} - 1)}{\delta_{IM} + \sigma_{IM}} \right] dr \qquad (6.11)$$

In Chapter 2 we presented evidence on the relevant U.S. supply and demand elasticities. We recall that $\delta_{EX} = 1.51$; $\delta_{IM} = 1.03$; $\sigma_{EX} = 10.0$; and $\sigma_{IM} = 8.5$. In 1971 total exports amounted to \$42.8 billion, while imports were \$45.5 billion. Inserting these data into equation 6.11 we predict that the U.S. trade balance will improve by \$5.3 billion as a result of the devaluation.

Of course, this estimate assumes that other things remain constant—which they will not—and that there are no further repercussions on incomes and prices. Accounts other than the trade account are neglected. Also, the estimate does not tell us how long it will take until the balance of payments will improve by that amount. This process may take anywhere from two to four years. However, men of affairs may not be willing to wait for such a long time period. When it turned out in February 1973 that the trade balance of the United States for the year 1972 showed a deficit of approximately 6.8 billion dollars, speculative movements of currency forced another devaluation of the U.S. dollar on February 12, 1973, this time by 10 percent.

In both instances, some countries did adjust their exchange rates at the same time as the dollar was devalued, and therefore the true change in exchange rates vis-à-vis all other currencies was different from the magnitude of the official dollar devaluations. It is very difficult indeed to sort out all the feedback effects set into motion by the dollar devaluations. Given the world wide importance of the U.S. dollar, only a global econometric model can give a precise answer as to the effect of the dollar devaluations.

TERMS OF TRADE EFFECTS

We have discussed so far the effects of an exchange-rate change on the balance of payments of a country. Now we will investigate other effects that are likely to be associated with an exchange-rate change. We begin with a discussion of the effects of an exchange-rate change on the international terms of trade. To simplify matters we will concentrate our attention on the effects of a devaluation.

The *terms of trade* denote the exchange ratio of exports to imports. We define

$$TOT = \frac{P_{EX}}{P_{IM}} \tag{6.18}$$

The terms of trade are said to improve if this ratio increases, because it enables the country to purchase a larger quantity of imports for a given volume of exports. Or, what amounts to saying the same thing, the higher the price received per unit of exports compared to the price paid for unit of imports, the better off the country will be.

It is important to state the price of both exports and imports in terms of the same currency, here dollars. In the typical case, depicted in Figures 6-4 and 6-5, both export and import prices increase. Whether the terms of trade will improve or deteriorate due to a devaluation is therefore open to question and will have to be investigated in detail.

The algebraic derivation of the formula showing the effects of an exchange-rate change on the terms of trade is carried out in the appendix to this chapter. Using our previous definition of the supply and demand elasticities of commodities, the formula showing the effects of exchange-rate changes dr on the terms of trade $dTOT$ reads:

$$\frac{dTOT}{dr} = \frac{\sigma_{IM}\sigma_{EX} - \delta_{IM}\delta_{EX}}{(\delta_{EX} + \sigma_{EX})(\delta_{IM} + \sigma_{IM})} \tag{6.19}$$

We see that the terms of trade will deteriorate $(-)$ subsequent to an exchange-rate devaluation $(-)$ if the right-hand term is positive, that is, if

$$\sigma_{EX}\sigma_{IM} > \delta_{EX}\delta_{IM} \tag{6.20}$$

We may illustrate this proposition by the four special cases shown in Figures 6-6 through 6-9.

Supply Elasticities Approaching Infinity (Figure 6-6)

Export prices P_{EX} stay constant, while import prices P_{IM} increase. The terms of trade $TOT = P_{EX}/P_{IM}$ will deteriorate. This is clear as the inequality 6.20 will be fulfilled as long as we have infinite supply elasticities and only finite demand elasticities.

Supply Elasticities Equal to Zero (Figure 6-7)

Export prices rise (Figure 6-7a) while import prices are unchanged. Inequality 6.20 is not fulfilled as the left-hand term is zero. The terms of trade will always improve.

Demand Elasticities Approaching Infinity (Figure 6-8)

Export prices rise, import prices stay constant, and inequality 6.20 is not fulfilled as the right-hand term is infinity. The terms of trade improve.

Demand Elasticities Equal to Zero (Figure 6-9)

Export prices remain unchanged, import prices increase, and consequently the terms of trade deteriorate. This is verified by the inequality 6.20, which is fulfilled as the right-hand term is zero.

We may conclude that the chances for a deterioration of the terms of trade after a devaluation increase as supply elasticities become larger and demand elasticities smaller. Under these circumstances a devaluation is costly to the country because of the deterioration in the terms of trade.

Using the same empirical estimates as previously utilized in connection with the balance-of-payments effects of the 1971 U.S. dollar devaluation, we estimate that the U.S. terms of trade deteriorate by .76 percent for every percentage point of devaluation. The 8.57 percent devaluation of 1971 would therefore lead to a worsening of the U.S. terms of trade by 6.52 percent. The 10 percent devaluation of 1973 would lead to a further deterioration of the terms of trade by 7.6 percent.

THE TERMS-OF-TRADE COSTS
OF A DEVALUATION

A country that lowers the value of its own currency in terms of foreign currencies by devaluation may worsen its own terms of trade as we have just demonstrated. In this section we will attempt to define the terms-of-trade *cost* of a devaluation in more precise terms. This discussion will also be of importance in later chapters when we will compare the costs of devaluation to the costs associated with alternative adjustment policies.

As a standard of reference we will use a balance-of-payments deficit of one dollar, and we will attempt to answer the question: "How much does it cost the country to eliminate the one-dollar deficit by devaluation?"

For convenience, we will subdivide the question into two components: we will determine by how much we have to devalue to eliminate the one-dollar deficit (dr/dB) and then calculate the effect of this devaluation on the terms of trade ($dTOT/dr$). Because this latter expression tells us how much the terms of trade change per unit, we have to multiply by the trade volume EX_0 to get the total cost of the exchange-rate change.

$$\frac{dTOT}{dB} = EX_0 \cdot \frac{dTOT}{dr} \cdot \frac{dr}{dB} \tag{6.21}$$

We may now insert equation 6.19 and the inverse of equation 6.11—assuming initially balanced trade—into this equation:

$$\frac{dTOT}{dB} = EX_0 \cdot \frac{(\sigma_{EX}\sigma_{IM} - \delta_{EX}\delta_{IM})}{(\delta_{EX} + \sigma_{EX})(\delta_{IM} + \sigma_{IM})}$$
$$\cdot \frac{-(\delta_{EX} + \sigma_{EX})(\delta_{IM} + \sigma_{IM})}{EX_0[\delta_{EX}(\sigma_{EX} + 1)(\delta_{IM} + \sigma_{IM}) + \sigma_{IM}(\delta_{IM} - 1)(\delta_{EX} + \sigma_{EX})]} \tag{6.22}$$

Collecting terms we obtain:

$$\frac{dTOT}{dB} = -\frac{\sigma_{EX}\sigma_{IM} - \delta_{EX}\delta_{IM}}{\delta_{IM}\delta_{EX}\sigma_{IM} + \delta_{IM}\delta_{EX}\sigma_{EX} + \delta_{IM}\sigma_{IM}\sigma_{EX} + \delta_{EX}\sigma_{IM}\sigma_{EX} + \delta_{IM}\delta_{EX} - \sigma_{IM}\sigma_{EX}} \tag{6.23}$$

This is clearly a formidable expression to evaluate. However, we should note that for empirical calculations we need only the four supply and demand elasticities of exports and imports. Estimates of supply elasticities cannot be obtained for most countries but are presumably very high. We will therefore assume as a first approximation that they approach infinity. For this case where $\sigma_{IM} \longrightarrow \infty$ and $\sigma_{EX} \longrightarrow \infty$, equation 6.23 simplifies[4] to:

$$\frac{dTOT}{dB} = -\frac{1}{\delta_{IM} + \delta_{EX} - 1} \qquad (6.24)$$

Equation 6.24 is an upper limit to equation 6.23. Empirical estimates of the demand elasticities are given in Table 2-1, and in Table 6-1 we calculate the terms-of-trade cost of an exchange-rate adjustment to a one-dollar deficit.

TABLE 6-1

COSTS OF DEVALUATION

Country	$-\delta_{IM}$ (1)	$-\delta_{EX}$ (2)	Cost of Adjustment to $1 Deficit (According to Equation 6.24) (3)
Canada	1.46	.59	0.95
Denmark	1.66	.56	0.82
Germany	.24	1.25	2.04
Italy	.13	1.12	4.00
Japan	1.72	.80	1.92
South Africa	.52	2.41	0.52
Sweden	.79	.47	3.85
Switzerland	.84	.58	2.38
United Kingdom	.21	1.24	2.22
United States	1.03	1.51	0.64

Source: Table 2-1 and equation 6.24.

According to these data, Italy and Sweden are faced with exchange-rate adjustment costs in the neighborhood of four dollars for each one-dollar deficit to be corrected. Other countries, such as Canada, Denmark, South Africa, and the United States, have considerably lower (less than one dollar per one-dollar deficit) adjustment costs. While we do not yet know anything

[4]We expand 6.23 by dividing by $\sigma_{EX}\sigma_{IM}$; then set $\sigma_{EX} = \sigma_{IM} = \infty$

$$\frac{dTOT}{dB} = -\frac{\dfrac{\sigma_{EX}\sigma_{IM}}{\sigma_{EX}\sigma_{IM}} - \dfrac{\delta_{EX}\delta_{IM}}{\sigma_{EX}\sigma_{IM}}}{\dfrac{\delta_{IM}\delta_{EX}\sigma_{IM}}{\sigma_{EX}\sigma_{IM}} + \dfrac{\delta_{IM}\delta_{EX}\sigma_{EX}}{\sigma_{EX}\sigma_{IM}} + \dfrac{\delta_{IM}\sigma_{IM}\sigma_{EX}}{\sigma_{EX}\sigma_{IM}} + \dfrac{\delta_{EX}\sigma_{IM}\sigma_{EX}}{\sigma_{EX}\sigma_{IM}} + \dfrac{\delta_{EX}\delta_{IM}}{\sigma_{EX}\sigma_{IM}} - \dfrac{\sigma_{EX}\sigma_{IM}}{\sigma_{EX}\sigma_{IM}}}$$

$$= -\frac{1-0}{0+0+\delta_{IM}+\delta_{EX}+0-1} = -\frac{1}{\delta_{EX}+\delta_{IM}-1}$$

about the costs associated with alternative adjustments, we might already conjecture that the high-adjustment-cost countries will be more reluctant than the low-adjustment-cost countries to use exchange-rate changes as a means of eliminating balance-of-payments deficits. On the other hand, these same countries will also be blessed by considerable gains to be made in case of exchange-rate appreciations to remedy balance-of-payments surplus positions.

PRICE, INCOME,
AND DISTRIBUTION EFFECTS

So far we have neglected completely any additional price, income, and income-distribution effects of a devaluation. Their complete analysis is extremely complex and calls for the use of a greatly expanded model. Many of the price and income effects of a devaluation can best be discussed with the analytical tools to be developed in Chapters 7 (price adjustment) and 8 (income adjustment). Without going into all possible ramifications of price and income effects, we will deal here briefly with the main tendencies that might be expected.

Price Effects

The primary effect of a devaluation is to increase the price (in terms of the home currency) of imported foreign commodities in the home country. To the extent that import prices enter into domestic price indices, we might expect these price indices to increase. Let us note that this effect in itself is a once-and-for-all change.

Secondary effects that are set into motion by this increase in the price level are difficult to evaluate. We will merely list the most important of these secondary effects:

1. As prices of imported inputs increase, cost of production goes up and hence other product prices may rise as well.

2. As the price level increases, labor unions may press for higher wages, thereby spreading the inflation to other sectors of the economy. Consequently increases in export prices will contribute to a deterioration of the balance of payments.

3. As the price level goes up, people will find that their real cash balances decrease, and in the attempt to restore their real balance positions they will spend less, thereby reducing inflationary pressures. But they will also bid up interest rates. Much will depend on the monetary policy pursued. If the money supply remains constant, the higher interest rates may lead to a decrease in investment activity. If we consider international capital move-

ments (to be discussed in Chapter 10), we might expect that the higher interest rates will attract foreign capital, thereby improving the balance of payments.

Income Effects

Income effects are greatly different under conditions of full employment and underemployment of resources. Under conditions of full employment a devaluation will succeed in increasing exports only if less is produced for domestic purposes. There will be no change in the aggregate employment and resource utilization level. Only the allocation pattern will change, that is, the division between domestic and export goods produced will be altered.

In the underemployment case we have a variety of income effects that may influence the trade balance.

1. The increased exports after a devaluation constitute an injection into the income stream that will set into motion a multiple income expansion (to be discussed in Chapter 8). As income expands, imports are likely to expand as well. This secondary effect has a negative influence on the balance of payments. That is, the real income changes will lessen the improvement in the balance of payments to be expected due to the devaluation.

2. The real balance effect discussed previously will lead to an attempt to build up cash balances after a devaluation and therefore result in less spending. National income will fall and the balance of payments will improve.

3. If the devaluation leads to a deterioration of the terms of trade, real income will fall. But the residents may attempt to react to this deterioration by spending money previously accumulated (dishoarding) and thereby increase income and imports, contributing to a deterioration of the balance of payments.

4. It is also possible that people, when faced with higher prices, will react by saving more and consuming less. This substitution effect will lower incomes and improve the balance of payments. It is clear that the sum total of these effects is highly uncertain.

Income-Distribution Effects

A devaluation is bound to change the income shares going to different economic groups. To the extent that different economic groups have different propensities to spend on imports, the trade balance will be affected.

1. It is a well-known proposition in international trade theory that the factor of production that is used intensively in an expanding industry will gain while the other factor will loose. If, for instance, the devaluation leads to increased exports and if exports are capital intensive, then it follows that owners of capital will gain. If their marginal propensity to import is greater

than that of labor, imports will rise, leading to a secondary deterioration in the balance of payments. Opposite conclusions obtain if the marginal propensity to import of labor-income recipients is greater or if exports are labor intensive.

2. Wages may lag behind prices, and as a country devalues, profits may therefore at first increase. Again everything will depend on the relevant marginal propensities to import. If they are greater for holders of capital than for wage earners, the balance of payments will deteriorate. Secondary effects may be due to a stimulation of investment brought about by the profit increase.

From this cursory examination it is clear that the final result of a devaluation will be uncertain, and that much will depend on a multitude of variables. Of particular importance in assessing the likely effects of a devaluation is the present state of the economy undergoing the exchange-rate change. In particular, the question whether the economy is in an underemployment, full-employment, and/or inflationary situation is of importance.

APPENDIX TO CHAPTER 6

The Effects of an Exchange-Rate Change on the Balance of Payments and the Terms of Trade

In this appendix we will derive algebraically equations 6.11 and 6.19, which show the effects of exchange-rate changes on the balance of payments and the terms of trade.

We define the demand δ and supply σ elasticities for commodities as usual:

$$\delta = -\frac{dQ^D \cdot P}{Q^D \cdot dP} \tag{6A.1}$$

$$\sigma = \frac{dQ^S \cdot P}{Q^S \cdot dP} \tag{6A.2}$$

For convenience purposes we will use a special type of demand and supply curves, which are characterized by a constant elasticity throughout their range. This specification will permit us to neglect differences between point and arc elasticities in our discussion. The format used is:

$$Q = CP^\epsilon \tag{6A.3}$$

where C is a constant and ϵ the elasticity. Let us show briefly that such a curve actually has the elasticity ϵ. First we take the derivative with respect to P:

$$\frac{dQ}{dP} = \epsilon C P^{\epsilon - 1} \qquad (6A.4)$$

Using the definition of the supply elasticity we obtain:

$$\sigma = \frac{P}{Q^S} \cdot \frac{dQ^S}{dP} = \frac{P}{CP^\epsilon} \epsilon C P^{\epsilon-1} = \epsilon \qquad \text{Q.E.D.} \quad (6A.5)$$

Let us define all quantity units in such a way that all prices, including the exchange rate, are initially equal to one.

Using the constant elasticity form we can define now the relevant supply and demand functions in terms of U.S. dollars, where EX is the U.S. export good, IM the U.S. import good, EX_0 and IM_0 are constants, and r is the £/$ exchange rate.

$Q_{EX}^S = EX_0 \cdot (P_{EX})^{\sigma_{EX}}$ (U.S. export supply curve) $\Big\}$ Export   (6A.6)

$Q_{EX}^D = EX_0 \cdot (P_{EX} \cdot r)^{-\delta_{EX}}$ (U.K. import demand curve for U.S. exports)   market   (6A.7)

$Q_{IM}^S = IM_0 \cdot (P_{IM} \cdot r)^{\sigma_{IM}}$ (U.K. export supply curve of U.S. imports) $\Big\}$ Import   (6A.8)

$Q_{IM}^D = IM_0 \cdot (P_{IM})^{-\delta_{IM}}$ (U.S. import demand curve)   market   (6A.9)

Let us start with the market for the U.S. export good described in equations 6A.6 and 6A.7. We transform them into logarithmic form:

$$\log Q_{EX}^S = \log EX_0 + \sigma_{EX} \log P_{EX} \qquad (6A.10)$$

$$\log Q_{EX}^D = \log EX_0 - \delta_{EX} \log P_{EX} - \delta_{EX} \log r \qquad (6A.11)$$

In equilibrium $Q_{EX}^S = Q_{EX}^D$ and therefore

$$\log EX_0 + \sigma_{EX} \log P_{EX} + \delta_{EX} \log P_{EX} = \log EX_0 - \delta_{EX} \log r \quad (6A.12)$$

$$(\delta_{EX} + \sigma_{EX}) \log P_{EX} = -\delta_{EX} \log r \qquad (6A.13)$$

Taking antilogs we obtain the equilibrium price for X:

$$P_{EX} = r^{-\delta_{EX}/(\delta_{EX} + \sigma_{EX})} \qquad (6A.14)$$

We substitute equation 6A.14 into 6A.6 to get the equilibrium quantity

$$Q_{EX} = EX_0 r^{-\delta_{EX}\sigma_{EX}/(\delta_{EX} + \sigma_{EX})} \qquad (6A.15)$$

In a similar manner we use 6A.8 and 6A.9 to derive the equilibrium price and quantity for the U.S. import market:

$$\log Q_{IM}^S = \log IM_0 + \sigma_{IM} \log P_{IM} + \sigma_{IM} \log r \qquad (6A.16)$$

$$\log Q_{IM}^D = \log IM_0 - \delta_{IM} \log P_{IM} \qquad (6A.17)$$

In equilibrium $Q_{IM}^D = Q_{IM}^S$ and consequently

$$\log IM_0 - \delta_{IM} \log P_{IM} = \log IM_0 + \sigma_{IM} \log P_{IM} + \sigma_{IM} \log r \qquad (6A.18)$$

$$-(\delta_{IM} + \sigma_{IM}) \log P_{IM} = \sigma_{IM} \log r \qquad (6A.19)$$

$$P_{IM} = r^{-\sigma_{IM}/(\delta_{IM} + \sigma_{IM})} \qquad (6A.20)$$

$$Q_{IM} = IM_0 r^{\delta_{IM}\sigma_{IM}/(\delta_{IM} + \sigma_{IM})} \qquad (6A.21)$$

We now know the equilibrium prices and quantities of both the export and the import commodity as a function of the exchange rate. Now we will investigate how the balance of payments (exports minus imports) is affected by changes in the exchange rate.

The U.S. balance of payments in terms of dollars is defined as:

$$B_{US}^\$ = Q_{EX}^\$ \cdot P_{EX}^\$ - Q_{IM}^\$ \cdot P_{IM}^\$ \qquad (6A.22)$$

That is, the U.S. balance of payments is the difference between export receipts and expenditures on imports. We may substitute equations 6A.14, 6A.15, 6A.20, and 6A.21 into equation 6A.22 to obtain the balance-of-payments reaction to exchange-rate changes in elasticity form.

$$B_{US}^\$ = EX_0 r^{(-\delta_{EX}\sigma_{EX} - \delta_{EX})/(\delta_{EX} + \sigma_{EX})} - IM_0 r^{(\delta_{IM}\sigma_{IM} - \sigma_{IM})/(\delta_{IM} + \sigma_{IM})} \qquad (6A.23)$$

or

$$B_{US}^\$ = EX_0 r^{-\delta_{EX}(\sigma_{EX} + 1)/(\delta_{EX} + \sigma_{EX})} - IM_0 r^{\sigma_{IM}(\delta_{IM} - 1)/(\delta_{IM} + \sigma_{IM})} \qquad (6A.24)$$

Differentiating with respect to r and remembering that $r = 1$ by assumption, we obtain the final equation:

$$\frac{dB_{US}^\$}{dr} = -\left[EX_0 \frac{\delta_{EX}(\sigma_{EX} + 1)}{\delta_{EX} + \sigma_{EX}} + IM_0 \frac{\sigma_{IM}(\delta_{IM} - 1)}{\delta_{IM} + \sigma_{IM}} \right] \qquad (6A.25)$$

This equation appears in the text as equation 6.11 and shows the effect of an exchange-rate change dr on the balance of payments dB in terms of the *home* currency. A similar expression may be derived for the effects of an exchange-rate change on the balance of payments in terms of *foreign* currency. This expression reads:

$$\frac{dB_{US}^\pounds}{dr} = -\left[EX_0 \frac{\sigma_{EX}(\delta_{EX} - 1)}{\delta_{EX} + \sigma_{EX}} + IM_0 \frac{\delta_{IM}(\sigma_{IM} + 1)}{\delta_{IM} + \sigma_{IM}} \right] \qquad (6A.26)$$

We will use 6A.25 throughout this book.

Next we will derive the formula for the effect of a change in the exchange rate on the terms of trade. The terms of trade *TOT* are defined as:

$$TOT = \frac{P_{EX}}{P_{IM}} \qquad (6A.27)$$

We substitute 6A.14 and 6A.20 into this equation:

$$TOT = \frac{P_{EX}}{P_{IM}} = r^{-\delta_{EX}/(\delta_{EX}+\sigma_{EX})+\sigma_{IM}/(\delta_{IM}+\sigma_{IM})}$$

$$= r^{(\sigma_{EX}\sigma_{IM}-\delta_{EX}\delta_{IM})/(\delta_{EX}+\sigma_{EX})(\delta_{IM}+\sigma_{IM})} \tag{6A.28}$$

We differentiate with respect to r while remembering that initially $r = 1$ by definition and obtain:

$$\frac{dTOT}{dr} = \frac{\sigma_{EX}\sigma_{IM} - \delta_{EX}\delta_{IM}}{(\delta_{EX} + \sigma_{EX})(\delta_{IM} + \sigma_{IM})} \tag{6A.29}$$

This equation shows the effect of an exchange-rate change on the terms of trade and appears in the main text as equation 6.19.

SUGGESTED FURTHER READINGS

ALEXANDER, SIDNEY S., "The Effects of a Devaluation on the Trade Balance," *IMF Staff Papers* (April 1952). Reprinted in R. CAVES and H. G. JOHNSON, eds., *AEA Readings in International Economics*. Homewood, Ill.: Richard D. Irwin, Inc., 1968.

ALLEN, WILLIAM R., "A Note on the Money Income Effects of Devaluation," *Kyklos* (Fasc. 3, 1956).

HABERLER, GOTTFRIED, "The Market for Foreign Exchange and the Stability of the Balance of Payments," *Kyklos* (Fasc. 3, 1949).

HARBERGER, ARNOLD, "Currency Depreciation, Income, and the Balance of Trade," *Journal of Political Economy* (February 1950). Reprinted in R. N. COOPER, ed., *International Finance*. Baltimore: Penguin Books, 1969; and in R. CAVES and H. G. JOHNSON, eds., *AEA Readings in International Economics*. Homewood, Ill.: Richard D. Irwin, Inc., 1968.

JONES, RONALD W., "Depreciation and the Dampening Effects of Income Changes," *Review of Economics and Statistics* (February 1960).

LAURSEN, S., and L. A. METZLER, "Flexible Exchange Rates and the Theory of Employment," *Review of Economics and Statistics* (November 1950).

MACHLUP, FRITZ, "The Terms of Trade Effects of Devaluation upon Real Income and the Balance of Trade," *Kyklos* (Fasc. 4, 1956).

SMITH, WARREN, "Effects of Exchange Rate Adjustments on the Standard of Living," *American Economic Review* (December 1954).

SOHMEN, EGON, *Flexible Exchange Rates*, rev. ed. Chicago: University of Chicago Press, 1969.

TSIANG, S. C., "The Role of Money in Trade-Balance Stability: Synthesis of the Elasticity and Absorption Approaches," *American Economic Review* (December 1961). Reprinted in R. CAVES and H. G. JOHNSON, eds., *AEA Readings in International Economics*. Homewood, Ill.: Richard D. Irwin Inc., 1968; and in R. N. COOPER, ed., *International Finance*. Baltimore: Penguin Books, 1969.

CHAPTER 7

Price Adjustment

In the last chapter we discussed in detail exchange-rate adjustment as a means of reestablishing external equilibrium. Exchange-rate adjustment is one type of a *switching policy* that alters the relative prices between domestic and foreign goods and thereby brings about a new balance in the international accounts. An alternative switching policy might rely on changing the relative price level between the countries that experience the external imbalance and by this altering the relative attractiveness of foreign and domestic goods in the countries. In this chapter we will deal with the international price-adjustment mechanism in the trade account of the balance of payments. We will assume that the transfer and capital accounts are unaffected. Also, exchange rates and real output levels are assumed to be constant. That is, we deal with a full-employment economy, in which all adjustment takes place via price-level changes.

THE EFFECTS OF A PRICE CHANGE
ON THE BALANCE OF TRADE

We will start with an analysis of the effects of a price change on the balance of trade. For purposes of simplicity, we will assume that the United States experiences a demand-pull inflation, and that the price level in the trading partners (exemplified by the United Kingdom) remains constant.

Figure 7-1 shows the market for the U.S. export good X. In Figure 7-1a we show the U.S. domestic market for the commodity. The supply curve S_X^{US} is drawn perfectly inelastic in the relevant range to show the prevailing

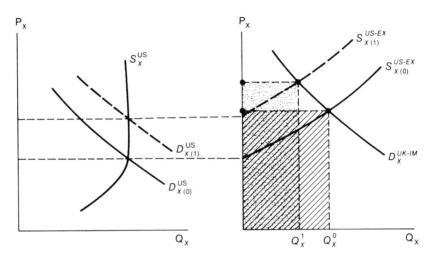

FIGURE 7-1a   **FIGURE 7-1b**

The Domestic and International Market for the U.S. Export Good

full-employment conditions. We assume that the demand curve for the export good shifts upward from $D_{X(0)}^{US}$ to $D_{X(1)}^{US}$. In Figure 7-1b we show the U.S. excess supply curve $S_{X(0)}^{US-EX}$, and the foreign demand curve D_X^{UK-IM} for commodity X. After the shift of the U.S. demand curve to the right, and the consequent leftward shift of the U.S. export supply curve from $S_{X(0)}^{US-EX}$ to $S_{X(1)}^{US-EX}$, the international price of the U.S. export good will increase from P_X^0 to P_X^1 (unless we face a perfectly elastic foreign demand curve). The quantity exported will decrease from Q_X^0 to Q_X^1 (unless the foreign demand curve is perfectly inelastic). Total U.S. export earnings will decrease if the foreign demand curve for the U.S. export good is elastic, stay constant if it is of unitary elasticity, and increase if it is inelastic.

Turning to the U.S. import commodity Y in Figure 7-2, we also see that the demand for the import good increases as a result of the general increase in demand in the U.S. (Figure 7-2a). Hence, the excess demand curve showing the U.S. import demand in international markets shifts from $D_{Y(0)}^{US-IM}$ to $D_{Y(1)}^{US-IM}$ (Figure 7-2b). The foreign supply curve S_Y^{UK-EX} is assumed to remain unchanged. Consequently, the price of the U.S. import commodity Y increases from P_Y^0 to P_Y^1. But let us note that this price increase is less than the price increase that would have resulted from the U.S. demand shift in the absence of international trade (from P_Y^0 to P_Y^2). Foreign trade mitigates the price increases due to the increase in demand. The quantity imported increases from Q_Y^0 to Q_Y^1, resulting in a certain increase in spending on imports.

The recent U.S. inflation offers a good example of the effects of inflation on import expenditures and export earnings. Figure 7-3a shows the

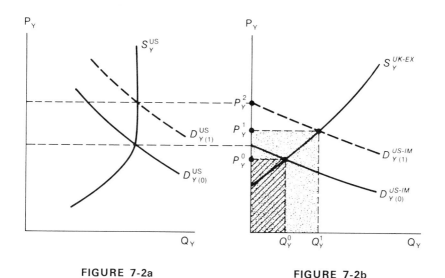

FIGURE 7-2a   **FIGURE 7-2b**

The Domestic and International Market for the U.S. Import Good

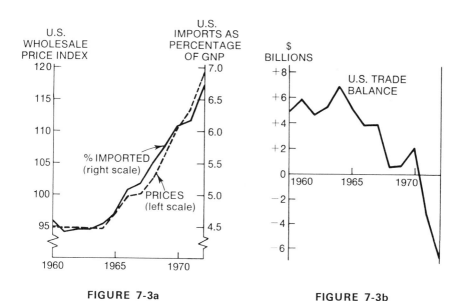

FIGURE 7-3a

The Relationship Between
U.S. Prices and Imports

SOURCE: Council of Economic Advisors,
Economic Report of the President, Washington, 1972.

FIGURE 7-3b

The U.S. Trade Balance

SOURCE: Federal Reserve Bank of St. Louis,
April 17, 1972.

development of the U.S. wholesale prices and imports as percentage of GNP. The graph shows that after virtually no change in the wholesale price index in the period 1960–64 the United States experienced a significant degree of inflation. As a result imports as a percentage of GNP, which were virtually constant at 4.5 percent during 1960–64, increased sharply in the second half of the sixties.

Figure 7-3b shows the development of the trade balance (exports minus imports, excluding services) during the same period. While the U.S. trade balance showed an average surplus of $5.4 billion during 1960–64, a process of steady deterioration started in 1965, leading to a deficit of $2.7 billion in 1971 and $6.8 billion in 1972.

MONETARY REPERCUSSIONS OF A
BALANCE-OF-PAYMENTS DISEQUILIBRIUM

We will now turn our attention to possible monetary changes introduced by an external disequilibrium. We will concentrate on the case of a U.S. balance-of-payments deficit and trace the monetary changes that are likely to occur.

Let us assume that the international supply of U.S. dollars increases as a result of the higher payments for imports made by U.S. residents. To simplify matters, we will assume that the total value of U.S. exports remains unchanged. Figure 7-4 shows the results of the rightward shift of the supply curve for U.S. dollars. If the balance of payments was initially in balance at the exchange rate r_0, the shift of the supply curve for dollars to the right will result in a balance of payments deficit equal to AB at the fixed exchange rate r_0.

Clearly, this excess spending abroad will have repercussions on the domestic money supply of the United States. The precise magnitude of the changes will depend to a large extent on the institutional arrangements that determine the U.S. money supply. For instance, if the United States were on a pure *gold specie standard*, with all circulating currency consisting entirely of gold, we would find that the U.S. domestic money supply would be reduced by the same amount as the U.S. deficit and the consequent gold outflow.

However, if the United States money supply is determined by the Federal Reserve operating through the commercial banking system with less than 100 percent reserve requirements, we find that the outflow of dollars represents a loss of *high powered money* or a reduction in the monetary base. If all commercial banks are fully loaned up, a multiple contraction process of the money supply will start, which will come to an end only after the money supply is reduced by the amount of the loss in base money times the

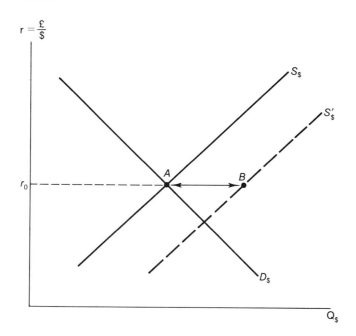

FIGURE 7-4

Balance of Payments Deficit Resulting from
an Increase in Payments for U.S. Imports

money multiplier.[1] But it is also possible that the domestic U.S. banking system has excess reserves available, and that therefore no multiple contraction process will be set into motion. Banks may instead reduce their excess reserves by the amount of the loss in high powered money. In that case, the Federal Reserve would have to take further actions if it wanted to contract the money supply in proportion to the change in high powered money due to the balance-of-payments deficit.

What course of action the Federal Reserve will in fact follow will often depend on the goals of its domestic monetary policy. If the Federal Reserve tries to stimulate the economy, it might well elect to neutralize the entire effects of the dollar outflow by appropriate policy actions, such as open market purchases of securities, a lowering of the discount rate, or a reduction of the reserve requirements. If the Federal Reserve were to follow such a neutralizing action, no further changes will occur. Let us assume here that the Federal Reserve will allow a change in the domestic money supply in

[1]See any elementary textbook for an exposition of the workings of the money multiplier; for instance: H. R. Heller, *The Economic System* (New York: The Macmillan Company, 1972), Chap. 14.

proportion to the change in high powered money due to the balance-of-payments deficit.

We will now continue with the analysis of the effects of the reduction in the U.S. domestic money supply. As individual economic units find that their money balances are below the desired level, they will attempt to replenish their balances. They can do this by reducing the amount of current spending on goods and services. Consequently, total expenditures will decrease. As a result of the reduction in expenditures, excess supplies of goods and services will appear, and in an attempt to reduce their inventories of unsold goods, sellers will lower their prices.[2] Eventually, as prices have fallen enough, the existing nominal money supply will have increased in value relative to goods and services, such that each individual economic unit will again hold its desired real money balances. The entire process will result in a lowering of the U.S. price level.

The effects just discussed will be amplified by interest-rate changes that are likely to take place. The initial decrease in the money supply will make loanable funds more scarce and hence will drive up the interest rate. This increase in the interest rate will discourage investment, and thereby further decrease aggregate demand. Prices will tend to fall.[3]

Consequently, we will find that the inflationary pressures that caused the initial disturbance will tend to be reduced, and in case of a pure gold standard or a faithful observance of the "rules of the game" by the Federal Reserve the external disequilibrium will be eliminated. The price mechanism, if allowed to be operational, will restore balance in the international accounts. However, there are generally considerable lags involved in the reaction of prices to changes in the money stock. Professor Friedman[4] estimates that it takes generally between one and two years until the changes in the money stock result in consumer price changes.

It is clear that the workings of the pure price mechanism can only rarely be observed in practice. Even during the heyday of the gold standard in the pre-World War I era price-level adjustments apparently played a minor role and international capital movements were relied upon to a considerable extent.[5] International capital movements will be discussed in Chap-

---

[2]Clearly, output changes may also occur at this stage. However, we assumed that real output remains constant, and that all adjustment is in the price variable.

[3]Though we assume throughout this chapter that no capital movements take place, we might note that the increase in interest rates might attract foreign funds and therefore help to eliminate the balance-of-payments deficit in a world where free capital movements are possible. The money supply would tend to increase again.

[4]Milton Friedman, "Have Monetary Policies Failed?" *American Economic Review*, 62, May 1972, p. 10–18.

[5]See, for instance, A. I. Bloomfield, *Monetary Policy Under the International Gold Standard* (New York: Federal Reserve Bank, 1959).

ter 10. Furthermore, in a modern economy we often encounter considerable inflexibility of prices and especially wages in a downward direction. Consequently, we will find that output changes are likely to accompany or even precede price level changes. Another important factor to be considered is the level of economic activity within the country. In times of full utilization of all resources, price changes will in fact occur. But in times of general resource underutilization, output changes are likely to be stronger and more immediate.

THE TERMS OF TRADE

The *terms of trade* are the exchange ratio between foreign and domestic goods and changes in the terms of trade are often used as an indicator of welfare changes that have occurred during a certain time interval. Here we will briefly discuss various definitions of the terms of trade and their significance for welfare comparisons.

Commodity Terms of Trade

The *commodity* terms of trade, often also referred to as the *gross barter* terms of trade, are simply the ratio of the quantity of import goods to the quantity of export goods:

$$TOT_c = \frac{Q_{IM}}{Q_{EX}} \qquad (7.1)$$

Instead of using physical quantities, it is often more convenient to use prices or price indices as an indicator. The price ratio is inversely related to the physical exchange ratio, and we obtain the *net barter* terms of trade:

$$TOT_c = \frac{P_{EX}}{P_{IM}} \qquad (7.2)$$

To calculate *changes* in the international exchange ratio that might have occurred, we can compare the price change in exports to the price change in imports, with the superscripts 0 and 1 indicating the base and end period.

$$\Delta TOT_c = \frac{P_{EX}^1/P_{EX}^0}{P_{IM}^1/P_{IM}^0} \qquad (7.3)$$

If export prices have increased more than import prices, making the ratio greater than one, we refer to this as a *favorable* movement in the terms of trade as our own goods are now worth more in international markets. Or, to put the same matter differently, it is an improvement because it takes now less of our export goods to purchase the same quantity of import goods as before. Conversely, a fall in the ratio is taken as an indication of an *unfavorable* movement or a deterioration of the terms of trade. The effects of changes in the exchange rate on the commodity terms of trade were discussed in detail in the previous chapter.

Income Terms of Trade

It has been pointed out that the commodity terms of trade may not be a good welfare indicator, as a deterioration of the commodity terms of trade does not necessarily mean that the nation is worse off. Changes in the *income terms of trade* measure the change in the commodity terms of trade corrected for changes in the quantity of exports:

$$\Delta TOT_Y = \frac{P^1_{EX}/P^0_{EX}}{P^1_{IM}/P^0_{IM}} \cdot Q^1_{EX}/Q^0_{EX} \tag{7.4}$$

The income terms of trade measure the purchasing power of exports in terms of imports, and therefore give a better indication of the change in welfare than the simple commodity terms of trade.

Also, the commodity terms of trade suggest that one country's gain must be another country's loss. Yet, we know from international trade theory that both trading partners will gain from trade—otherwise no trade would take place at all. While the commodity terms of trade for a pair of countries (or groups of countries) will always move in opposite directions, the income terms of trade may show an improvement for all countries.

The Factorial Terms of Trade

A closely associated concept are the *factorial terms of trade*, which focus on the amount of resources required to produce the traded commodities. For instance, let us assume that the country experiences a reduction in the real cost of producing the export commodity due to some technological improvement. Then export prices might fall, and the terms of trade deteriorate. Clearly, this does not mean that the country is worse off. It may, in fact, be better off after the change. To remedy this defect, the *single factorial* terms of trade were devised, which take account of the change in factor use, F, that occurs during the period of comparison:

$$\Delta TOT_{SF} = \frac{F^0_{EX}}{F^1_{EX}} \cdot \frac{P^1_{EX}/P^0_{EX}}{P^1_{IM}/P^0_{IM}} \tag{7.5}$$

This single factorial terms-of-trade index gives a good indication of the change in the *real cost* of obtaining the import goods.

But for international welfare comparisons, it is necessary to take account also of the foreign changes in factor productivity, and for this purpose the *double factorial* terms of trade are particularly useful.

$$\Delta TOT_{DF} = \frac{F_{EX}^0/F_{EX}^1}{F_{IM}^0/F_{IM}^1} \cdot \frac{P_{EX}^1/P_{EX}^0}{P_{IM}^1/P_{IM}^0} \tag{7.6}$$

This measure gives an indication of the change in the quantity of factors used to produce the export commodity in exchange for the quantity of factors used in the import commodity. By this, it denotes the changes in the real production effort in the two countries.

Real Cost Terms of Trade

Some economists would argue that even the double factorial terms of trade do not give a complete picture of the change in the real effort involved, as the disutility of labor might have changed as well. Clearly, such considerations will render the terms of trade concept largely useless for empirical purposes, as it would be a vexing problem indeed to calculate the disutility of the labor effort. Conceptually it is easy to arrive at the *real cost* terms of trade. It is done by simply multiplying the double factorial terms of trade by change in the disutility, *DU*, that takes place in the factor *F*:

$$\Delta TOT_{RC} = \frac{DU_{EX}^0}{DU_{EX}^1} \cdot \Delta TOT_{DF} \tag{7.7}$$

Utility Terms of Trade

The economic purist might even be interested in the *utility* terms of trade, which take account also of any changes in the utility, *U*, derived from the export and import commodities:

$$\Delta TOT_U = \frac{U_{EX}^1/U_{EX}^0}{U_{IM}^1/U_{IM}^0} \cdot \Delta TOT_{RC} \tag{7.8}$$

or

$$\Delta TOT_U = \frac{P_{EX}^1/P_{EX}^0}{P_{IM}^1/P_{IM}^0} \cdot \frac{F_{EX}^0/F_{EX}^1}{F_{IM}^0/F_{IM}^1} \cdot \frac{DU_{EX}^0}{DU_{EX}^1} \cdot \frac{U_{EX}^1/U_{EX}^0}{U_{IM}^1/U_{IM}^0} \tag{7.9}$$

Clearly, this idealized concept is hardly useful for empirical calculations.
To derive the *total gains* (or losses) from a change in the terms of trade

of a country, one has to multiply the change in the terms-of-trade index, which gives the *per unit* change, by the trade *volume*. This number will then give an indication of the total gains or losses in dollar terms.

The Data

Table 7-1 shows the terms of trade for the developed and the developing countries of the world (United Nations definition). The terms of trade for some individual countries are also listed. The data refer to the terms of trade averaged over the 1962–65 period, using the years 1950–53 as a base of 100. While the commodity terms of trade of developed and developing countries moved in opposite direction, the income terms of trade indicate that both the developed and the developing countries as groups were able to increase the purchasing power of their exports. Both groups gained. But it is also true

TABLE 7-1

TERMS OF TRADE

(indices for 1962–65 average, with 1950–53 average as base = 100)

Country	Commodity Terms of Trade $\dfrac{P_{EX}}{P_{IM}}$	Income Terms of Trade $\dfrac{P_{EX}}{P_{IM}} Q_{EX}$
Developed Countries (Average)	*109.8*	*236.5*
Canada	97.6	170.0
France	108.7	254.1
Germany	131.9	511.8
Italy	99.0	448.6
Japan	107.0	666.6
Netherlands	103.8	284.2
United Kingdom	121.6	168.5
United States	115.1	189.6
Developing Countries (Average)	*90.7*	*156.8*
Argentina	91.2	175.9
Ghana	80.2	135.8
India	110.5	142.7
Kenya	83.7	162.7
Nigeria	93.4	178.8
Pakistan	108.8	155.2
Peru	80.6	220.8
Phillipines	81.3	160.9

Note: The averages for developed and developing countries contain a larger sample of countries than listed here.

Source: T. Wilson, R. Sinha, and J. Castree, "The Income Terms of Trade of Developed and Developing Countries," *Economic Journal*, December 1969.

that the income terms of trade showed a larger improvement for the developed countries than for the developing countries.

SUGGESTED FURTHER READINGS

BLOOMFIELD, ARTHUR I., *Monetary Policy Under the International Gold Standard.* New York: Federal Reserve Bank, 1959.

HARBERGER, ARNOLD C., "Some Evidence on the International Price Mechanism," *Journal of Political Economy* (1957). Reprinted in R. N. COOPER, ed., *International Finance*, Chap. 7. Baltimore: Penguin Books, 1969.

HUME, DAVID, "Of the Balance of Trade," (1752). Reprinted in R. N. COOPER, ed., *International Finance*, Chap. 1. Baltimore: Penguin Books, 1969.

KEMP, MURRAY, "Technological Change, the Terms of Trade, and Welfare," *Economic Journal* (September 1955).

MEADE, JAMES E., *The Balance of Payments*, Part IV. London: Oxford University Press, 1951.

TRIFFIN, ROBERT, "The Myth and Realities of the So-called Gold Standard," *The Evolution of the International Monetary System.* Princeton: Princeton University Press, 1964. Reprinted in R. N. COOPER, ed. *International Finance*, Chap. 2. Baltimore: Penguin Books, 1969.

YEAGER, LELAND B., *International Monetary Relations*, Chaps. 9 and 14. New York: Harper & Row, 1966.

CHAPTER 8

Income Adjustment

Ever since the advent of "Keynesian" economics, the role of income adjustments to autonomous disturbances has received much attention. One of the basic assumptions of the pure income adjustment model is that the general price level will remain unaffected and may therefore be neglected in the analysis. We are dealing with an economy where resources are not fully employed, and where output may be expanded and contracted at constant costs. There is no upward pressure on prices.

Keynes himself restricted most of his analysis to a closed economy and consequently did not provide a comprehensive theory of the balance of payments. But his followers extended the analysis to build a "Keynesian" theory of balance-of-payments adjustment.

The Keynesian theory of balance-of-payments adjustment concentrates attention on the effects of income changes on the balance of payments. But in the more elaborate models, which include foreign repercussions, we do find income both as a dependent and an independent variable. The analysis starts by assuming an initial disturbance in one of the national income accounts, and then traces the effect of this disturbance on the external accounts of the country experiencing the imbalance. But due to the fact that we are dealing with an open economy, foreign countries also—previously in equilibrium—will be affected and through the changes introduced in their external accounts, *their* national income may be altered. The change in foreign national income in turn affects secondarily the external accounts of the original country with subsequent repercussions on domestic incomes.

THE BASIC MODEL

In order to show the differences between income and relative price adjustment, we will begin our analysis with a simple Keynesian model, where the exchange rate is fixed and sufficient excess capacity exists to permit output changes at constant prices. Also, we will neglect at the outset the monetary sector.

In such a simple economy the national income is determined by the sum of consumption, investment, governmental, and foreign spending on goods and services minus the amount that is imported (equation 8.1). Consumption is a function of income (8.2). The marginal propensity to consume is denoted by c. Autonomous components are indicated by the superscript 0. Investment (8.3), governmental expenditures (8.4), and exports (8.5) are determined autonomously. Imports are assumed to have an autonomous and income determined component (equation 8.6), with m indicating the marginal propensity to import. Note that C, I, and G include domestic spending on both home and foreign-produced commodities. We will assume throughout that all relevant marginal propensities remain constant.

$$Y = C + I + G + EX - IM \tag{8.1}$$

$$C = C^0 + cY \tag{8.2}$$

$$I = I^0 \tag{8.3}$$

$$G = G^0 \tag{8.4}$$

$$EX = EX^0 \tag{8.5}$$

$$IM = IM^0 + mY \tag{8.6}$$

To simplify matters somewhat we will refer to the sum of all domestic spending on consumption, investment, and government commodities as domestic absorption

$$A = C + I + G \quad \text{and} \tag{8.7}$$

$$A^0 = C^0 + I^0 + G^0 \tag{8.8}$$

The only component of domestic absorption that is a function of income is consumption. Amounts not consumed are saved, and hence we are able to define the *marginal propensity to save s* as[1]

$$s = 1 - c \tag{8.9}$$

[1]If we were to expand our model slightly and also make investment and governmental spending functions of national income, we would be able to define the *marginal propensity to absorb a* as the sum of the marginal propensities to consume, invest, and

The national economy will be in equilibrium if

$$Y = C + I + G + EX - IM \tag{8.1}$$

or

$$Y = A + B, \tag{8.10}$$

where

$$B = EX - IM \tag{8.11}$$

B is the external trade balance and in the absence of a monetary sector equivalent to the balance of payments. The entire economy is in balance when national income equals absorption plus the trade balance. That is, if the trade balance is zero, the equality of income and absorption is assured in equilibrium.

NATIONAL INCOME MULTIPLIERS

We will investigate now how the level of national income Y will change in response to an autonomous disturbance, that is, a change in A^0, EX^0, or IM°.[2] Inserting equations 8.2 through 8.9 into equation 8.1, we obtain

$$Y = A^0 + EX^0 - IM^0 + aY - mY \tag{8.12}$$

or for small changes

$$dY = dA^0 + dEX^0 - dIM^0 + adY - mdY \tag{8.13}$$

---

engage in governmental expenditures. In this expanded model we would then identify the *marginal propensity of nonabsorption* (1-*a*) or the *marginal propensity to hoard h*. To keep our terminology from being unduly complicated we will restrict ourselves to the simpler model, which does not recognize induced changes in investment and governmental expenditures. As both the marginal propensities to invest and to engage in governmental expenditures are zero, the marginal propensity to absorb is equal to the marginal propensity to consume, and similarly the marginal propensity to hoard is equal to the marginal propensity to save. None of the substantive conclusions of the model are affected by this simplification, and in circumstances where it seems appropriate to assume that the marginal propensities to invest and to engage in governmental spending are positive, it is easy to make the necessary substitutions.

[2]Note how an autonomous change in *IM* affects income. Money income consists of spending on *domestically* produced current, final output, that is, basically $C + I + G + EX$. The only reason *IM* is in equation 8.1 is to subtract it out after its value has been included under *C*, *I*, *G*, and *EX*. If *IM* increases, we simply enlarge $C + I + G + EX$ and then subtract it out. The only way a change in *IM* can change income is by changing the *C*, *I*, *G*, and *EX* expenditures on *domestic* output. For example, an autonomous rise in spending on foreign goods might be accompanied by some corresponding fall in consumption spending on domestic goods.

Collecting terms and using equation 8.9 we arrive at the familiar *foreign trade multiplier.*

$$dY = \frac{1}{s + m}(dA^0 + dEX^0 - dIM^0) \qquad (8.14)$$

Let us note that the foreign trade multiplier $1/(s + m)$ is smaller than the conventional multiplier $1/s$ for a closed economy. The multiplier shows the national income changes that will result *automatically* from any autonomous disturbance originating in the domestic or foreign trade sector.

We are also able to show the effects of an autonomous disturbance graphically. We use the simplified national income equilibrium condition, which sets total leakages equal to total injections. Assuming that we can neglect the governmental sector for the time being (or, alternatively, that taxation is included in saving S and governmental expenditures in investment I) the equilibrium condition reads:

$$S + IM = I + EX \qquad (8.15)$$

In Figure 8-1 we show the saving (S), import (IM), investment (I) and export

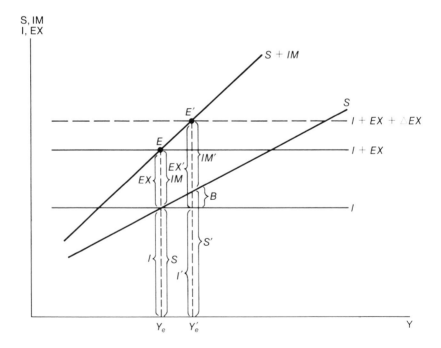

FIGURE 8-1

Automatic Effects of Export Increase

(EX) functions, as well as the initial equilibrium point E that results in a national income of Y_e. Now let us assume that an autonomous change in exports occurs, which shifts the export function by the amount ΔEX (dashed line). The new equilibrium point is given by E' and equilibrium national income will be Y'_e.

BALANCE-OF-PAYMENTS MULTIPLIERS

We note, however, that although at the new equilibrium point total injections $EX' + I'$ are equal to total leakages $IM' + S'$, the equality of exports and imports is no longer assured. In our example, EX' exceeds IM' by the amount B—the balance-of-payments surplus. As balance-of-payments equilibrium is not guaranteed with national income equilibrium, we have to investigate how the balance of payments will react to autonomous disturbances.

We defined the balance of payments previously as

$$B = EX - IM \tag{8.11}$$

For small changes we get

$$dB = dEX - dIM. \tag{8.16}$$

Substituting equations 8.5 and 8.6 into this equation we obtain:

$$dB = dEX^0 - dIM^0 - m\,dY \tag{8.17}$$

and further substitution of 8.14 yields

$$dB = dEX^0 - dIM^0 - \frac{m}{s+m}(dA^0 + dEX^0 - dIM^0). \tag{8.18}$$

$$dB = \left(1 - \frac{m}{s+m}\right)dEX^0 - \left(1 - \frac{m}{s+m}\right)dIM^0 - \frac{m}{s+m}dA^0 \tag{8.19}$$

$$dB = \frac{s}{s+m}(dEX^0 - dIM^0) - \frac{m}{s+m}dA^0. \tag{8.20}$$

This formula gives the balance-of-payments multipliers and allows us to determine the effects of any autonomous change on the balance of payments. Let us note that the multipliers are different depending on the origin of the disturbance. For autonomous changes that have their origin in the external accounts, the multiplier is $s/(s+m)$. That is, the balance of payments will not be affected at all by a change in EX^0 or IM^0 if the marginal propensity to save is zero. The other extreme is reached when the marginal propensity to import is equal to zero, resulting in a multiplier of one and con-

sequently a change in the balance of payments that is equal to the size of the
initial disturbance in the foreign sector.

For autonomous disturbances in domestic absorption ($dA^0 = dC^0 + dI^0 + dG^0$) the balance-of-payments multiplier is $m/(s + m)$. This multiplier
is zero if the marginal propensity to import is zero and equal to one if the
marginal propensity to save is zero. The size of the automatic balance-of-
payments multiplier depends crucially on the origin of the disturbance.

Unless s is zero in cases of external account disturbances or m is zero
for domestic disturbances, there will be a residual imbalance in the trade
account even when national income has reached a new equilibrium. Some
economists have therefore argued that the income adjustment mechanism is
an incomplete adjustment process, and has to be supplemented by either
price or exchange-rate changes. Here we will adopt a slightly different approach and analyze what action the policy maker should take to bring about
complete balance-of-payments equilibrium while relying solely on income
changes.

Foreign Sector Disturbances

Let us assume that there is an initial disturbance in the *foreign* sector that
results in a residual balance-of-payments disequilibrium after the automatic
adjustment mechanism has taken its course. To eliminate the remaining
external imbalance, we will assume that the policy maker will change the
level of domestic absorption. It is obvious that the government has the power
to determine governmental expenditures G. It also has the power to set
taxes and thereby to influence consumption and investment activity. In any
case, it is possible for the government to bring about changes in domestic
absorption A.

From equation 8.20 we know the relationship between absorption A
and the balance of payments B. If we have a residual balance-of-payments
surplus, the government will have to increase domestic absorption by

$$dA = \frac{s + m}{m} dB \tag{8.21}$$

to eliminate the balance-of-payments surplus dB. Substituting the source of
the original disturbance in the foreign sector dEX^0 from equation 8.20 we
obtain

$$dA = \frac{s + m}{m} dB = \frac{s + m}{m} \frac{s}{s + m} (dEX^0 - dIM^0) = \frac{s}{m} (dEX^0 - dIM^0) \tag{8.22}$$

Naturally, this government-induced change in absorption will have multiplier repercussions on national income, which we can calculate by using equation 8.14:

$$dY = \frac{1}{(s + m)} \frac{s}{m} (dEX^0 - dIM^0) \qquad (8.23)$$

Finally we may add the automatic changes in national income due to the workings of the foreign trade multiplier of equation 8.14 and the policy-induced changes that are necessary to bring about balance-of-payments equilibrium (8.23). Thus we derive the total national income change associated with a return to domestic and international balance after a disturbance that originates in the foreign trade sector:

$$dY_{total} = dY_{automatic} + dY_{policy\ induced}$$

$$= \left[\frac{1}{s + m} + \frac{s}{(s + m)m} \right] (dEX^0 - dIM^0)$$

$$dY_{total} = \frac{1}{m} (dEX^0 - dIM^0) \qquad (8.24)$$

Let us note that this formula showing the total income changes required to eliminate a balance-of-payments disequilibrium applies only to autonomous disturbances originating in the *external* sector.

Figure 8-2 illustrates the case just discussed, again under the assumption that both the marginal propensity to invest and to engage in governmental spending are zero. The economy is described by the following equations:

$$S + IM = I + EX \qquad (8.25)$$
$$S = .2 Y \qquad (C = .8 Y) \qquad (8.26)$$
$$IM = .1 Y \qquad (8.27)$$
$$I = 200 \qquad (8.28)$$
$$EX = 100 \qquad (8.29)$$

Balance-of-payments equilibrium prevails if

$$EX = IM \qquad (8.30)$$

Initially, the economy is in equilibrium at

$$S + IM = I + EX \qquad (8.31)$$
$$.2 Y + .1 Y = 200 + 100$$
$$.3 Y = 300$$
$$Y = 1,000$$

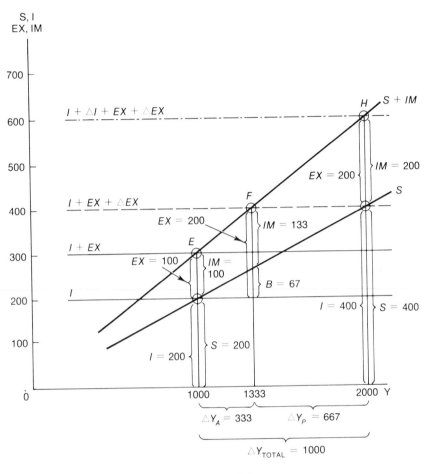

FIGURE 8-2

Total Income Change Required to Restore External and Internal Balance
after Disturbance in Exports

NOTE: $s = .2$; $m = .1$.

Now let us assume that exports increase by $\Delta EX^0 = 100$. Using the previously derived equation 8.14 we derive the automatic change in national income

$$\Delta Y_a = \frac{1}{s + m} \Delta EX^0 = 3.33 \cdot 100 = 333 \qquad (8.32)$$

In Figure 8-2 we show the increase of ΔEX^0 and the consequent move from equilibrium point E to F, resulting in an income change from 1,000 to 1,333.

But at this new income level, external balance is no longer maintained. Exports are now equal to 200, but imports at an income level of 1,333 are only 133. Hence, a balance-of-payments surplus of 67 exists. Formally, we can use equation 8.20 to calculate this surplus.

$$\Delta B = \frac{s}{s + m} \Delta EX^0 = \frac{.2}{.2 + .1} \Delta EX^0 = .67 \cdot 100 = 67 \qquad (8.33)$$

An expansionary economic policy can eliminate the balance-of-payments surplus by increasing national income and thereby inducing higher imports. For instance, an increase in absorption by \$200 will increase national income by \$667, which will result in \$67 more imports and thereby the elimination of the balance-of-payments surplus.

Formally (according to equation 8.22), we calculate the absorption increase required to eliminate the surplus generated by the autonomous disturbance in the foreign sector:

$$\Delta A = \frac{s}{m} \Delta EX^0 = \frac{.2}{.1} \Delta EX^0 = 2 \cdot 100 = 200 \qquad (8.34)$$

This increase in absorption will expand national income (according to equation 8.14) by

$$\Delta Y_p = \frac{1}{s + m} \Delta A = \frac{1}{.2 + .1} \Delta A = 3.33 \cdot 200 = 667 \qquad (8.35)$$

This is the *policy-induced* income increase that will eliminate the remaining external imbalance.

The total increase in income will be equal to the sum of ΔY_a and ΔY_p, that is: $\Delta Y_t = \Delta Y_a + \Delta Y_p = 333 + 667 = 1,000$. This value could have been obtained directly by using the total multiplier from equation 8.24:

$$\Delta Y_t = 1/m \cdot \Delta EX^0 = (1/.1) \cdot 100 = 1,000$$

The new equilibrium point is labeled H in Figure 8-2. At that new equilibrium point external balance is restored, as $EX = IM = 200$, and overall balance is maintained: $S + IM = I + EX = 600$. The new level of national income is given by:

$$S + IM = I + EX$$

$$.2 Y + .1 Y = 400 + 200$$

$$.3 Y = 600$$

$$Y = 2,000$$

Domestic Sector Disturbances

For disturbances occurring in the domestic sector we have to repeat the calculation due to the fact that the balance-of-payments disequilibrium is of a different size (cf. equation 8.20).

We will now retrace all the steps covered in our discussion of a disturbance having its origin in the foreign sector for a disturbance in the domestic sector. The following steps are involved:

1. Calculate the automatic national income changes induced by the domestic disturbance dA^0:

$$dY_{automatic} = \frac{1}{s + m} dA^0 \tag{8.36}$$

2. Determine the size of the balance-of-payments disequilibrium dB:

$$dB = -\frac{m}{s + m} dA^0 \tag{8.37}$$

3. Determine the change in absorption dA that the government has to bring about to eliminate the disequilibrium dB:

$$dA = \frac{s + m}{m} dB = -\frac{(s + m)m}{m(s + m)} dA^0 = -1dA^0 \tag{8.38}$$

4. Find out the effect of this policy-induced change dA on income by using equation 8.14:

$$dY_{policy\ induced} = -\frac{1}{s + m} dA^0 \tag{8.39}$$

5. Calculate the sum of the automatic and policy-induced income changes:

$$dY_{total} = dY_{automatic} + dY_{policy\ induced} = \left(\frac{1}{s + m} - \frac{1}{s + m}\right) dA^0 = 0 \tag{8.40}$$

The not-too-surprising result is that the national income will be unchanged. It is clear that a balance-of-payments disturbance that has its origin in an autonomous change in domestic consumption, investment, or government spending can be eliminated by simply inducing a change of equal magnitude but opposite sign in domestic absorption. The two multipliers from the initial disturbance and the policy action will cancel each other exactly, leaving the national income level unchanged. Table 8-1 summarizes the important multipliers.

TABLE 8-1

SOURCE OF INITIAL DISTURBANCE

	Change in Domestic Absorption	Change in Exports	Change in Imports
	dA°	dEX°	dIM°
1. Automatic income adjustment dY_a	$\dfrac{1}{s+m}$	$\dfrac{1}{s+m}$	$-\dfrac{1}{s+m}$
2. External imbalance remaining dB	$-\dfrac{m}{s+m}$	$\dfrac{s}{s+m}$	$-\dfrac{s}{s+m}$
3. Change in absorption required to restore external balance dA	-1	$\dfrac{s}{m}$	$-\dfrac{s}{m}$
4. Effect of dA on national income dY_p	$-\dfrac{1}{s+m}$	$\dfrac{s}{m(s+m)}$	$-\dfrac{s}{m(s+m)}$
5. Total income change required to eliminate initial disturbance dY_t	0	$\dfrac{1}{m}$	$-\dfrac{1}{m}$

For policy purposes it is important to know that a balance-of-payments disequilibrium that has its origin in the domestic sector (dA°) can be eliminated at no cost to the country by using income adjustment policies. But we should be careful to point out that the "no cost" conclusion holds only with reference to the initial equilibrium. If, for instance, a country is initially in underemployment equilibrium and an autonomous increase in investment spending results in a balance-of-payments deficit, we show that a return to the old national income level will eliminate the deficit. But in comparison to the higher income level that had been achieved as a result of the first increase in investment spending, the reduction in national income required to restore external balance is costly.

On the other hand, a balance-of-payments disequilibrium that has its origin in the international accounts and is eliminated via income changes will result in a cost of $1/m$ dollars per dollar deficit or a gain of $1/m$ dollars per dollar surplus eliminated.

The next step in the analysis is to include the effect of foreign repercussions. That is, we will no longer assume that our exports are determined autonomously, but instead that they are a function of the income level in the other country. But the income level of the other country in turn depends on their exports to our country. By using simultaneous equations, we are able to model these interrelated changes that occur in both countries. The detailed algebraic calculations are carried out in the appendix to this chapter. Suffice it to say that the results are perfectly analogous to the case of autonomously determined exports just discussed. The conclusions are that (1) a disturbance originating in the home sector of the country under consideration can be eliminated at zero cost by returning to the initial equilibrium, and (2) the costs of remedying a $1 balance of payments deficit that has its origin in the foreign trade sector is equal to the reciprocal of the country's marginal propensity to import: $1/m$.

Empirical Evidence

Here we will present some empirical estimates of income adjustment costs for disturbances originating in the foreign sector. Let us emphasize again that these estimates pertain only to the "pure" income adjustment case, where all prices and the exchange rate remain constant. Table 8-2 gives estimates of the marginal propensity to import and the cost of eliminating a $1 deficit in the balance of payments that had its origin in the external sector.

TABLE 8-2

INCOME ADJUSTMENT COST TO A $1 DEFICIT CAUSED BY A DISTURBANCE IN THE FOREIGN SECTOR

Country	Marginal Propensity to Import	Marginal Adjustment Cost in Dollars $(1/m)$
Canada	.19	$ 5.21
Denmark	.38	$ 2.65
Germany	.15	$ 6.49
Italy	.35	$ 2.90
Japan	.13	$ 7.58
South Africa	.15	$ 6.54
Sweden	.38	$ 2.65
Switzerland	.56	$ 1.79
United Kingdom	.32	$ 3.13
United States	.05	$22.22

Source: Marginal propensities are calculated according to the formula: $mpm = e_y \cdot apm$. Income elasticities are from H. S. Houthakker and S. P. Magee, "Income and Price Elasticities in World Trade," *Review of Economics and Statistics*, Vol. 51 (May 1969); and average propensities to import from IMF, *International Finance Statistics*, (May 1970).

We should note that as the adjustment costs are inversely related to the marginal propensity to import and a high marginal propensity to import generally is associated with a relatively large foreign trade sector, it follows that open economies can use income adjustment at relatively low cost. Most of the world's small countries are in this category. Conversely, relatively closed economies with low marginal propensities to import—like the United States—face very high income adjustment costs to external disturbances. For this latter group of countries adjustments in exchange rates, price levels, or capital movements may well represent less expensive and hence more efficient alternatives.

Data for most of the underdeveloped nations would probably not be very meaningful, as actual imports are likely to be considerably below the level that would prevail in the absence of import controls and restrictions. Hence, the free-market multipliers calculated here are not too representative of the true adjustment costs.

APPENDIX TO CHAPTER 8

Income Adjustment with Foreign Repercussions, Stability, and Interest-Rate Changes

THE TRADITIONAL FOREIGN TRADE MULTIPLIERS

The model of income adjustment incorporating foreign repercussions is formally analogous to the simpler model discussed in Chapter 8. Using the same notation and utilizing subscripts 1 and 2 to denote the two countries, we calculate the national income multipliers incorporating foreign repercussions.

We have the two equations determining national income of the two countries:

$$Y_1 = A_1^0 + a_1 Y_1 + EX_1^0 - IM_1^0 - m_1 Y_1 \tag{8A.1}$$

$$Y_2 = A_2^0 + a_2 Y_2 + EX_2^0 - IM_2^0 - m_2 Y_2 \tag{8A.2}$$

But we also know that in the two country case

$$EX_1^0 = IM_2 = (IM_2^0 + m_2 Y_2) \tag{8A.3}$$

$$EX_2^0 = IM_1 = (IM_1^0 + m_1 Y_1) \tag{8A.4}$$

Substituting we obtain:

$$Y_1 = A_1^0 + a_1 Y_1 - IM_1^0 - m_1 Y_1 + IM_2^0 + m_2 Y_2 \tag{8A.5}$$

$$Y_2 = A_2^0 + a_2 Y_2 - IM_2^0 - m_2 Y_2 + IM_1^0 + m_1 Y_1 \tag{8A.6}$$

and for changes:

$$dY_1 = dA_1^0 - dIM_1^0 + dIM_2^0 + a_1 \, dY_1 - m_1 \, dY_1 + m_2 \, dY_2 \quad (8A.7)$$

$$dY_2 = dA_2^0 - dIM_2^0 + dIM_1^0 + a_2 \, dY_2 - m_2 \, dY_2 + m_1 \, dY_1 \quad (8A.8)$$

and

$$dY_1 = \frac{1}{1 - a_1 + m_1} (dA_1^0 - dIM_1^0 + dIM_2^0 + m_2 \, dY_2) \quad (8A.9)$$

$$dY_2 = \frac{1}{1 - a_2 + m_2} (dA_2^0 - dIM_2^0 + dIM_1^0 + m_1 \, dY_1) \quad (8A.10)$$

Substituting equation 8A.10 into 8A.9 and writing s for $(1-a)$ we obtain:

$$dY_1 = \frac{1}{s_1 + m_1} \left[dA_1^0 - dIM_1^0 + dIM_2^0 + \frac{m_2}{s_2 + m_2} \right.$$
$$\left. \times (dA_2^0 - dIM_2^0 + dIM_1^0 + m_1 \, dY_1) \right] \quad (8A.11)$$

After solving for dY_1:

$$dY_1 = \frac{1}{s_1 m_2 + s_2 m_1 + s_1 s_2} [(s_2 + m_2) dA_1^0$$
$$+ m_2 \, dA_2^0 - s_2 \, dIM_1^0 + s_2 \, dIM_2^0]. \quad (8A.12)$$

Similarly, we obtain for country 2:

$$dY_2 = \frac{1}{s_1 m_2 + s_2 m_1 + s_1 s_2} [(s_1 + m_1) dA_2^0$$
$$+ m_1 \, dA_1^0 - s_1 \, dIM_2^0 + s_1 \, dIM_1^0]. \quad (8A.13)$$

These are the *national income multipliers with foreign repercussions*. They show the changes in national income that result automatically from autonomous changes having their origin in the domestic or foreign trade sectors of both countries 1 and 2.

The effects of the same autonomous changes on the balance of payments are:

$$dB_1 = dEX_1 - dIM_1 = dIM_2^0 + m_2 \, dY_2 - dIM_1^0 - m_1 \, dY_1 \quad (8A.14)$$

Substituting 8A.12 and 8A.13 into this equation we obtain

$$dB_1 = dIM_2^0 - \frac{m_2 s_1}{D} dIM_2^0 - \frac{m_1 s_2}{D} dIM_2^0 - dIM_1^0 + \frac{m_2 s_1}{D} dIM_1^0$$
$$+ \frac{m_1 s_2}{D} dIM_1^0 + \frac{m_2(s_1 + m_1)}{D} dA_2^0 - \frac{m_1 m_2}{D} dA_2^0$$
$$+ \frac{m_1 m_2}{D} dA_1^0 - \frac{m_1(s_2 + m_2)}{D} dA_1^0 \quad (8A.15)$$

where $D = s_1 m_2 + s_2 m_1 + s_1 s_2$. Combining terms we arrive at the standard *balance-of-payments multiplier with foreign repercussions*:

$$dB_1 = \frac{s_1 s_2}{s_1 m_2 + s_2 m_1 + s_1 s_2} \left[dIM_2^0 - dIM_1^0 + \frac{m_2}{s_2} dA_2^0 - \frac{m_1}{s_1} dA_1^0 \right].$$
(8A.16)

The same formula holds for the balance of payments of country 2 with subscripts reversed.

The two important formulas for our purposes are equation 8A.12, which shows the automatic multiplier repercussions resulting from an autonomous change on national income of country 1, and equation 8A.16, which shows the automatic multiplier repercussions due to an autonomous change on the balance of payments of country 1.

CALCULATIONS OF THE COST OF TOTAL INCOME ADJUSTMENTS

The total cost of a national income adjustment can be calculated from the above model in the same manner as it was done for the simple case in the main body of Chapter 8. It involves the following five steps: (1) the calculation of the *automatic national income changes*, dY_1^q, resulting from the foreign trade multiplier after an exogenous disturbance; (2) the calculation of the *balance-of-payments disequilibrium*, dB_1, resulting from the same disturbance; (3) *the determination of dA_1*, that is, the change in domestic consumption, investment, and government expenditures required to restore external balance; (4) the *effect on national income*, dY_1^p, of this policy-induced change; and (5) the calculation of the *total effect on national income*, dY_1^t, which is the sum of the automatic income changes, dY_1^q, and the policy-induced income changes, dY_1^p.

In this model all these calculations have to be made for each of four possible disequilibrium sources: disturbances in the domestic sectors of country 1 and country 2 as well as the foreign sector of each of the two countries. To simplify matters we follow the scheme discussed above and present the calculations in summary form in Table 8A-1.

In spite of the forbidding appearance of this summary of the total national income cost calculations, we find the results extremely simple.

Taking foreign repercussions into account we find that *national income adjustment costs to external disequilibria caused by disturbances originating in the country's foreign sector—either at home or abroad—are equal to the inverse of the marginal propensity to import times the disturbance.*

The interpretation of these results is perfectly analogous to those obtained in the case of no foreign repercussions. The total costs of both the automatic income changes caused by a disturbance originating in the *foreign* trade sector and the policy-induced income changes designed to maintain external balance are equal to $1/m$ per dollar disturbance. It is immaterial whether these disturbances are originating in the foreign sector of the home country or the other country.

The significance of the $1/m$ multiplier should be emphasized. This simple multiplier shows the *total* cost of income adjustment to a disturbance in the foreign trade sector. All the lengthy traditional foreign multipliers show

TABLE 8A-1

	(a) Disturbance in Domestic Sector of Country 1 dA_1^0	(b) Disturbance in Domestic Sector of Country 2 dA_2^0	(c) Disturbance in Foreign Sector of Country 1 dIM_1^0	(d) Disturbance in Foreign Sector of Country 2 $dIM_2^0 = dEX_1^0$
(1) Automatic national income changes: dY_1^a (equation 8A.12)				
$dY_1^a =$	$\dfrac{s_2 + m_2}{D} dA_1^0$	$\dfrac{m_2}{D} dA_2^0$	$-\dfrac{s_2}{D} dIM_1^0$	$\dfrac{s_2}{D} dIM_2^0$
(2) Balance-of-payments disequilibrium: dB_1 (equation 8A.16)				
$dB_1 =$	$-\dfrac{s_2 m_1}{D} dA_1^0$	$\dfrac{s_1 m_2}{D} dA_2^0$	$-\dfrac{s_1 s_2}{D} dIM_1^0$	$\dfrac{s_1 s_2}{D} dIM_2^0$
(3) Determination of dA_1 (equation 8A.16 backwards)				
$dA_1 =$	$\dfrac{D}{s_2 m_1} dB_1$ $= -1 \cdot dA_1^0$	$\dfrac{D}{s_2 m_1} dB_1$ $= \dfrac{s_1 m_2}{s_2 m_1} dA_2^0$	$\dfrac{D}{m_1 s_2} dB_1$ $= -\dfrac{s_1}{m_1} dIM_1^0$	$\dfrac{D}{m_1 s_2} dB_1$ $= \dfrac{s_1}{m_1} dIM_2^0$
(4) Effect on national income: dY_1^p (equation 8A.12)				
$dY_1^p =$	$\dfrac{s_2 + m_2}{D} dA_1$ $= -\dfrac{s_2 + m_2}{D} dA_1^0$	$\dfrac{s_2 + m_2}{D} dA_1$ $= \dfrac{s_1 m_2(s_2 + m_2)}{s_2 m_1 D} dA_2^0$	$\dfrac{s_2 + m_2}{D} dA_1$ $= -\dfrac{s_1(s_2 + m_2)}{m_1 D} dIM_1^0$	$\dfrac{s_2 + m_2}{D} dA_1$ $= \dfrac{s_1(s_2 + m_2)}{m_1 D} dIM_2^0$
(5) Total effect on national income: dY_1^t (sum of 1 and 4)				
$dY_1^t =$	$\left(\dfrac{s_2 + m_2}{D} - \dfrac{s_2 + m_2}{D}\right) dA_1^0$ $= 0$	$\left(\dfrac{m_2}{D} + \dfrac{s_1 m_2(s_2 + m_2)}{s_2 m_1 D}\right) dA_2^0$ $= \dfrac{m_2}{s_2 m_1} dA_2^0$	$\left[-\dfrac{s_2}{D} - \dfrac{s_1(s_2 + m_2)}{m_1 D}\right] dIM_1^0$ $= -\dfrac{1}{m_1} dIM_1^0$	$\left[\dfrac{s_2}{D} + \dfrac{s_1(s_2 + m_2)}{m_1 D}\right] dIM_2^0$ $= \dfrac{1}{m_1} dIM_2^0$

an incomplete—albeit automatic—adjustment to the disturbance. The total income adjustment cost, that is, the adjustment costs associated with a return to internal as well as external equilibrium, are given by the simple $1/m$ multiplier. This multiplier applies to both the case with no foreign repercussions as well as with foreign repercussions.

Second, we obtain the familiar result that *a disturbance originating in the country's own level of domestic absorption, A_1, will have no effects on national income if eliminated by an income adjustment policy that merely reverses the original disturbance.* The country will return to both the domestic and international situation prevailing before the initial disturbance.

Third, a disturbance due to a change in absorption of the *foreign* country, A_2, if eliminated by income adjustments of country 1 will result in a change in Y_1 that is equal to $dY = m_2/m_1 s_2 dA_2^0$. That is, the larger the foreign country's marginal propensity to import, m_2, the larger will be the adjustment cost for country 1. Conversely a larger propensity to import in country 1 or higher propensity to save in country 2 will lower the adjustment cost for country 1.

STABILITY

A dominant feature of the foreign repercussions model is that the income of one country is influenced by the income of the other country. Thus the question arises whether this feedback mechanism is consistent with a stable equilibrium or whether the feedback effects will be such that they instigate wider and wider fluctuations of national income. Naturally, many different dynamic models may be specified, and we will discuss only one simple version.

Equation 8A.5 shows the relationship between country 1's income and that of country 2. Neglecting all other variables we obtain the following relationship between Y_1 and Y_2.

$$Y_1 = \frac{m_2}{s_1 + m_1} \, Y_2 \qquad (8A.17)$$

Similarly, we can express Y_2 as a function of Y_1 as given in equation 8A.6.

$$Y_2 = \frac{m_1}{s_2 + m_2} \, Y_1 \qquad (8A.18)$$

In order to be able to show both functions in the same graph, 8A.18 can be rewritten as

$$Y_1 = \frac{s_2 + m_2}{m_1} \, Y_2 \qquad (8A.19)$$

Equations 8A.17 and 8A.19 are shown in Figure 8A-1. The slopes of the functions are the coefficients of the equations.

To investigate the stability conditions we start at an arbitrary income level Y_1^A in Figure 8A-1a. Looking at point A on the line $Y_2 = f(Y_1)$, we are able to determine the income level in country 2 that is consistent with Y_1^A. This income level is found to be Y_2^A.

But given that country 2 will have an income level Y_2^A, we find that

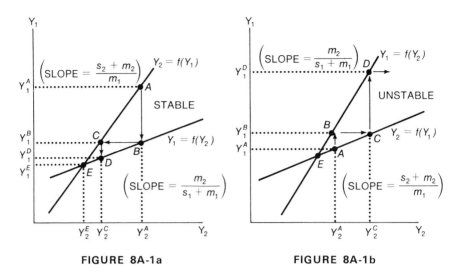

FIGURE 8A-1a   FIGURE 8A-1b

Stability Problems in Foreign Repercussions Models

$Y_1 = f(Y_2)$ yields point B and a new income level for country 1: Y_1^B. Now that the income level of country 1 has changed, country 2's will have to change as well. We move to point C. The process continues until point E is reached, where no further income changes will take place. We have reached a stable equilibrium as a small displacement will tend to return us to the equilibrium point.

In Figure 8A-1b we draw the slopes of the two functions differently. Again starting with an arbitrary income level Y_1^A, we find that we move from point A to B, C, D, and beyond. It turns out that the equilibrium point E is unstable.

We will obtain a stable equilibrium whenever the slope of $Y_2 = f(Y_1)$ is steeper than the slope of $Y_1 = f(Y_2)$, as shown in Figure 8A-1a. If the reverse holds true, no stable equilibrium exists.

Hence, the stability condition is that in the neighborhood of E the following inequality holds:

$$\frac{s_2 + m_2}{m_1} > \frac{m_2}{s_1 + m_1} \qquad (8A.20)$$

or

$$(s_2 + m_2)(s_1 + m_1) > m_1 m_2 \qquad (8A.21)$$

This stability condition is always fulfilled as long as the marginal propensities to save s are positive.

THE EFFECT OF INTEREST-RATE CHANGES

In our previous discussion we assumed that—along with all other prices—interest rates remained constant throughout. As a last extension of the income adjustment model and a first link to the discussion of international capital movements to be taken up in the following chapter, we will turn our attention now to the effect of induced interest-rate changes on the size of the national income multipliers. All other prices are still assumed to be constant. To keep the analysis as simple as possible, we will employ again the no-foreign-repercussions model. The extensions to the model incorporating foreign repercussions are obvious.

We will use the following model:

$$S + IM = I + EX \quad \text{(commodity equilibrium)} \qquad (8A.22)$$

$$S = S(Y) \quad \text{(saving function)} \qquad (8A.23)$$

$$IM = IM(Y) \quad \text{(import function)} \qquad (8A.24)$$

$$I = f(i) \quad \text{(investment function)} \qquad (8A.25)$$

$$EX = EX^0 \quad \text{(autonomously determined exports)} \quad (8A.26)$$

$$M_S = M_D \quad \text{(monetary equilibrium)} \qquad (8A.27)$$

$$M_S = M_S^0 \quad \text{(autonomously determined money supply)} \qquad (8A.28)$$

$$M_D = L(i, Y) \quad \text{(speculative and transactions demand for money)} \qquad (8A.29)$$

Let us assume that an initial disturbance takes the form of an auto-nomous increase in exports. The increased exports will result in a multiple national income expansion. But as income goes up, the amount of money demanded for transactions purposes increases as well. Given a constant money supply, the increase in transaction funds can come only from a decrease in speculative money balances. As funds available for speculative money balances are decreased, the interest rate goes up, and consequently investment will decrease and cause a reduction in national income below that which would otherwise prevail. Hence, the national income multiplier will be smaller than it would be if we would ignore interest-rate changes.

Formally, this result is obtained as follows. We first substitute the appropriate expressions into the equilibrium conditions (8A.22) and (8A.27) to obtain

$$S(Y) + IM(Y) = I(i) + EX^0 \qquad (8A.30)$$

$$M_S^0 = L(i, Y) \qquad (8A.31)$$

Differentiating totally we get:

$$\frac{dS}{dY} dY + \frac{dIM}{dY} dY = \frac{dI}{di} di + dEX^0 \qquad (8.A32)$$

$$\frac{\partial L}{\partial i} di + \frac{\partial L}{\partial Y} dY = 0 \qquad (8A.33)$$

Solving for di:

$$di = -\frac{\partial L/\partial Y}{\partial L/\partial i} dY \qquad (8A.34)$$

Inserting this expression in 8A.32 yields

$$dY\left(\frac{dS}{dY} + \frac{dIM}{dY} + \frac{dI}{di} \cdot \frac{\partial L/\partial Y}{\partial L/\partial i}\right) = dEX^0 \qquad (8A.35)$$

Writing s and m for the marginal propensities to save and to import, 8A.35 can be simplified to

$$dY = \frac{1}{s + m + \frac{dI}{di} \cdot \frac{\partial L/\partial Y}{\partial L/\partial i}} dEX^0 \qquad (8A.36)$$

This is the national income multiplier analogous to 8.14 but allowing for interest-rate effects.

Typically, we would expect to find that an increase in interest rates will lower investment and the speculative demand for money:

$$\frac{\partial I}{\partial i} < 0; \quad \frac{\partial L}{\partial i} < 0$$

As $\partial L/\partial Y$ is positive, the entire expression $(dI/di)(\partial L/\partial Y)/(\partial L/\partial i)$ will be positive as well, lowering the value of the entire multiplier. It is interesting to discuss some borderline cases.

The Keynesian Liquidity Trap

This case obtains when the speculative demand for money is infinitely elastic with respect to the interest rate. In terms of the traditional Hicks-Hansen *IS-LM* diagram of Figure 8A-2, we have a horizontal *LM* curve. In this case $\partial L/\partial i$ in equation 8A.37 approaches infinity and the multiplier will be equal to $dY = 1/(s + m) dEX$. That is, if no interest-rate changes are induced because we have an infinitely elastic money supply (liquidity trap), the foreign trade multiplier will be the same as discussed in the main section of this chapter. The same result follows if the monetary authorities expand the money supply sufficiently to accommodate the increased demand for money, thereby holding interest rates constant.

Interest Inelastic Investment

If investment is not influenced by interest-rate changes, dI/di equals zero. In this case, which is illustrated in Figure 8A-3, there will be an increase in the interest rate, but it has no effect on investment, and hence the national income multiplier is not affected either.

No Speculative Demand for Money

If there is no speculative demand for money (as in the typical classical model), $\partial L/\partial i$ equals zero and the entire multiplier becomes zero. If there are no speculative balances to begin with, transactions balances cannot increase given a fixed money supply. But as the transaction balances are unchanged, income cannot change either. We are in the vertical (classical) portion of the *LM* curve (Figure 8A-4) where interest-rate changes are so strong that they negate any income changes.

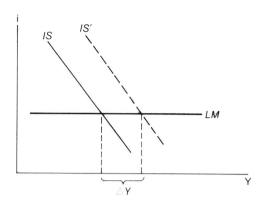

FIGURE 8A-2

The Liquidity Trap Case

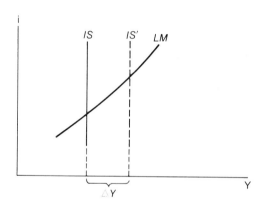

FIGURE 8A-3

Interest Inelastic Investment Case

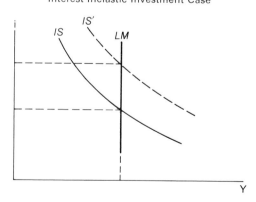

FIGURE 8A-4

No Speculative Demand for Money Case

This will conclude our present discussion of the effects of interest-rate changes. The relationship between interest rates and international capital movements is discussed in Chapter 10.

SUGGESTED FURTHER READINGS

BLACK, JOHN, "A Geometric Analysis of the Foreign Trade Multiplier," *Economic Journal* (June 1957).

BRONFENBRENNER, MARTIN, "The Keynesian Equations and the Balance of Payments," *Review of Economics and Statistics* (June 1940).

HOLZMAN, FRANKLIN, and ARNOLD ZELLNER, "The Foreign Trade and Balanced Budget Multipliers," *American Economic Review* (March 1958).

LANGE, OSCAR, "On the Theory of the Multiplier," *Econometrica* (July–October 1943).

MACHLUP, FRITZ, *International Trade and the National Income Multiplier*. Philadelphia: The Blakiston Co., 1943.

METZLER, LLOYD, "Underemployment Equilibrium in International Trade," *Econometrica* (April 1942).

NEISSER, HANS, and FRANCO MODIGLIANI, *National Incomes and International Trade*. Urbana, Ill.: University of Illinois, 1953.

ROBINSON, ROMNEY, "A Graphical Analysis of the Foreign Trade Multiplier," *Economic Journal* (September 1952).

CHAPTER 9

The Transfer Problem

In the past few chapters we concentrated on the economic effects of adjustment in the goods-and-services account. We will now turn our attention to the effects of transfers. But before doing so, it is necessary to say a few words about the relationship between international transfers and capital movements.

TRANSFERS AND CAPITAL MOVEMENTS

The terms *transfer* and *capital movement* are used with a number of different connotations in economics. Here we use the word *transfer* to mean a movement of economic assets from one country to another without the receipt of a *quid pro quo*; that is, without the receipt or expectation of a future receipt of a real or financial asset in exchange. A transfer is a gift. After the transfer has been made, no future obligations exist between the donor and recipient.

A *capital·movement*, by contrast, creates an obligation. There is an expectation that in the future the recipient will reimburse the lender for the funds received.

In addition, interest or dividends may accrue to the owner of the capital. Analytically, we can treat a capital movement as two transfers: a movement of the original capital and a "return" flow of principal and/or interest in some future time period.

REAL AND FINANCIAL TRANSFERS

Another important distinction to be kept in mind is whether the transfer or capital movement involves real or financial assets. A *real transfer* consists of the shipment of goods and services without receipt of a *quid pro quo*. No international payments are involved, and the supply of and demand for foreign currencies is generally not affected. For balance-of-payments purposes real transfers are not very interesting as no monetary imbalances are created. But the manner in which the real commodities are acquired and disposed of may through induced changes influence the external accounts indirectly. In the following sections we will neglect these possible repercussions.

Financial transfers consist of movements of financial claims without the receipt of a *quid pro quo*. That is, financial assets are donated to a foreign recipient—either a government or a private economic unit—without any expectation of future repayment. It is important how these financial assets are raised in the donating country and how they are used in the recipient country. If, for example, the donated funds consist of newly printed currency and go into governmental stockpiles of foreign currency in the recipient country nothing much will change. But if the funds are raised by taxation or a reduction of spending in the donating country and if they are spent by the foreign recipient—be it a public agency or a private individual—we will find that there are repercussions on the balance of payments and other economic magnitudes. In particular, the question whether a financial transfer of say $100 million from the United States to the United Kingdom will result in the subsequent movement of $100 million of commodities from the U.S. to the U.K. has attracted much attention. If it should turn out that an amount of real resources exactly equal to the financial transfer moves between the donating and recipient countries, we speak of the transfer as being *effected*. If real goods and services amounting to less than the financial transfer move, the transfer is *undereffected*, and if more real goods and services than the amount of the transfer move, the transfer is *overeffected*.

Viewed from a slightly different vantage point, a transfer that is effected will result in no balance-of-payments problems, as the financial flows are precisely matched by trade flows. The balance of payments will remain in equilibrium and no further adjustments are called for. Of course, once the transfer payments cease, all international transactions will return to their old values.

It may be instructive to follow in detail the various entries to be made in the balance-of-payments accounts for both a real and a financial transfer. In addition, we will draw the distinction between an effected and an undereffected transfer. In all cases, we will deal with the balance of payments of the donating country and use the official-settlements concept (see Chapter 4) as measuring the size of the balance-of-payments imbalance.

Table 9-1 shows the entries into the balance of payments of a country donating $1,000 in goods and services to another country. The credit entry

TABLE 9-1

A REAL TRANSFER

	Credit	Debit	
Goods and Services	1,000		
Transfers		1,000	
Capital			OSB = 0
Reserves			

OSB = Official-settlements balance

is the export of the goods and services and the offsetting debit entry is made in the transfer account. The official-settlements balance (*OSB*) is unaffected.

Table 9-2 records the initial entries to be made in case of a cash grant

TABLE 9-2

AN UNEFFECTED FINANCIAL TRANSFER

	Credit	Debit	
Goods and Services			
Transfers		1,000	
Capital			OSB = −1,000
Reserves	1,000		

to another country. Let us assume for convenience that the cash grant consists of gold or foreign currency. The transfer reduces the international reserves of the donating country by the amount of the transfer (credit entry) and the offsetting debit entry is made in the transfer account. We see that the official-settlements balance is in deficit by $1,000. The transfer is not effected at all.

If now the recipient country (see Table 9-3) uses the funds received for purchases of goods and services in the donating country, the donor's balance of payments will show the new exports of $1,000 and a corresponding entry in the international reserve account. The official-settlements balance will again show a balance of zero. The transfer is now fully effected. Of course, it is possible that an increase in exports and a decrease in imports together are responsible for the effecting of the transfer. The example merely illustrates one possible set of developments.

If instead of paying the transfer payment out of its own international

TABLE 9-3

AN EFFECTED FINANCIAL TRANSFER

	Credit	Debit	
Goods and Services	1,000		
Transfers		1,000	
Capital			OSB = 0
Reserves	1,000	1,000	

reserve holdings the donating country gives its own currency or other short-term assets to the other country, the entries that were made in our previous example in the reserve account will now be made in the capital account. In that case, the official-settlements balance will not be changed at all, as all credit and debit entries are made "above" the line. But if we were to utilize the net liquidity concept of the balance of payments, which considers short-term capital movements as being "below" the line (see Chapter 4) we would find that the net liquidity balance would be affected in the same way as the official-settlements balance.

The transfer problem is illustrated graphically in Figure 9-1, where we

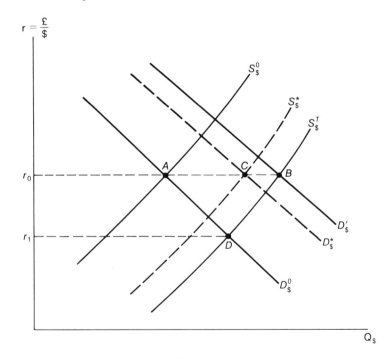

FIGURE 9-1

The Transfer Problem

show the familiar supply and demand curves for currency, here U.S. dollars. The initial supply and demand curves are labeled $S_\$^0$ and $D_\$^0$, resulting in equilibrium at the exchange rate r_0. Let us assume that the United States will now engage in a transfer payment equal to AB, increasing the dollar supply by that amount. That is, the dollar supply curve will shift to $S_\$^T$. The transfer is effected if simultaneously the demand for dollars due to foreign purchases in the United States increases by the same amount AB, shifting the demand curve for dollars to $D_\$'$ and resulting in a new equilibrium point B. The exchange rate will then remain at r_0. Clearly, it is not necessary that the entire shift is in the demand curve. A smaller increase in demand will be sufficient *if* the supply curve undergoes a leftward shift from its position $S_\$^T$. This might occur because Americans now have less to spend and consequently will reduce their imports. Such a possibility is shown by the dashed supply and demand curves $S_\$^*$ and $D_\$^*$. The combination shown is brought about by an increase in the dollar volume of exports by AC and a decrease in the dollar volume of U.S. imports by BC. The determination of the precise magnitude of the shifts will occupy our attention later in this chapter.

THE TRANSFER UNDER FLEXIBLE EXCHANGE RATES

Let us begin our analysis of the effect of transfers under the assumption that exchange rates are freely flexible, while prices and output levels remain constant. We will also assume that capital movements are nonexistent. In terms of Figure 9-1, we have an initial situation given by the dollar supply and demand curves $S_\$^0$ and $D_\$^0$. The transfer will shift the dollar supply curve to $S_\$^T$, and consequently the exchange rate will fall from r_0 to r_1. This fall in the exchange rate will bring about an increase in the physical quantity of exports and a decrease in the quantity of import goods. Consequently, the quantity of dollars demanded will increase due to the increase in export volume, and the quantity of dollars supplied will increase if the underlying import demand curve is elastic. (See Chapter 6 for a full discussion of the problems that may arise in case the demand curve for imports is inelastic.) A new equilibrium point is reached at D, where the value of U.S. exports is increased and that of imports decreased. The opposite holds true for the recipient country, where the exchange rate appreciates and the value of exports falls while imports go up.

With flexible exchange rates no balance-of-payments equilibrium problem will ever arise as the value of the currency will adjust to accommodate any transfer desired. Yet, there remains the problem whether the value of the real goods and services transferred is equal to the amount of the initial monetary transfer. In terms of the currency of the donating country it certainly is, as the initial monetary payment of let us say $100 million that the United

States makes is matched by an increase in exports and decrease in imports measured in terms of U.S. dollars. However, as we have seen, the U.S. dollar will depreciate in value as a result of the transfer, and in terms of *foreign* currency the value of goods and services that change hands is (with the exception of certain borderline cases) smaller than the value of the initial transfer payment. Here we are faced with the familiar index number problem of having to decide in terms of which yardstick—domestic or foreign currency—to evaluate the transfer. If we deal with an economy as large as the United States, there is some justification to opt for the use of the domestic currency. On the other hand, if the country under consideration is as small as Luxembourg or Iceland, the use of foreign units of exchange as a measuring rod is often more realistic.

Furthermore, there may be income and price changes associated with the devaluation, and the supply and demand curves of Figure 9-1 may undergo secondary shifts. Here we will not be concerned with these problems. We assume that the government adopts a policy that effectively neutralizes the secondary impact of the transfer on incomes and prices.

THE TRANSFER UNDER CONDITIONS OF PRICE FLEXIBILITY

Next we will investigate the effects of a transfer under classical assumptions: we will postulate that prices are fully flexible, but that exchange rates and output levels remain fixed. The economy is assumed to be operating at the full employment level. We will also assume that the amount transferred is raised by taxation and redistributed in the recipient country.

Under these assumptions, the question whether the transfer will be effected or not has a simple answer. The transfer will reduce aggregate expenditures in the donor country by the amount of the transfer, while expenditures in the recipient country increase by the same amount. The donor country's balance of payments is improved by the reduction in its expenditures on imports and the increase in exports due to the increased expenditures of the recipient country. (All reckoned in terms of the currency of the donor country if we are to analyze its balance of payments.) Formally, we may state the change in the balance of payments of the donor country as:

$$dB = dEX - dIM - T \tag{9.1}$$

$$dB = m_2 T - m_1(-T) - T \tag{9.2}$$

$$dB = (m_1 + m_2 - 1) T \tag{9.3}$$

Where B is the balance of payments of the donating country, m_1 the marginal propensity to import of the donating country, m_2 that of the recipient country, and T the transfer.

That is, the transfer will result in no effect on the balance of payments if the sum of the marginal propensities to import is equal to one. In that case the transfer will be fully effected. The transfer will be undereffected (over-effected) if the sum of the marginal propensities is smaller (larger) than one. In these cases balance-of-payments deficits (surpluses) remain, which have to be rectified by exchange rate changes, income adjustment, or some other method. Secondary costs may be associated with these adjustments required to restore external balance.

TRANSFERS AND INCOME ADJUSTMENTS

The third set of assumptions that is widely used for analysis of the effects of a transfer are the Keynesian assumptions of stable prices and ex-change rates as well as excess capacity that permits output and income changes to occur. We discussed the income adjustment mechanism in Chapter 8 and will draw heavily upon the conclusions arrived at in that chapter.

If the transfer represents the only disturbance to be analyzed, it is possible to replace the various sources of autonomous disturbances that we analyzed in Chapter 8 by the effects of the transfer. Let α_1 represent the pro-portion of the transfer by which absorption in country 1 is reduced; α_2 the proportion of the transfer by which absorption in country 2 is increased; μ_1 the proportion of the transfer by which imports in country 1 are reduced; and μ_2 the proportion of the transfer by which imports in country 2 are in-creased. Then we have

$$dA_1^0 = -\alpha_1 T \tag{9.4}$$

$$dA_2^0 = \alpha_2 T \tag{9.5}$$

$$dIM_1^0 = -\mu_1 T \tag{9.6}$$

$$dIM_2^0 = \mu_2 T \tag{9.7}$$

These expressions may then be substituted into equations 8A.12 and 8A.13 to obtain the effect of the transfer on the national incomes in the two coun-tries:

$$dY_1 = \frac{1}{m_1 s_2 + m_2 s_1 + s_1 s_2}$$
$$\times [(s_2 + m_2)dA_1^0 + m_2 dA_2^0 - s_2 dIM_1^0 + s_2 dIM_2^0] \tag{8A.12}$$

$$dY_2 = \frac{1}{m_2 s_1 + m_1 s_2 + s_1 s_2}$$
$$\times [(s_1 + m_1)dA_2^0 + m_1 dA_1^0 - s_1 dIM_2^0 + s_1 dIM_1^0] \tag{8A.13}$$

Writing $D = m_1 s_2 + m_2 s_1 + s_1 s_2$ and making the necessary substitutions we obtain

$$dY_1 = \frac{1}{D}[-(s_2 + m_2)\alpha_1 + m_2\alpha_2 + s_2\mu_1 - s_2\mu_2]T \qquad (9.8)$$

$$dY_2 = \frac{1}{D}[-m_1\alpha_1 + (s_1 + m_1)\alpha_2 + s_1\mu_1 + s_2\mu_2]T \qquad (9.9)$$

We are now able to derive the effect of the transfer on the balance of payments of the donating country, in our example country 1, by using the familiar balance-of-payments equation.

$$dB_1 = dEX_1 - dIM_1 - T \qquad (9.10)$$

$$dB_1 = dIM_2^0 + m_2 dY_2 - dIM_1^0 - m_1 dY_1 - T \qquad (9.11)$$

Substituting 9.8 and 9.9 into this equation we obtain:

$$dB = \left[\frac{s_1 s_2}{D}\mu_1 + \frac{s_1 s_2}{D}\mu_2 + \frac{m_1 s_2}{D}\alpha_1 + \frac{m_2 s_1}{D}\alpha_2 - 1\right]T \qquad (9.12)$$

The term in brackets will decide whether the transfer will be effected or not. If it is larger than zero, the transfer is overeffected, if it is equal to zero it is effected, and if it is smaller than zero it is undereffected.

WHY SHOULD A TRANSFER BE EFFECTED?

Unless the transfer is exactly effected, further adjustments of exchange rates, prices, or incomes are called for. That these adjustments may be associated with costs has been pointed out previously. If these secondary adjustment costs are positive, the total cost of a transfer to the donating country will exceed the budgeted cost of the transfer. It should be noted that these secondary adjustment costs may amount to a multiple of the budgeted transfer payment. Hence, countries that may expect that the transfer payments made to other countries will be undereffected may find it advisable to take steps designed to minimize these additional balance-of-payments adjustment costs. The tying of foreign aid is one instrument by which the relevant marginal propensities to import in equation 9.12 may be increased and may help to keep the costs of the transfer to the donating country down. Of course, tied grants are a less efficient way to receive aid from the viewpoint of the recipient country. The costs of these inefficiencies on the recipient side will have to be balanced against the savings in adjustment cost to the donor country if we want to arrive at a global assessment of the costs and benefits of tied foreign aid.

All we said in the previous three chapters regarding the costs and benefits associated with exchange rate, price level, and income adjustments is also valid for disturbances that have their origin in transfer payments. First we have to determine the effect of the transfer on the exchange rate, price, and income level, and then we can utilize the analysis of Chapters 6, 7, and 8 to determine the costs and benefits that accrue to the transferring and the recipient country.

TRANSFER DATA

Figure 9-2 shows the amounts of the private and governmental transfer payments made by the United States in the post-World War II period. Clearly, it is not possible to determine in each instance whether the transfer was actually effected or not. On the one hand it may be argued that the generally sizeable U.S. surplus on trade account was due in large measure to

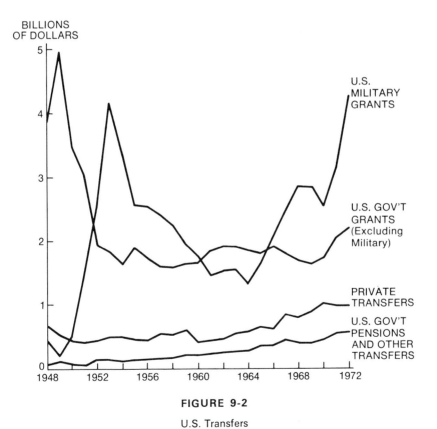

FIGURE 9-2

U.S. Transfers

SOURCE: Survey of Current Business, June 1972, p. 30 and October 1972, p. 27.

the generous transfer payments made to foreigners, which enabled them to purchase American goods. On the other hand, the overall U.S. balance of payments during most of the period was in deficit (according to most standard measures), and it may be argued that a large part of that deficit was due to the fact that the transfer payments were undereffected. If this second view is accurate, then the United States was actually forced to bear a burden *in excess* of the amount of the actual transfer payments made because a balance-of-payments deficit was created, which called for further income, price, and/or exchange-rate adjustments. These adjustments then imposed a secondary cost on the U.S. economy.

SUGGESTED FURTHER READINGS

JONES, RONALD, "The Transfer Problem Revisited," *Economica* (May 1970).

JOHNSON, HARRY G., "The Transfer Problem and Exchange Stability," *Journal of Political Economy* (June 1956). Reprinted in R. E. CAVES and H. G. JOHNSON, eds., *AEA Readings in International Economics*. Homewood, Ill.: Richard D. Irwin, Inc., 1968.

KEYNES, JOHN M., "The German Transfer Problem," *Economic Journal* (March 1929). Reprinted in H. S. ELLIS and L. A. METZLER, eds., *AEA Readings in the Theory of International Trade*. Homewood, Ill.: Richard D. Irwin Inc., 1950.

MACHLUP, FRITZ, *International Payments, Debts, and Gold*, Chaps. 15–19. New York: Charles Scribner's Sons, 1964.

METZLER, LLOYD A., "The Transfer Problem Reconsidered," *Journal of Political Economy* (June 1942). Reprinted in H. S. ELLIS and L. A. METZLER, eds., *AEA Readings in the Theory of International Trade*. Homewood, Ill.: Richard D. Irwin, Inc., 1950.

MIKESELL, RAYMOND F., *The Economics of Foreign Aid*. Chicago: Aldine Publishing Co., 1968.

OHLIN, BERTIL, "The Reparation Problem," *Economic Journal*, (June 1929). Reprinted in H. S. ELLIS and L. A. METZLER, eds., *AEA Reading in the Theory of International Trade*. Homewood, Ill.: Richard D. Irwin, Inc., 1950.

SAMUELSON, PAUL A., "The Transfer Problem and Transport Costs," in R. E. CAVES and H. G. JOHNSON, eds., *AEA Readings in International Economics*, Homewood, Ill.: Richard D. Irwin, Inc., 1968 (abridged version of two articles in the *Economic Journal*, June 1952 and June 1954.)

CHAPTER 10

Capital Movements

In the first chapter of this book we introduced the rationale for capital movements: the gains to be reaped by improving the intertemporal allocation of resources. At that juncture it was assumed that a movement of real capital goods was to follow the financial capital movements. In Chapter 9 we pointed out that there is no certainty that a real commodity movement will accompany or follow a financial movement. Capital movements may be viewed as a two-way transfer, consisting of an initial flow from the lending to the borrowing country and a subsequent return flow of principal and interest. Analytically, it is therefore possible to treat a capital flow as two separate transfers—one from the lender to the borrower and one (or several) payments in the opposite direction. In each case, we will be faced with a "transfer problem," and all that has been said about the problem of effecting a one-way transfer will also apply to the two-way capital movements. Here we will not repeat the discussion of Chapter 9 but concentrate instead on other important aspects of international capital movements. But before analyzing the causes and effects of international capital movements it will be necessary to draw some basic distinctions between direct investment, long-term capital, and short-term capital flows.

DIRECT INVESTMENT

The term *direct investment* is generally applied to international movements of capital in which the investor acquires some degree of control over the decisions of the enterprise in which the funds are invested. Where exactly such control starts is difficult to ascertain, and U.S. balance-of-payments statistics use an arbitrary cutoff point by labeling every foreign asset as a direct investment (rather than a portfolio investment) whenever Americans own at least 10 percent of the controlling interest. For foreign direct investment in the United States a cutoff of 25 percent foreign ownership is used.

First of all, let us direct our attention to some of the reasons why direct foreign investment takes place at all. At first glance, we might expect that local entrepreneurs with their more intimate knowledge of market conditions, local customs, language, and laws and the existence of established business connections will have a competitive advantage in operating a firm. Furthermore, foreign investors will be faced with higher costs of international travel, communication, and transportation for their management and perhaps some of the resources as well.

There are many powerful reasons why these obstacles may prove insufficient to stop foreign investment, though not all reasons listed will apply in each circumstance. First, a foreign branch or subsidiary will bring a firm engaged in international trade closer to its foreign markets, resulting in lower transport cost. Second, tariff walls will be scaled because goods are no longer shipped across national borders. It is said that the substantial increase in U.S. investment in the countries of the European Common Market was prompted in large measure by the fact that a large, tariff-free market was created by the formation of the customs union with a common external tariff. Third, a firm may be able to operate closer to the source of essential raw materials. This argument is especially persuasive in the case of mineral and petroleum industries. Fourth, the foreign country may offer cheap labor sources, which may be of considerable advantage in labor-intensive production processes. Fifth, a firm may have a certain degree of monopoly power due to patents or advanced technology. According to this argument, we would expect little direct foreign investment in perfectly competitive industries, such as farming. This argument also explains why we observe direct investment going in both directions between two countries. Industries that are heavily based on patents, like the chemical industry, offer an example. All these and many other factors may be influential in making direct foreign investment a profitable proposition.

The book value of U.S. direct investments abroad amounted to $94.0 billion in 1972, accounting for 47 percent of the value of all U.S. assets abroad. Figure 10-1 shows the U.S. direct investments abroad and foreign direct investment in the United States.

The bulk of U.S. direct investment abroad at the end of 1972 was in Canada with $25.8 billion dollars. The European countries together account for another $30.7 billion. Direct investment in Japan amounted to $2.2 billion. Among the less-developed regions, Latin America is the leader with $16.6 billion, and other foreign countries account for $13.9 billion.

Direct investment in the United States in mostly undertaken by large

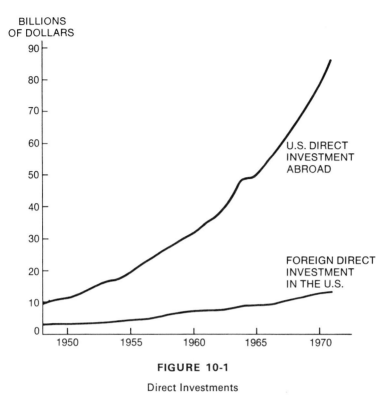

FIGURE 10-1

Direct Investments

SOURCE: *Historical Statistics of the United States* and Survey
of Current Business, October 1972, p. 21.

foreign companies. Of the total of $14.4 billion of foreign direct investment in the United States at the end of 1972, $10.4 billion came from Europe, $3.6 billion from Canada, and a mere $0.3 billion from the entire rest of the world.

We should note that the balance-of-payments accounts report only part of the change in the international direct position of a country. The book value of direct foreign investments changes due to (1) the familiar balance-of-payments flows recording international capital flows; (2) the reinvestment of foreign earnings that are not repatriated but instead invested again in overseas ventures; (3) asset valuation adjustments due to asset price changes; and (4) changes in the value of foreign assets due to exchange-rate adjustments. Table 10-1 shows the main components of the annual changes in U.S. direct investments abroad for the period 1966–71.

In addition, foreign subsidiaries and branches may raise capital directly in the foreign countries in which they operate, but those funds also represent liabilities to foreigners. The net investment position is unaffected.

Figure 10-2 gives the rates of return on all U.S. foreign direct investment and, for comparison, the rates of return in domestic manufacturing industries (excluding petroleum). We note that there are no basic discrepancies between the two rates during the period studied. The differences

TABLE 10-1

CHANGES IN U.S. DIRECT INVESTMENT
(millions of dollars)

	1966	1967	1968	1969	1970	1971
Change in direct investment	5,325	4,692	5,492	6,033	7,074	7,823
Balance-of-payments flows	3,661	3,137	3,209	3,254	4,445	4,765
Reinvested earnings	1,739	1,598	2,175	2,604	2,885	3,116
Valuation adjustments	−75	−43	108	175	−256	−58

Source: *Survey of Current Business*, October 1971, p. 27 and October 1972, p. 20.

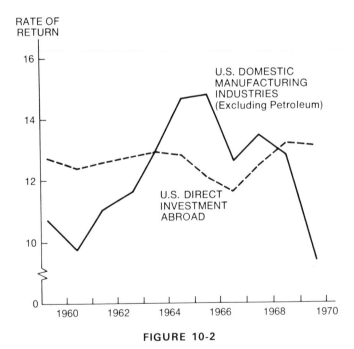

FIGURE 10-2

Rates of Return on U.S. Direct Investments Abroad
and in Domestic Manufacturing Industries

NOTE: Return on direct investments represents earnings plus interest (on intercompany accounts) applied to book value at beginning of year. Return on domestic manufacturing represents net income applied to net worth at beginning of year.

SOURCE: *Survey of Current Business,* October 1971.

shown are mainly due to the timing of the business cycles abroad and in the United States.

LONG-TERM CAPITAL

International capital movements that do not result in any control over foreign investments are called *portfolio investments*. They consist basically of two categories: (1) international equity investments that do not qualify as direct investments because Americans hold less than 10 percent of the controlling interest; and (2) international loans and bonds with more than one-year maturity. Financial assets with less than one-year maturity are classified as short-term capital.

Here we will pay particular attention to international long-term *bonds*, which pay a fixed amount of interest per year. International capital markets form a link between the domestic capital markets of those nations that allow free international capital movements. At present, there are some 20 nations that permit free international capital movements. In the period immediately following World War II, the New York bond market dominated the international scene. Foreign issues floated in the New York market amounted to about half a billion dollars in the first half of 1963. At that time, the continuing U.S. balance-of-payments deficit prompted the administration to adopt an *interest-equalization tax* of 15 percent, which was applied to all borrowings by developed countries other than Canada. This tax effectively barred the developed countries—mainly Europe—from direct access to the United States capital markets, and bond issues floated in the U.S. by these countries declined from $536 million in 1963 to zero in 1970. Figure 10-3 shows the main borrowers in the United States capital market as Canada, international organizations, and less-developed countries.

Due to the exclusion of borrowers from the developed countries from the New York capital market, new markets rapidly developed in Europe. Figure 10-4 shows the annual volume of new international bond issues in European capital markets. Most of these bonds are *Eurobonds*, a term applied to international bond issues that are underwritten by an international bank consortium and sold in several countries simultaneously. Of the aggregate $4.4 billion dollars of international bonds issued in European capital markets in 1971, $3.5 billion were of the Eurobond variety. The remaining $0.9 billion were regular foreign bonds that were sold in just one foreign country. Most of these international bonds are denominated in U.S. dollars, and the second most important currency in international bond markets is now the German mark. But more and more other currencies are starting to be used as markets deepen and currencies become stronger.

A substantial number of bonds carried a provision which allowed the

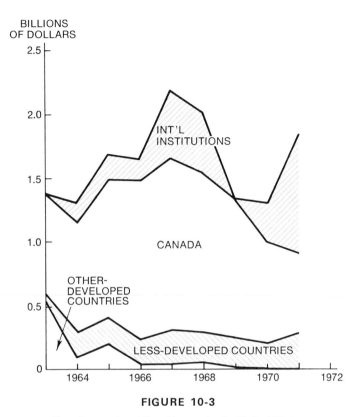

FIGURE 10-3

New International Bond Issues in the United States

SOURCE: International Monetary Fund, *1971 Annual Report,* Washington, D.C., and World Bank, *1972 Annual Report,* Washington, D.C., 1972.

lender to demand repayment in one or even several other currencies. These so-called *currency option bonds* provide an effective hedge against possible losses to be suffered by the lender in case of exchange rate changes. Naturally, the borrower assumes this additional risk.

We should also note that the majority of all borrowing by international institutions—like the International Bank for Reconstruction and Development, the Asian Development Bank, and similar organizations—ultimately benefits the less-developed countries as these funds are merely channeled through these international organizations before reaching the ultimate borrowers in the less-developed countries. These international organizations play an important role in the financing of development projects by making their expertise and reputation available with the result that less-developed countries are able to borrow more funds than they would be able to raise in their own behalf.

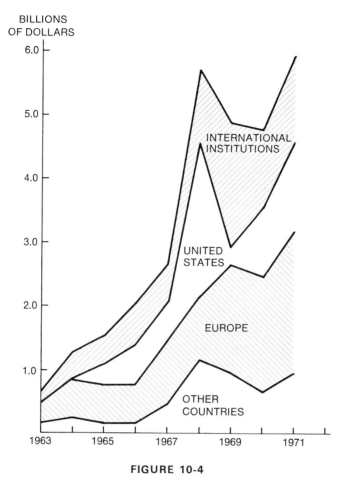

FIGURE 10-4

New International Bond Issues in Europe

SOURCE: International Monetary Fund, *1971 Annual Report,* Washington,
D.C., and World Bank, *1972 Annual Report,* Washington, D.C., p. 93.

SHORT-TERM CAPITAL

Much of the distinction between long-term and short-term capital
movements is arbitrary. The official dividing line is drawn at a bond maturity
date of one year. However, there may well be purchasers of long-term bonds
who do not intend to hold these bonds for more than a few weeks, while
others may continue to keep their funds perpetually invested in short-term
bonds, buying new short-term bonds each time the old ones mature. Of
course, it is difficult to identify these motivations and hence an arbitrary dividing line of one-year maturity has been established in the official accounts.

Short-term capital consists of currency, demand and time deposits with commercial banks, Treasury bills, commercial paper, and similar financial obligations with less than one-year maturity. Clearly, short-term capital is more liquid than the long-term capital discussed in the previous section. Some of the short-term assets like currency and demand deposits are properly classified as money, while others constitute near-money. Here, then, lies an important distinction between short- and long-term capital movements: short-term capital movements are likely to have a direct effect on the money stock; long-term capital movements do not. For example, if a person decides to move $1 million from his checking account with an American Bank into an account with a German Bank, the monetary base in the United States will shrink by $1 million. In addition, there may be a multiple contraction of the money supply in the United States as banks that have no free reserves will have to call in some of their outstanding loans. The details of the multiple contraction process of the money supply are described in most elementary textbooks.[1] These monetary effects may have repercussions on the level of employment, income, and prices in both countries.

On the other hand, the new deposit with the German bank may be the basis for a multiple expansion process of German marks, if the German bank exchanges its dollars against marks at the German Central Bank. This assumes, of course, that the German Central Bank does not take steps to effectively neutralize the effect of the transactions on the German money supply.

Rather than converting the dollars into another currency, the German bank might simply hold on to the new dollar deposits. The German bank now holds dollars, but because the funds are held by a European bank, these dollars are referred to as *Eurodollars*. The initial impetus to the Eurodollar market was given by the Soviet Union, which did not want to hold her dollar balances in U.S. banks for fear that these funds might be blocked by governmental action. As interest rates on Eurodollars—which are not subject to the same regulations as U.S. bank deposits—rose, American and foreign companies channeled dollars to European banks rather than depositing them with U.S. banks. To a large extent, the great increase in the Eurodollar market in 1969 resulted from the fact that U.S. banks were prevented from paying competitive interest rates to their depositors due to interest-rate ceilings imposed by the Federal Reserve Board. Consequently, these funds were deposited with European Banks, some of them being subsidiaries or branches of U.S. banks. These Eurodollar deposits earned higher interest rates than could be paid legally in the United States. In turn, the U.S. banks that had lost the deposits to their own European branches borrowed the funds back.

---

[1] H. R. Heller, *The Economic System* (New York: The Macmillan Company, 1972), Chap. 14; or P. A. Samuelson, *Economics*, 8th ed. (New York: McGraw-Hill Book Company, 1970), Chap. 16.

The result was a large circular flow of dollar deposits, which increased the nominal size of the Eurodollar market substantially. The removal of interest-rate ceilings for certain large time deposits in the second half of 1969 and the imposition of reserve requirements on foreign branches of U.S. banks in 1970 largely eliminated the incentive to go through these complicated book-keeping procedures just to pay a market rate of interest on deposits. Figure 10-5 illustrates the relationship between high Eurodollar interest rates and

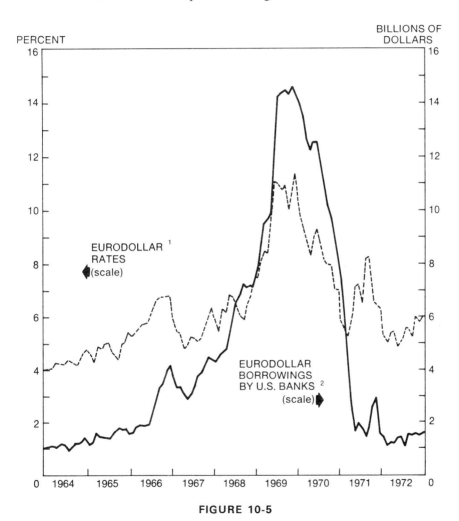

FIGURE 10-5

Eurodollar Borrowings by U.S. Banks and Eurodollar Rates

NOTES: [1]Monthly averages of Friday figures for 90-day Eurodollar rates.
[2]Monthly averages of Wednesday figures. Eurodollar borrowings represent gross liabilities of U.S. banks to their foreign branches.
SOURCE: Federal Reserve Bank of St. Louis.

the borrowings by U.S. banks in the Eurodollar market made necessary by the prior outflow of U.S. funds to Europe in search for higher interest rates than could be paid legally by U.S. banks under the interest rate ceilings imposed by the Federal Reserve Bank (Regulation Q). But despite the decreased role played by U.S. banks, the Eurodollar market continues to expand. External liabilities of banks in eight reporting European countries amounted to $97.9 billion at the end of 1971 (see Figure 10-6).

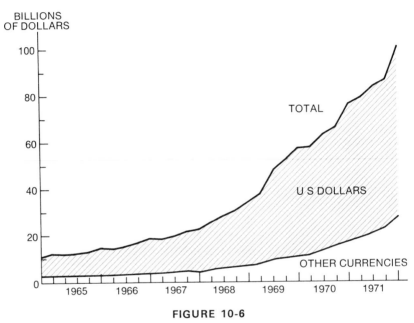

FIGURE 10-6

Size of the Euro-Currency Market (in billions of dollars)

SOURCE: Bank for International Settlements, *42nd Annual Report,* Basle, 1972.

Due to the fact that many of the recorded financial flows in the Eurodollar market are circular in nature, the gross data overestimate the actual importance of the market as a source of new funds. After eliminating redeposits of funds, the size of the Eurocurrency market is estimated to be about $71 billion, with Eurodollars accounting for $54 billion at the end of 1971.

In spite of the fact that movements are under way to increase the extent of governmental control, the Eurodollar market provides an important link between the various national capital markets. It also offers an interesting example as to how international borrowers and lenders reacted to the imposition of controls to the U.S. market by shifting the center of activity to Europe.

INTEREST RATES AND CAPITAL FLOWS

We will now turn to a theoretical analysis of international capital movements. Two main factors will be considered: interest-rate differentials and risk diversification. We will treat all capital as a homogeneous unit. Given our previous discussion of direct investments, long-term, and short-term capital movements, this is clearly a gross oversimplification. However, the unified analysis will permit us to avoid unnecessary repetition. If we wish to argue that there is no such thing as one unified capital market, but instead a multitude of separate markets, we can apply the following analysis separately to each one of these markets.

Capital markets may be analyzed in terms of the supply of and demand for loanable funds. As higher interest rates are offered, people will forego present consumption and offer their funds in capital markets, leading to an upward-sloping supply of loanable funds curve as depicted in Figure 10-7a. The quantity of loanable funds (LF) demanded increases as the price of capital in the form of interest to be paid falls, resulting in a downward sloping demand curve for loanable funds. From the domestic supply and demand curves for loanable funds, we may derive the excess supply and demand curves for loanable funds, which indicate the amounts that are available for international lending or are demanded in free international capital markets at various interest rates. Figure 10-7b shows a set of hypothetical excess supply and demand curves for loanable funds for the United States. For simplicity's sake we will assume that there is a fixed exchange rate between the

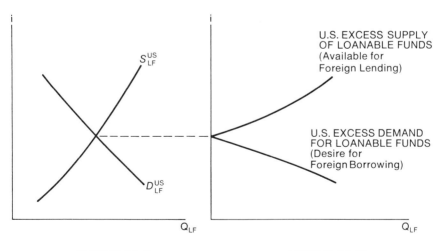

Fi GURE 10-7a   **FIGURE 10-7b**

Supply and Demand for Loanable Funds

various currencies in international capital markets. Or, even simpler, that we are dealing with a domestic and an overseas market for dollar funds, such as the Eurodollar market.

Let us assume that the excess supply and demand curves for loanable funds in the United States and in the Eurodollar market are as given in Figure 10-8. In the absence of international capital flows, the interest rate in the United States, i^{US}, will be below that prevailing in the European market, i^{E}. As soon as international capital movements are allowed, the United States will lend capital equal to OF in the Eurodollar market. The old interest-rate differential will be eliminated and a new common interest rate i^{W} will be established. Let us note that once the common interest rate is established the international capital flows will *not* cease, as they are necessary to keep the interest rates equal to each other. If capital flows would cease, the old inter-est-rate differential would be reestablished in this simple flow model.

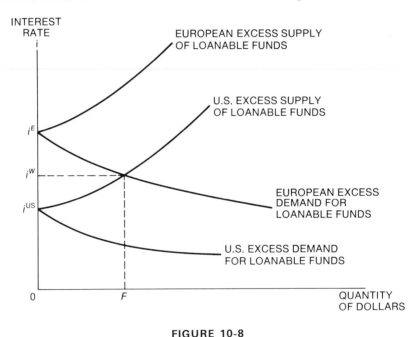

FIGURE 10-8

The International Loanable Funds Market

STOCK-FLOW ADJUSTMENTS

The next step in our analysis is to combine the simple flow model of capital movements with a rudimentary stock adjustment model. As capital flows into Europe, the *stock* of capital there will be increased. But as the stock of capital becomes larger, less and less attractive investment projects will be available. Consequently, the demand for new funds will decrease, leading to a downward shift of the excess demand (and excess supply) curve for Euro-dollars. Let us assume for simplicity's sake that the excess supply of loanable funds from the U.S. is perfectly elastic at the interest rate i^{US}. As the European capital stock increases, the interest-rate differential that gave rise to the capital flows will be eliminated, and we will reach a new equilibrium as we attain the desired stock of capital both in Europe and the United States.

The stock-flow adjustment process is further illustrated in Figure 10-9,

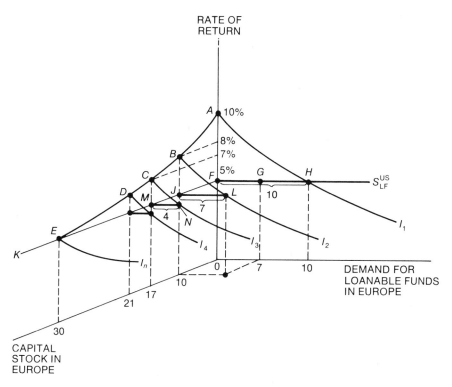

FIGURE 10-9

Stock-Flow Adjustment

where we show the hypothetical excess demand for loanable funds by Europe on the horizontal axis to the right, the interest rate on the vertical axis, and the European capital stock along the third axis. Let us assume that initially Europe has no capital at all and that the United States has an infinitely elastic supply of capital at an interest rate of 5 percent. Capital stock depreciation is neglected.

In year 1 we assume that Europe has a demand curve for loanable funds as indicated by I_1. At an interest rate of 5 percent Europe will want to borrow FH (= 10) units of capital. This is the capital inflow into Europe in year 1. At the beginning of year 2, Europe has a stock of capital of 10 units. Let us assume that the new excess demand curve for loanable funds starts at point B and is indicated by I_2. Again Europeans will borrow in the U.S. capital market, this time JL or FG (= 7) units. These 7 units of new funds are added to the European capital stock, which amounts to 17 units at the beginning of year 3. We now reach point C on the demand for capital curve. The new demand curve for loanable funds is shown by I_3, and the process is repeated. Eventually, Europe will have accumulated so much capital that there is no further new demand for loanable funds. This point is reached in Figure 10-9 at point E, where the rate of return on capital in Europe coincides with the rate of interest that has to be paid for new funds borrowed from the United States. Hence, no new borrowing will take place: long-term equilibrium is reached with a total capital stock of 30 units in Europe. The balance of payments will show no further capital flows, and the balance of international indebtedness will show a net debtor position for Europe and a net creditor position for the United States.

PORTFOLIO MODELS

A question that has been left unanswered so far is what determines the desired stocks of foreign assets that investors wish to hold. In addition to the interest-rate differential mentioned already, two other factors are generally considered: a wealth constraint and a risk factor. The treatment of the wealth constraint is fairly straightforward when we deal with private capital movements, but more elusive in case of government capital. Here we will deal mainly with the risk factor.

Investors prefer a low-risk asset over a high-risk asset if both offer the same rate of return. Conversely, for a given risk exposure, they prefer a higher rate of return over a lower rate of return. In Figure 10-10 we show the rate of return i along the vertical axis and the standard deviation σ of the selected portfolio as a measure of the risk associated with the portfolio along the horizontal axis. As long as a higher interest rate is desirable and higher risk is undesirable, we will find that indifference curves showing the various rate of return and risk combinations between which the investor is indifferent will slope upward to the right. One possible set is shown by the indifference curves I_0, I_1, and I_2 in Figure 10-10. In the same graph we plot the rates of return and risks associated with various possible portfolios; each portfolio being represented by a dot. The collection of all *efficient* portfolios, in that they offer the highest rate of return for any given degree of risk (or vice versa) is

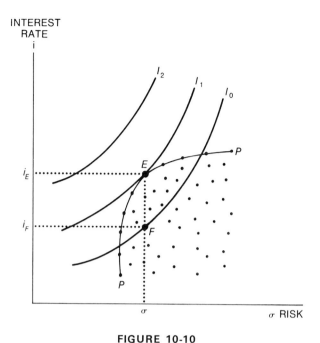

FIGURE 10-10

The Optimal Portfolio

shown by the frontier *PP*. A portfolio, such as *F*, allows the investor to reach the indifference curve I_0. Clearly, portfolio *E* yields a higher degree of satisfaction in that it permits the attainment of a higher rate of return for the same degree of risk. We can reach the higher indifference curve I_1. On the other hand, given the portfolio frontier *PP*, indifference curve I_2 is not attainable.

We start by demonstrating that with portfolio diversification it is possible to reduce the risk while attaining the same expected rate of return. For instance, let us assume that the rate of interest that can be obtained by investing in securities *A* or *B* is equal to 5 percent in both cases. That is, the expected rate of return will be 5 percent regardless of how much is invested in each security. We will assume that the variance σ^2 for each security is equal to 10. If the entire wealth is invested in one security, this will also be the variance of the portfolio. The variance of a diversified portfolio is determined according to the following formula:[2]

$$V(i_{A, B}) = P_A^2 \sigma_A^2 + 2P_A P_B \sigma_{A,B} + P_B^2 \sigma_B^2 \qquad (10.1)$$

[2]See W. F. Sharpe, *Portfolio Theory and Capital Markets* (New York: McGraw-Hill Book Company, 1970), Part I, for an introduction to portfolio selection theory.

where P stands for the proportion of the portfolio held in the respective asset, σ^2 is the variance, and $\sigma_{A,B}$ the covariance of the rates of return. Assuming that the covariance between the rates of return of the two securities is .3, formula 10.1 yields a variance of 5.15 for a portfolio containing both assets in the same proportion. This is clearly lower than the variance of 10 obtainable by investing in one security only.

International investors have a choice between investing in their home country alone or diversifying their portfolio internationally. Foreign assets will become more attractive if they (1) offer a higher rate of return, (2) offer a lower risk factor, and (3) have a low degree of correlation between the rates of return at home and abroad. Table 10-2 shows the rates of return and standard deviations obtainable by investing in diversified portfolios of common stocks in eleven industrialized countries, as well as the correlation coefficient between the rates of return of the different foreign portfolios and the United States.[3] The various combinations of rates of return and standard deviations

TABLE 10-2

RATES OF RETURN AND STANDARD DEVIATION FROM INVESTING
IN FOREIGN CAPITAL MARKET AVERAGES
1959–1966

	Rate of Return (Per cent per Annum) (1)	Standard Deviation (2)	Correlation of Foreign Rate of Return with US Rate of Return (3)
Australia	9.44	34.87	0.0585
Belgium	1.09	37.56	0.1080
Canada	5.95	41.19	0.7025
France	4.27	49.60	0.1938
Germany	7.32	94.69	0.3008
Italy	8.12	103.33	0.1465
Japan	16.54	92.52	0.1149
Netherlands	5.14	86.34	0.2107
South Africa	8.47	61.92	−0.1620
United Kingdom	9.59	65.28	0.2414
United States	7.54	47.26	1.0000

Source: H. G. Grubel, "Internationally Diversified Portfolios," *American Economic Journal*, December 1968, p. 1304.

[3] From H. G. Grubel, "Internationally Diversified Portfolios," *American Economic Review*, December 1968. Grubel assumes that the investor holds a portfolio that is equivalent to the basis of the various stock market indicators (like Standard and Poor's in the U.S.) in the different countries.

for each national portfolio are also depicted in Figure 10-11. It is possible to calculate the rates of return and standard deviations that would have accrued to investors who incorporated foreign assets into their portfolios. The set of efficient portfolios, in the sense that they maximize the rate of return for any given standard deviation, can be calculated, and an efficient portfolio frontier be graphed. This is done in Figure 10-11, where we also show the rate of

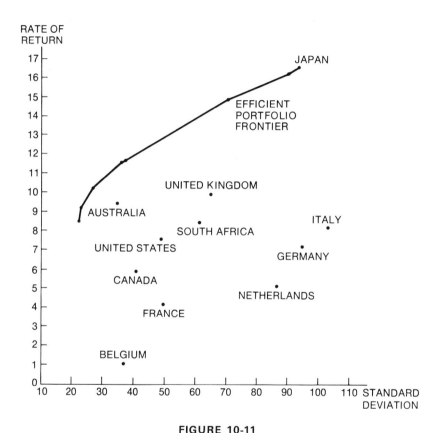

FIGURE 10-11

The Set of Attainable Portfolios

SOURCE: Adapted from H.G. Grubel, "Internationally Diversified Portfolios," *American Economic Review,* December 1968, p. 1299–1314.

return and standard deviation of the various national portfolios. It is evident that the diversified portfolios allow the investor to attain higher rates of return for a given degree of risk or a lower degree of risk for a given rate of return, and therewith to reach higher levels of satisfaction as illustrated in Figure 10-10.

For instance, by investing in an average portfolio in the United States, a rate of return of 7.54 percent could have been obtained, with a standard deviation of 47.26 during the period 1959–66. An investor who would have diversified his portfolio internationally could have obtained a rate of return of approximately 12.6 percent while maintaining the same degree of risk by selecting a portfolio located on the frontier *PP*.

Portfolio adjustment models of international capital flows are stock adjustment models. But, as we pointed out earlier, the balance-of-payments data represent annual flows. Some investigators have used stock adjustment models to estimate annual balance of payments flows, while others have used flow models. Table 10-3 summarizes the results of some of the most important empirical studies.

TABLE 10-3

EFFECT OF A 1 PERCENT INCREASE IN U.S. INTEREST RATES ON THE CAPITAL ACCOUNTS
(millions of dollars per year)

Item	Investigator	Stock Effect	Flow Effect
U.S. short-term assets	Branson	−468	
	Branson (m)	−210	
	Kenen		−1,080
	Prachowny		−680
U.S. long-term assets	Branson	−315	
	Branson (m)	−800	
	Miller-Whitman	−1,073	−84
	Prachowny		−496
U.S. short-term liabilities	Branson	260	
	Branson (m)	449	
	Kenen		1,040
U.S. long-term liabilities	Branson	693	
	Branson (m)	2,000	
	Prachowny		400

(m) indicates that monthly data were used in the estimates.

Source: Edward Leamer and Robert Stern, "Problems in the Theory and Empirical Estimation of International Capital Movements," National Bureau of Economic Research, *Conference on International Mobility and Movement of Capital*, Washington, D.C., 1970. The sources cited refer to W. H. Branson, *Financial Capital Flows in the United States Balance of Payments* (Amsterdam: North-Holland Publishing Co., 1968); P. B. Kenen, "Short Term Capital Movements and the U.S. Balance of Payments," in *The United States Balance of Payments*, Hearings before the Joint Economic Committee, (Washington, D. C.,1963); M. F. J. Prachowny, *A Structural Model of the U.S. Balance of Payments* (Amsterdam: North-Holland Publishing Co., 1969).

All data refer to annual balance-of-payments flows caused by a 1 percent increase in U.S. interest rates. The estimates vary widely, with the high estimates generally being four or five times as large as the low estimates for any individual account. Many problems are associated with the estimation of reliable capital flow coefficients. Among the problems encountered is the presence of speculators, especially in periods of uncertainty as to future exchange rates; the imposition of capital controls and capital rationing by governments; data inadequacies; lags in the reaction of investors and speculators; and the specification of the proper functional form of the regression coefficients.

Clearly, much work remains to be done both in the theoretical formulation and the empirical estimation of international capital movements. It is an area where a multitude of factors impinges on each decision, and at various times the weight attributed to the different factors is apt to change radically in the investor's decision calculus. Rather than dealing with the economic forces as they are at one point in time, the researcher has to take into account the expectations of the investors as to what the economic situation is likely to be some time in the future. Reasonable men will differ in their estimates of the future course of economic activity, and hence unexpected variations in international capital flows will occur.

SUGGESTED FURTHER READINGS

BELL, PHILIP W., "Private Capital Movements and the U.S. Balance of Payments Position," in U. S. Congress, Joint Economic Committee, *Factors Affecting the United States Balance of Payments.* Washington, D.C., 1962.

BRANSON, WILLIAM, *Financial Capital Flows in the U.S. Balance of Payments.* Amsterdam: North-Holland Publishing Co., 1968.

BRYANT, RALPH C., and PATRIC H. HENDERSHOTT, "Financial Capital Flows in the Balance of Payments of the U.S.," *Princeton Studies in International Finance:* Princeton, N.J.: Princeton University Press, 1970.

FRIEDMAN, MILTON, "The Euro-Dollar Market: Some First Principles," *Review,* Federal Reserve Bank of St. Louis (July 1971).

GRUBEL, HERBERT G., "Internationally Diversified Portfolios," *American Economic Review* (December 1968).

HELLER, H. ROBERT, "Foreign Bond Issues in Europe," *Lloyds Bank Review* (October 1967).

HODJERA, ZORAN, "Short-Term Capital Movements of the United Kingdom," *Journal of Political Economy* (July 1971).

LEAMER, EDWARD E., and ROBERT M. STERN, "Problems in the Theory and Empirical Estimation of International Capital Movements," F. MACHLUP, W. SALANT, and L. TARSHIS, eds. *International Mobility and Movement of Capital,* New York: National Bureau of Economic Research, 1972, p. 171–206.

SHARPE, WILLIAM F., *Portfolio Theory and Capital Markets.* New York: McGraw-Hill Book Company, 1970.

CHAPTER 11

International Reserves

In the last few chapters we analyzed various alternative adjustment possibilities that are open to a country faced with a balance-of-payments disequilibrium. In this chapter we will discuss an alternative to international adjustment: the financing of an imbalance by international reserves. We will first look at the purpose and function of international reserves, discuss its various sources of supply, and then analyze the factors determining the demand for international reserves by a country.

THE FUNCTION
OF INTERNATIONAL RESERVES

Most individual economic units find it advantageous to hold part of their aggregate wealth in the form of liquid assets. These liquid reserves derive their usefulness from their general acceptability by other economic units. By holding inventories of liquid assets, costly and frequent adjustments to nonsynchronized patterns of payments and receipts can be avoided.

The authorities responsible for national economic policy hold international reserves for the same purpose: to avoid having to incur adjustment costs to every international imbalance. A country that is faced with an imbalance in its international accounts (Chapter 5) has a choice of adjusting via exchange-rate changes (Chapter 6), price-level changes (Chapter 7), income changes (Chapter 8), or by capital movements (Chapter 10). Typically, these adjustments are associated with costs. The financing of an existing imbalance by the build-up or depletion of international reserves offers an alternative to having to adjust to every international imbalance.

In Figure 11-1 we show the familiar U.S. currency-market diagram.

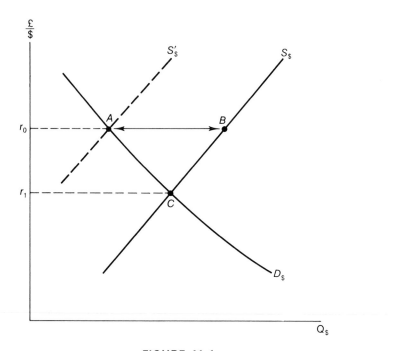

FIGURE 11-1

Exchange Rate Adjustment and Financing of a Disequilibrium

The supply and demand curves for dollars are indicated, and the exchange rate is assumed to be initially at r_0. At that exchange rate, the U.S. balance of payments shows a deficit equal to AB. Exchange-rate adjustment will lead to a new equilibrium exchange rate of r_1. Income (or price-level) adjustment can be accomplished by lowering the domestic income (or price) level until $S_\$$ has shifted sufficiently far to the left to eliminate any existing deficit at the exchange rate r_0. Such a possibility is indicated by the new dollar supply curve $S'_\$$, leading to equilibrium at point A. Of course, a combination of demand and supply shifts is also possible as a remedy to the disequilibrium situation.

Instead of undertaking any of these adjustments, the monetary authorities can maintain the exchange rate r_0 by simply buying up the excess supply of dollars AB. The resources that the authorities have at their disposal for the purpose of foreign exchange market intervention are their international reserves.

International Reserves Defined

International reserves may be defined as the resources at the disposal of the monetary authorities for purposes of intervention in the foreign exchange market. To give empirical meaning to this concept, it is necessary to define somewhat more precisely the qualities that assets must possess to qualify as international reserves. Two criteria are most commonly used: the assets have to be liquid and they must be unconditionally available to the monetary authorities. The types of assets that qualify under this operational definition may vary from time to time. At present there is wide agreement that the four following assets should properly be regarded as constituting a country's international reserves: (1) governmental gold holdings; (2) governmental holdings of convertible foreign currencies; (3) the Reserve Position with the International Monetary Fund (IMF); and (4) the country's holdings of IMF Special Drawing Rights (SDR). Figure 11-2 shows the composition of the

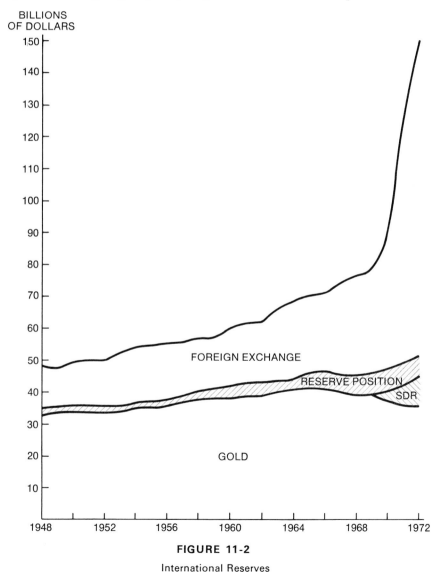

FIGURE 11-2

International Reserves

SOURCE: IMF, *International Financial Statistics,* various issues.

world's international monetary reserves for the period 1948–72. These international reserve assets may be supplemented by various types of near-reserves, which include other precious metals, inconvertible foreign currency, the Credit Tranches with the IMF, and borrowing arrangements made with other countries or international institutions. We will now turn to a closer analysis of the four main sources of international reserve assets.

SOURCES OF INTERNATIONAL RESERVES

Gold

Gold is the most traditional component of international reserves. It has been used as a monetary metal and reserve asset for centuries and continues to play an important role on the international monetary scene. In 1939 world gold production amounted to $1.19 billion. This level of output was not reached again until 1960. In 1970, gold production of the western world had increased to $1.45 billion, $1.13 billion of which was produced by South Africa. The International Monetary Fund estimates that of the total $1.45 billion of newly mined gold available, $.27 billion were added to world monetary gold stocks, $.98 billion went for industrial and artistic uses, and $.20 billion into private hoards. In 1970, there were no gold sales by the Soviet countries in international markets.

Due to the increasing demand for gold by the private sector, total holdings by monetary authorities have remained virtually constant in the last decade, after increasing only slightly during the decade of the fifties as shown in Figure 11-3. The most significant development throughout the period has been the redistribution of gold from the United States to other countries and international organizations. In 1948, the United States held $24.4 billion of the world's monetary gold stock of $34.5 billion, or over 70 percent of the world's gold supply. By the end of 1972, the U.S. gold stock had decreased to $10.5 billion or approximately 27 percent of the total of $38.8 billion held by monetary authorities. Table 11-1 shows the gold holdings of some selected countries as of December 31, 1972.

At this time it seems unlikely that gold will constitute a significant addition to world monetary reserves in the foreseeable future. Before March 17, 1968, the gold price was maintained at $35 per ounce by official governmental intervention in the gold market. At that date, a two-tier system was established, which essentially segregated the private gold market from the official market for monetary gold. In the official market the gold price was kept at $35 per ounce until it was changed as part of the Smithsonian Agreement of December 18, 1971, to $38 per ounce. Soon thereafter, on February 12, 1973, the official gold price was changed to $42.22 per fine ounce.

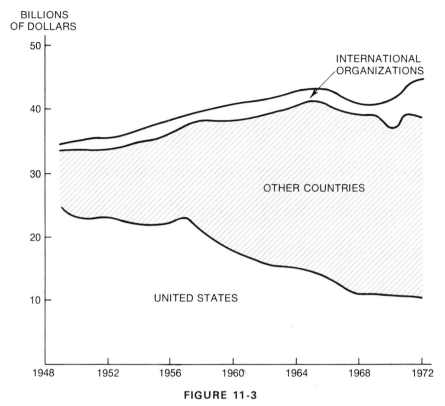

FIGURE 11-3

World Monetary Gold Stock

SOURCE: IMF, *International Financial Statistics,* various issues.

The gold price in private markets is determined by the forces of supply and demand for the metal. The continuing inflationary process in the United States and Europe and the associated decrease in the value of the respective currencies contributed greatly to the sharp increase in the gold price during 1972 and 1973 (See Figure 11-4). In May 1973 gold traded at prices above $125 in European gold markets. American citizens are still barred from purchasing any gold—unless it is for industrial, artistic, or numismatic purposes.

Foreign Exchange

Convertible foreign currencies are another component of international reserves. We stated previously that international reserves are held by the monetary authorities for intervention purposes in the foreign exchange market. It is natural that countries will hold balances of foreign currencies with which they can directly intervene in the foreign exchange market. The currencies

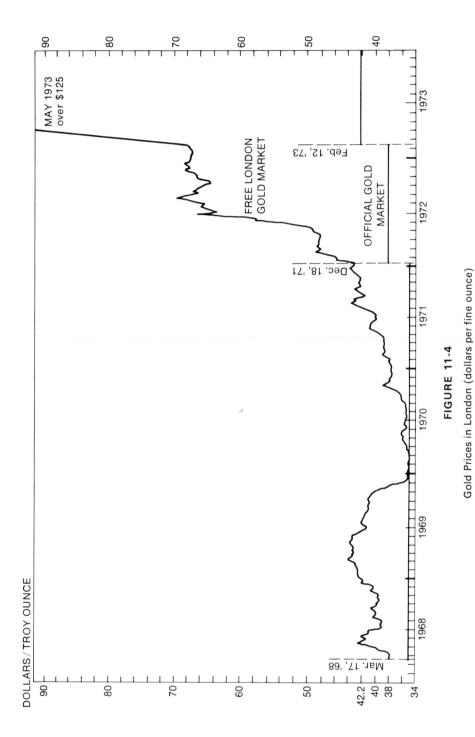

FIGURE 11-4

Gold Prices in London (dollars per fine ounce)

SOURCE: *Finance and Development*, Vol. 9, December 1972, p. 10–11, and *IMF Survey*, Vol. 2, February 26, 1973, p. 55.

that are widely held by other countries as part of their international monetary reserves are generally referred to as *key currencies* or *reserve currencies*. Traditionally the British Pound Sterling played an important reserve currency role, but since World War II the U.S. dollar has assumed the dominant role. Sterling is held in significant quantities only by the Commonwealth countries, and Britain has agreed to abandon its reserve currency role as one of the conditions of entry into the European Economic Community. In recent years, several other European currencies have assumed a minor role as reserve currencies. Among them the German mark is the most prominent. To enable other countries to accumulate foreign exchange as a *net* addition to their international reserves, the key currency countries have to run a balance-of-payments deficit on the official settlements basis (see Chapter 4).

Figure 11-5 shows the total foreign exchange reserve holdings of all countries. The components represented by net liabilities of the United States

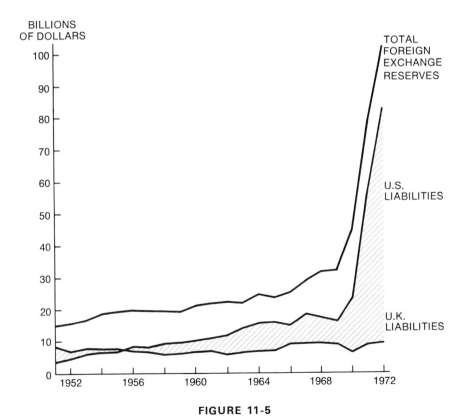

FIGURE 11-5

Foreign Exchange Reserves

SOURCE: IMF, *International Financial Statistics,* various issues.

and the United Kingdom are shown as well. The residual is accounted for partly by other currencies and partly by the *Eurodollar multiplier* process. During the late 1960s yields obtainable in the Eurodollar market became substantial and several central banks did deposit some of their official dollar holdings with private banks, generally through the intermediary of the Bank for International Settlements. The commercial banks in turn did lend the dollars to private individuals, some of whom converted them into other European currencies. In the process, the central banks reacquired the dollars, which they again counted as part of their international reserves as they constituted a new dollar inflow from their viewpoint. Hence, a multiple expansion of dollar reserves ensued, which resulted in total dollar assets reported by foreign central banks in excess of dollar liabilities reported by the United States. These practices have been discontinued in the meantime.

Foreign official dollar holdings increased spectacularly as a result of the 1971 and 1973 dollar crises. In both instances, the weeks immediately preceding the dollar devaluations saw large speculative dollar outflows out of the United States. The two countries that absorbed the largest inflows of dollars were Japan and Germany. (See also Table 11-1)

IMF Reserve Position

The International Monetary Fund was established in 1944 and one of its main functions is to provide a source of international reserves for its member countries. Upon becoming a member, a country is assigned a *quota* that establishes the basis for the country's rights and voting privileges with the IMF[1]. Once the quota is established, the country has to make a *subscription* payment to the IMF that is equal to its quota. Twenty-five percent of the subscription is payable in gold, and the remaining 75 percent in the country's own currency. By this device the IMF acquires an initial stock of member countries' currency, which it can lend to countries that find themselves in balance-of-payments difficulties.

A country that draws from the IMF will in fact *purchase* foreign currencies in exchange against its own currency. The total amount of currencies held by the IMF remains constant and only its composition changes. A country is expected to repay the drawn foreign currencies by *repurchasing* its own currency within a reasonable time period, normally three to five years.

---

[1] The basic formula that was used to determine a country's initial quota at the Bretton Woods Conference establishing the IMF was: Two percent of a nation's national income in 1940, plus 5 percent of its gold and U.S. dollar balances on July 1, 1943, plus 10 percent of its average annual imports in 1934–38; the total being increased in the same ratio as that which the country's average annual exports in 1934–38 bore to its national income. Since then, the formula has been revised. In practice the IMF does not apply the formula mechanically, establishing a quota by negotiation with the member country. The formula merely serves as a basis for the discussion.

For our purposes the most important measure of a country's borrowing rights from the IMF is its *reserve position*. The reserve position of a member is the net result of a country's initial gold subscription paid to the IMF, minus any subsequent drawings, plus the amount repaid, and any loans made to the IMF by the country. In addition, the reserve position may be influenced by the service charges assessed. In total, the reserve position shows the amount of reserves that are available from the IMF to a member country on an essentially automatic basis and constitutes therefore part of the country's international reserves. Table 11-1 shows the Reserve Position of some selected countries, and Figure 11-6 shows its historical development.

TABLE 11-1

INTERNATIONAL RESERVES
(December 31, 1972; millions of dollars)

Country or Region	Gold	Foreign Exchange	Reserve Position	Special Drawing Rights	Total
Austria	792	1,690	144	93	2,719
Belgium	1,638	1,104	560	568	3,870
Canada	834	4,368	343	505	6,050
Denmark	69	637	71	78	855
France	3,826	5,059	499	630	10,015
Germany	4,336	16,825	1,238	893	23,415
Italy	3,130	2,220	359	371	6,079
Japan	801	16,483	620	461	18,365
Netherlands	2,059	1,420	601	705	4,785
Norway	37	1,117	75	95	1,325
Sweden	217	1,144	98	116	1,575
Switzerland	3,158	4,330	non-member		7,488
United Kingdom	800	4,062	127	656	5,645
United States	10,487	241	465	1,958	13,150
Latin America	1,165	8,080	390	615	10,250
Middle East	1,085	6,100	135	135	7,450
Asia (exc. Japan)	720	5,345	214	532	6,810
Africa	1,121	5,480	300	349	7,250
World Total	38,780	101,665	6,867	9,431	156,745

Source: IMF, *International Financial Statistics*, May 1973.

In addition to the automatic borrowing rights described above, the IMF allows its members to draw an amount equivalent to their quota as a *credit tranche*. These borrowings are conditional in character in that the IMF has to approve of them. Consequently, they are not normally included in the calculation of the country's international reserves. Also, the IMF imposes an

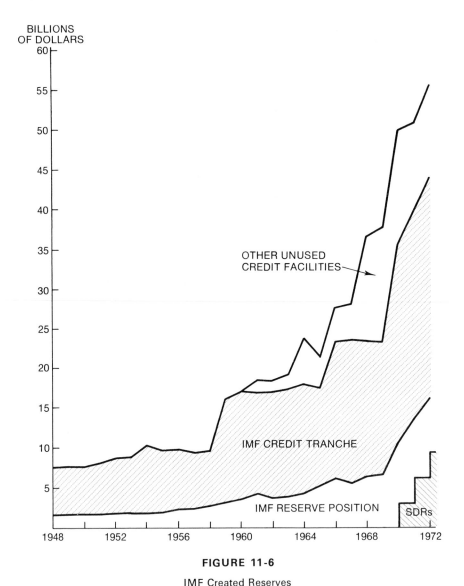

FIGURE 11-6

IMF Created Reserves

SOURCE: IMF, Annual Report 1972, and *International Financial Statistics,*
various issues.

interest charge on any member who draws in the credit tranche. The charge
increases with the amount drawn and the time for which the IMF credit is
utilized. The maximum interest rate is 6 percent. The precise technical arrangements of the transactions between the IMF and a member country are

rather complicated and the interested reader is referred to the more specialized literature on the subject.[2]

Special Drawing Rights

In 1968 the Articles of Agreement of the IMF were amended to allow for
the provision of *Special Drawing Rights* (SDR) in addition to the facilities of
the general account. These SDR's are allocated to countries in proportion to
their quotas. Any new SDR allocations must first be proposed by the man-
aging director of the IMF, concurred to by a majority of the IMF's executive
directors, and approved by an 85 percent majority of all votes of the IMF's
Board of Governors.[3] On January 1, 1970, a total of $3.4 billion SDR's were
allocated by the IMF, and at the beginning of 1971 and 1972 additional
allocations of $3.0 billion each were made. Due to the sharp increase in total
world reserves in 1972, no SDR allocations were made in 1973.

Special Drawing Rights may be used by any country in times of balance-
of-payments deficit, provided that the country's holdings do not fall short
of 30 percent of its allocation averaged over a five-year period. The maximum
amount of SDR's that countries are obliged to accept is limited to three
times their allocation. Countries earn 1.5 percent interest on their SDR holdings above their allocation and pay the same rate on SDR's used. Table 11-1
shows the December 1972 SDR holdings for some selected countries.

The main difference between the IMF general account and the Special
Drawing Rights lies in the fact that in the general account the IMF does not
engage in new asset creation, while it does so in the case of SDR's. In the
general account the IMF makes currencies previously paid in one member
country available to other member countries. In the case of the SDR account,
the IMF creates an entirely new reserve asset that constitutes a net addition
to world reserves.

Near Reserves

There is a whole spectrum of other assets that surrounds the international reserves as defined in our narrow sense. In addition to the already
mentioned IMF credit tranche, which does not count as part of the unconditionally available reserves, several countries have arranged for bilateral
swap agreements. Swap agreements are understandings between the monetary
authorities of different countries to exchange each other's currencies in times
of balance-of-payments pressures. If, for instance, the U.S. Federal Reserve

---

[2]Most of the basic concepts are explained in *Introduction to the Fund* (Washington,
D.C.: International Monetary Fund, 1964).

[3]For a detailed discussion of SDR's see: Joseph Gold, *Special Drawing Rights:
Character and Use*, IMF Pamphlet Series #13, Washington, D.C., 1970.

swaps $500 million for German marks, the U.S. resources for currency market intervention are boosted by $500 million. The total swap agreements in existence between the United States and other countries as of March 1973 are shown in Table 11-2.

TABLE 11-2

FEDERAL RESERVE RECIPROCAL CURRENCY
SWAP ARRANGEMENTS
(in millions of dollars)

Institution	Amount of facility on July 11, 1973
Austrian National Bank	250
National Bank of Belgium	1,000
Bank of Canada	2,000
National Bank of Denmark	250
Bank of England	2,000
Bank of France	2,000
German Federal Bank	2,000
Bank of Italy	2,000
Bank of Japan	2,000
Bank of Mexico	180
Netherlands Bank	500
Bank of Norway	250
Bank of Sweden	300
Swiss National Bank	1,400
Bank for International Settlements:	
Swiss francs/dollars	600
Other authorized European currencies/dollars	1,250
TOTAL	17,980

Source: *IMF Survey*, July 23, 1973.

In addition, the *Bank for International Settlements* in Basle stands ready to help countries with short-term financing of balance-of-payments deficits.

There are also many foreign assets held by the governmental authorities of a country that do not qualify as *liquid* international reserves because they are not close substitutes for gold or key currencies. Long-term bonds and equities denominated in foreign currencies as well as all types of foreign real assets are examples. The total amount of international reserves obtainable on short notice through these channels cannot be measured with any degree of accuracy.

To sum up: From the wide spectrum of international reserve assets either owned by or available to the monetary authorities of a country, we single out one group as constituting a country's liquid international reserves. These liquid international reserves consist of internationally acceptable means of payment that are unconditionally available to the monetary authorities. The assets that qualify under this definition of liquid international reserves are official holdings of gold, convertible foreign exchange, and the IMF resources in the form of the reserve position and Special Drawing Rights.

THE DEMAND
FOR INTERNATIONAL RESERVES

Having discussed the various sources of supply of international reserves, we will now direct our attention to the factors influencing the demand for international reserves. In particular, we will discuss (1) the national wealth constraint; (2) the opportunity cost of holding reserves; (3) the size of external imbalances; (4) alternative adjustment cost; and (5) the speed of the adjustment process.

The Wealth Constraint

We mentioned already that international reserves are part of the nation's total assets. National wealth provides the *constraint* on a country's reserve holdings. As national wealth increases, the constraint increases as well and we might expect that countries will—*ceteris paribus*—want to increase their reserve holdings.

In Figure 11-7 we measure the dollar volume of international reserves along the vertical axis and the value of all other assets along the horizontal axis. The total resource constraint is shown by the line *BW*. The amount of the nation's assets that will be devoted to reserves is determined by the tangency to an indifference curve showing the country's preference for reserve holdings. In Figure 11-7, equilibrium is attained at *E*, with the country devoting *OR* of its wealth to international reserves and *OA* to other assets. It has been estimated that the wealth elasticity of the demand for international reserves is approximately unity. That is, a one percent increase in national wealth will result in a one percent increase in the quantity of reserves demanded.[4] We will now turn to an analysis of the various factors that determine the fraction of their national wealth that countries devote to international reserves.

[4]H. Robert Heller, "Wealth and International Reserves", *Review of Economics and Statistics*, May 1970.

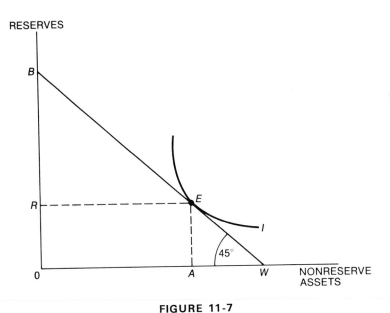

FIGURE 11-7

The Wealth Constraint to Reserves

Opportunity Costs of Holding Reserves

When a nation decides to devote part of its national resources to international reserves, it will incur opportunity costs of holding these reserves. If the assets were devoted to alternative uses, such as investment in machinery and equipment, they would yield a return to the nation. The relevant concept for measuring the opportunity cost of holding international reserves is the difference between the *marginal social rate of return on capital* and the *rate of return earned on reserves*. Unfortunately, no precise quantitative estimates of the marginal social rate of return on capital are available.

The opportunity cost of holding reserves is reduced by the amount that governments are able to earn on their reserve holdings. There are two components to this rate of return on reserves: annual yield and capital gains (or losses). In general, the annual yield of the gold stock is zero, and it might even be argued that it is negative when account is taken of the costs associated with the safekeeping of the gold. Capital gains due to the increase in the gold price have been made in connection with the December 1971 increase in the official gold price from $35 to $38. For the United States this capital gain amounted to $875 million, and for all monetary authorities taken together to some $3.1 billion, as shown in Table 11-3. Similar gains were made after the 1973 change in the official gold price.

TABLE 11-3

CAPITAL GAINS AND LOSSES DUE TO EXCHANGE RATE
AND GOLD PRICE CHANGES OF DECEMBER 18, 1971
(in millions of predevaluation dollars)

Country	Gold	Foreign Exchange
Australia	+35	−211
Austria	+62	−105
Belgium	+132	−56
Canada	+68	−322
Denmark	+5	−44
France	+302	−281
Germany	+349	−970
Israel	+4	−53
Italy	+247	−239
Japan	+58	−1,088
Norway	+3	−78
Sweden	+17	−57
Turkey	+11	−49
United Kingdom	+66	−402
United States	+875	+22
World total	+3,095	−6,095

Source: IMF, *International Financial Statistics*, May 1972.

Countries may attempt to earn some interest on their reserves by holding them in the form of interest-yielding time deposits, U.S. Treasury bills, or other interest-paying obligations. Naturally, in case of a revaluation or devaluation of key currency, paper gains or losses in terms of the home currency will be made. The gains and losses associated with the general exchange rate realignment of 1971 are also shown in Table 11-3. But it should be noted that the value of the foreign exchange reserve assets in terms of their purchasing power in the country of issue—generally the United States—remained constant. No interest is earned on unused portions of the reserve position with the IMF, and a modest 1.5 percent is paid for SDR balances held in excess of the allocation received. The value of SDR's is stated in terms of gold, and hence an increase in the official gold price will also result in a capital gain on SDR balances held.

Size of External Imbalances

In Chapter 5 we dealt with the sources of external imbalances and also determined the size of imbalances faced by various countries. This analysis need not be repeated here. Because reserves are held as a buffer stock that permits the financing of temporary imbalances, it is clear that countries that experience larger imbalances also have greater need to hold international reserves.

We should point out, however, that the simple measurement of past imbalances is liable to give a biased estimate of the size of the imbalances. The measurement of the imbalances is, of course, *ex post* and takes account of any adjustment measures taken and their effect on the size of the imbalances. That is, in the absence of corrective measures the imbalances would presumably be larger than the actually measured imbalances. Only in times of absolute *laissez faire* will the actually occurring imbalances be an accurate measure of the size of the imbalances. Of course, if the exchange rate is allowed to fluctuate, adjustment will be automatic and instantaneous.

Alternative Adjustment Costs

A country will want to hold a larger volume of reserves if the benefits to be expected from these reserve holdings are larger. The benefits of reserves are to be found in the avoidance of adjustments that would have to be undertaken in the absence of reserves. The larger the adjustment costs that can be avoided, the greater the benefits to be attributed to the reserves.

In this book we have focused attention on the cost of income-switching policies (Chapters 6 and 7) and income-adjustment policies (Chapter 8). In both cases we attempted to provide an empirical estimate of the main adjustment costs associated with a $1 improvement in the balance of payments. Assuming infinite supply elasticities, the terms-of-trade costs of exchange-rate or price-level changes was estimated at

$$MC_S = \frac{1}{\delta_{IM} + \delta_{EX} - 1} \tag{6.24}$$

and the cost of income adjustment to a $1 deficit was found to be

$$MC_Y = \frac{1}{m} \tag{8.24}$$

for disturbances originating in the foreign sector. A country will find it advantageous to adjust to balance-of-payments imbalances whenever the marginal cost of adjustment is smaller than the marginal cost incurred by financing and vice versa. Under ideal circumstances the country will use a policy mix such that the marginal cost of adjustment and the marginal cost of financing are equal to each other: $MC_{adj.} = MC_{fin.}$. The avoidance of an adjustment cost may be seen as a benefit of reserve holdings. Hence, we may restate the optimality condition as: $MC_{fin.} = MB_{nonadj.}$. Figure 11-8 shows the marginal benefits from nonadjustment by utilizing reserves and the marginal costs of

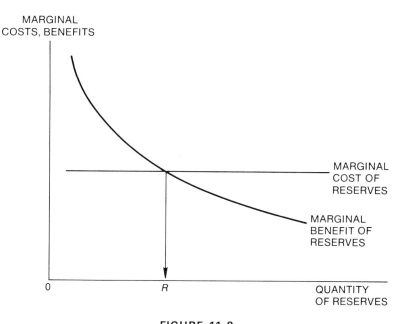

FIGURE 11-8

The Optimal Reserve Level

holding reserves. It is assumed that the marginal costs of holding reserves stay constant while the marginal benefits from additional reserve stocks decrease. This decrease is due to the fact that—even if the marginal adjustment costs referred to earlier stay constant—we find that the probability of large imbalances is smaller than the probability of small imbalances. Hence, additional reserves have a lower probability of being actually used and therewith confer lower benefits upon the country. The optimal reserve level is attained when the marginal costs of additional reserves are equal to the marginal benefits. In Figure 11-8 this level is reached at point *R*.

Table 11-4 shows empirical estimates of the optimal international reserve levels which countries may want to hold for precautionary motives— that is, to be able to finance the short-term fluctuations which may occur. These calculations do not take into account reserves that countries might want to hold to ward off speculative attacks against their own currency nor do they permit the long-term financing of fundamental disequilibria. The data refer to the early sixties and show two alternate optimal reserve levels —one if exchange rate changes are considered the relevant alternative and one under the assumption that income adjustments are the other policy considered.

TABLE 11-4

OPTIMAL INTERNATIONAL RESERVES
(millions of dollars)

Country	Optimal Reserve Level With Exchange Rate Adjustment	Optimal Reserve Level With Income Adjustment
Canada	398.7	699.9
Denmark	119.1	191.0
Germany	2,293.2	3,172.8
Italy	1,464.8	1,337.0
Japan	1,005.3	1,472.6
South Africa	268.3	680.4
Sweden	307.6	276.1
Switzerland	457.8	416.7
United Kingdom	2,447.1	2,751.8
United States	2,259.3	6,720.7

Source: M. Kreinin and H. R. Heller, "Adjustment Costs, Optimal Currency Areas, and International Reserves", in W. Sellekaerts, ed., *Essays in Honor of Ian Tinbergen*, (New York: Macmillan International), 1973.

Speed of Adjustment

So far we have neglected the speed with which countries adjust to balance-of-payments disequilibria. We implicitly assumed that all adjustment is instantaneous. However, adjustment takes time, and one of the functions of international reserves is to allow the monetary authorities to select the most appropriate adjustment policy and to let this policy work itself out—a process that may take considerable time.

It follows that countries that hold relatively low international reserves will have to take policy actions designed to correct the imbalance faster than a country that has a large cushion of reserves that may last for many years or even decades. For instance, the United States was able to run a balance-of-payments deficit in every year between 1950 and 1971 except for 1957 (calculated on the liquidity basis) before devaluating the dollar in December 1971. The United States was able to run these prolonged deficits because she had a large stock of international reserves at the beginning of the period and because foreign central banks were willing to acquire the obligations of the U.S. government. Peter B. Clark[5] has provided some evidence that the amount of reserves that a country holds depends on the speed with which it adjusts to balance-of-payments imbalances. This trade-off between reserves and speed of adjustment is another important factor in a country's decision as to how much reserves it should hold.

[5]Peter B. Clark, "Demand for International Reserves: A Cross-Country Analysis," *Canadian Journal of Economics*, November 1970.

SPECULATION
AND THE CONFIDENCE PROBLEM

International reserves are held for the purpose of financing balance-of-payments disequilibria and to avoid having to undertake immediate adjustment measures. In an international monetary system where the exchange rate is pegged at a certain value and is changed only in case of a fundamental disequilibrium, changes in the level of international reserves also serve as an indicator of the size of the imbalances that were actually financed. As a country's reserves decline continuously it is easy to see that eventually the reserves will be exhausted and other corrective actions have to be taken. Often an exchange-rate adjustment (devaluation in case of a deficit) is the least-expensive policy alternative. However, the exchange-rate adjustment also offers an opportunity for speculators to make a quick capital gain by shifting their funds into a currency that is expected to appreciate or to sell short the currency expected to be devalued. In either case, a profit will be made by the speculator at little risk of capital loss because an appreciation of the deficit currency is highly unlikely.

In a world of free capital movements, sizeable sums of money can cross national borders in a very short period of time and thereby aggravate the disequilibrium problem. The result is a series of international monetary crises in anticipation of every change in official exchange rates. For example, in the three and a half months between March 31, 1971 and the August 15, 1971 suspension of the dollar convertibility and subsequent dollar devaluation, U.S. liquid liabilities to foreigners increased by $14.4 billion. The funds left the United States largely in the anticipation of a capital gain to be made by shifting the funds into other currencies, whose value was expected to appreciate. An example in the opposite direction is provided by the German mark. From the beginning of 1971 until the cessation of official intervention in the foreign exchange market on May 10, 1971, and the subsequent floating of the mark, heavy capital inflows into Germany took place. The result was a $5.2 billion increase in official international reserves, $2.6 billion of which entered Germany in the last three days. The free mark appreciated as predicted by the speculators, and between May 10 and the end of July German foreign exchange reserves declined by some $1.6 billion as some speculators took their profits. Others did hold on to their marks in anticipation of further exchange rate increases—a well-founded expectation as Figure 11-9 shows.

The story was repeated in 1973, when the German monetary authorities purchased $5.9 billion in the first week of February alone in order to keep the mark from appreciating vis-à-vis the dollar. A week later, the dollar was devalued by ten percent and the German Central Bank took a capital loss of over $2 billion on the nation's foreign exchange reserves which it manages. Private speculators, of course, gained.

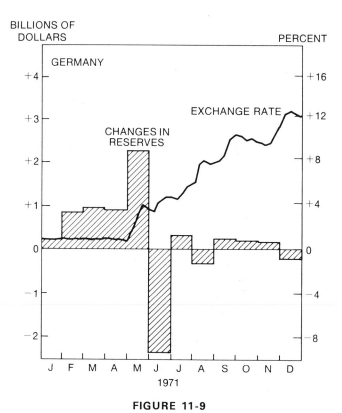

FIGURE 11-9

Changes in Exchange Rates and Official Reserve Transactions

SOURCE: *Federal Reserve Bulletin,* March 1972, p. 234.

In countries with no restrictions on free capital movements and pegged exchange rates, it is to be expected that massive flows of speculative capital will take place in anticipation of exchange-rate changes. The experience of virtually all countries during the brief interval of floating exchange rates (August 15–December 18, 1971, for most countries; May 10–December 18, 1971, for Germany and the Netherlands) shows that the large speculative capital flows experienced before the floating were drastically reduced during the time that exchange rates were free to respond to market forces. There is also a mounting volume of evidence that indicates that speculative activity in free exchange-rate markets during the late 1930s and in Canada during much of the fifties was in fact stabilizing.[6]

[6]See for example: Stanley Black, "International Money Markets and Flexible Exchange Rates," *Staff Economic Studies*, Washington, D.C.: Board of Governors of the Federal Reserve System, 1972, and John Pippenger, "The Canadian Experience with Flexible Exchange Rates," *American Economic Review*, May 1967.

Figure 11-9 illustrates the point that exchange-rate changes and reserve changes are essentially substitutes for each other. During the time of fixed exchange rates before May 10, 1971, German reserves increased. After that date, reserves stayed virtually constant (neglecting the return flow of speculative capital after the exchange rate appreciated), while most of the adjustment took place via exchange-rate changes. A new par value of the German mark was established on December 18, 1971 as part of the Smithsonian Agreement. As it turned out, this attempt to fix new exchange rates by official actions did not survive for more than 14 months. On February 12, 1973 the dollar was devalued for a second time, and the mark was allowed to appreciate again on June 29, 1973.

INTERNATIONAL TRANSACTIONS BALANCES

We have established that international reserves are held by the monetary authorities for purposes of intervention in the foreign exchange market. In addition to these official uses, there exists a private demand for international means of payment because international transactions have to be paid for. For this purpose commercial banks hold working balances of foreign currencies to effect foreign currency transactions for their customers and to provide short-term financing for international commercial transactions.

Table 11-5 shows the total foreign exchange holdings of the commercial banks of all western countries. To give an idea of the relative adequacy of these foreign exchange balances for the financing of an increasing international trade volume, world imports and the ratio between banks' foreign exchange holdings and imports is shown as well. Judging from these data, the adequacy of commercial banks' foreign exchange balances increased considerably since 1950.

TABLE 11-5

FOREIGN EXCHANGE TRANSACTION BALANCES
(in billions of dollars)

Year	Foreign Exchange Holding by Commercial Banks	World Imports	Foreign Exchange to-Import Ratio
1950	3.3	58.3	0.057
1955	4.5	88.3	0.051
1960	9.4	118.8	0.079
1965	21.2	174.2	0.122
1970	65.0	293.9	0.221

Source: IMF, *International Financial Statistics*, 1966/67 Supplement and May 1972.

SUGGESTED FURTHER READINGS

CLARK, PETER B., "Demand for International Reserves: A Cross-Country Analysis," *Canadian Journal of Economics* (November 1970).

———, "Optimum International Reserves and the Speed of Adjustment," *Journal of Political Economy* (March 1970).

CLOWER, ROBERT, and RICHARD G. LIPSEY, "The Present State of International Liquidity Theory," *American Economic Review* (May 1968).

GOLD, JOSEPH, *Special Drawing Rights: Character and Use.* Washington, D.C.: IMF Pamphlet Series #19, 1970.

GRUBEL, HERBERT G., "The Demand for International Reserves," *Journal of Economic Literature* (December 1971).

HELLER, H. ROBERT, "Optimal International Reserves," *Economic Journal* (June 1966).

———, "The Transactions Demand for International Means of Payment," *Journal of Political Economy* (January 1968).

———, "Wealth and International Reserves," *Review of Economics and Statistics* (May 1970).

INTERNATIONAL MONETARY FUND, *International Reserves: Need and Availability.* Washington, D.C., 1970, especially the articles by Jurg Niehans and Egon Sohmen.

KELLY, MICHAEL G., "The Demand for International Reserves," *American Economic Review* (September 1970).

KREININ, MAX, and H. ROBERT HELLER, "Adjustment Costs, Optimal Currency Areas, and International Reserves," in W. SELLEKAERTS, ed., *Essays in Honor of Ian Tinbergen.* New York: Macmillan International, 1973.

CHAPTER 12

The International
Monetary System

The purpose of this chapter is twofold: For one, we will give a summary of the main strands of thought which run through the entire book. When dealing with a specific aspect of international monetary economics, it is easy to loose sight of the overall framework into which a particular part of the analysis belongs. In the individual chapters we took a close look at the trees that make up the forest of international monetary economics. In this chapter we will take a look at the entire forest.

Second, we will draw some new inferences about the efficiency of alternative international monetary systems. That is, we will address ourselves to the question whether one or the other international monetary system is more efficient and outline the basic characteristics of an optimal international monetary system.

EXTERNALITIES
IN INTERNATIONAL TRANSACTIONS

Most international commercial and financial transactions are undertaken by individual economic units for the purpose of their own gain. We showed in Chapter 2 how welfare maximization by households and profit maximization by firms serves as the motivating force behind international transactions. Gains from specialization and exchange may be identified. Free international exchange of goods and services leads to a more efficient resource allocation in the production of commodities and increases the utility that can be derived from the commodity bundle produced during the current period.

These international transactions are recorded in the goods-and-services account of the balance of payments discussed in Chapter 4. The capital account of the balance of payments records the transactions that involve the transfer of titles of ownership or financial assets. Capital-account transactions lead under competitive conditions to an optimization of intertemporal production and consumption patterns. Individual economic units may reap additional gains from intertemporal optimization made possible on a world-wide basis through capital movements.

In a static world equilibrium is reached after all economic units have a chance to make an initial adjustment. After this initial adjustment is completed, maximum world welfare in the Pareto sense is achieved, provided the side conditions about competitive markets and absence of externalities are fulfilled.

Most of the problems on the international monetary scene are problems of adjustment to new disturbances. If there were no new disturbances, the pure theory of international specialization and exchange would be adequate to handle most problems of analysis.

First, it is necessary to identify the sources of the international disturbances. We did this in Chapter 5, where we discussed the main sources of international economic instability.

Second, we must recognize that disturbances that have their origin in one sector may affect other sectors as well.

Third, adjustment—although leading to an optimal allocation of resources in the long run—is costly in the short run. There are two types of costs to contend with: (1) the costs of information gathering and decision making associated with the adjustment to the new economic realities; and (2) the loss of value of capital assets in those industries that are hurt by the adjustment. This loss pertains not only to those resources that are specialized in their present employment—as is true about certain embodied human skills and capital equipment—but also to factors that are mobile between different employments.[1] Of course, these latter losses may be balanced by gains made to other factors.

The short-run costs of information, decision making, and loss in capital values associated with the adjustment must be counterbalanced against the long-run gains to be made from more efficient resource allocation. As the time horizon under consideration increases, gains are likely to outweigh costs. Hence, we may establish the important proposition that it will generally pay to adjust to long-run disturbances.

---

[1] The Heckscher-Ohlin theory, for instance, states that a factor of production that is used intensively in the contracting industry will loose not only in relative but also in absolute term. Cf. H. R. Heller, *International Trade: Theory and Empirical Evidence*, 2nd ed. (Englewood Cliffs, N.J.: Prentice-Hall, Inc., 1973), Chap. 11.

The same does not necessarily apply to short-term, reversible patterns. For instance, a country might experience an inflow of short-term capital due to some unusual conditions in its capital markets. Consequently, the exchange rate might appreciate. It would be costly indeed for the entire trade sector to have to adjust to the new exchange rate if the capital flow might be reversed within a year or two. Many of these changes in capital markets might be a result of governmental policy action, and hence it is not possible for speculators to correctly predict the course of future economic events—unless they are apt at outguessing the government officials.

Hence, an important role of an efficient international monetary system consists in the minimization of the adjustment costs to any type of disturbance.

ADJUSTMENT ALTERNATIVES

In the main body of the book we discussed several of these alternative adjustment methods. Chapter 6 dealt with exchange-rate adjustment, Chapter 7 with price-level adjustment, Chapter 8 with income adjustment, and Chapter 10 with capital movements. Chapter 11 offered an alternative to adjustment: the financing of imbalances by the use of international reserves. In most cases the alternatives open to the policy maker confronted with a balance-of-payments disequilibrium were discussed in their pure forms. That is, we assumed that all other variables either remained constant or that the policy maker took appropriate actions to keep them constant by pursuing a policy of active neutralization of any secondary effects. Here we will address ourselves briefly to some of the important links between the various adjustment methods.

So far, economists have not succeeded in building one grand model in which all cross effects can be shown and analyzed. There is not only the practical problem of designing such a large model but in all likelihood such a general theoretical model will not allow us to make any specific predictions. In most cases the answer to a question such as "What will happen to incomes, prices, and capital movements if we devalue the currency?" will be "Anything is possible." We would have to know the specific size of the various parameters to make any predictions about the final outcome. But this requires us to build a complete econometric model of the entire world, a task that is still well beyond the ambitions of most economists. Some efforts have been made to construct rudimentary models, in which the entire world is reduced to a few regions, such as the United States, Europe, and the rest of the world. But even these crude models typically do not contain capital movements and exchange-rate changes. Project LINK is an attempt to connect various national econometric models. Much work remains to be done.

Here we will investigate some of the important linkages between various adjustment models discussed in their pure form in the previous chapters. We will not be able to offer a complete taxonomy on all possible combinations. Instead we will merely analyze some of the linkages that do exist and therewith call attention to some of the cross effects and interactions that must be taken into account in an analysis of the complete system.

The Price-Income Link

One of the most widely discussed relationships in economics is the link between changes in the aggregate level of real income and the rate of change in the general price level. The Phillips curve, which describes this relationship, has also been used in connection with wage rate changes and similar variables.

The basic postulate of Keynesian economics is that as long as there is general unutilized capacity in all relevant factor markets, output increases are possible at constant prices. Of course, this assumes that the marginal productivity of all factors is also constant. But as the output level of the economy approaches capacity, bottlenecks develop. Some sectors may have already reached the capacity barrier, while other sectors are still characterized by unused capacity. In such a situation prices will tend to change along with output changes. The closer we get to the capacity barrier, the more pronounced the price changes will be compared to the income changes. If the capacity barrier is reached, further increases in aggregate demand will result solely in prices increases, and we have a pure inflationary situation. In Figure 12-1 the three possibilities of pure output expansion—without inflation, bottleneck inflation, and pure inflation—are illustrated by a Phillips curve.

In an economy that is trying to eliminate a balance-of-payments surplus with income adjustment methods, we might expect that also price increases will take place as the capacity barrier is reached. These price increases will have their own effect on the balance of payments. The relationship between price changes and the balance of payments has been investigated in Chapter 7. It is easily seen that a situation might arise where the income expansion will help to eliminate the balance-of-payments surplus while the accompanying inflation will make it worse. The final outcome is uncertain. By the simple combination of income and price effects we have arrived at a situation where we no longer can predict with *a priori* reasoning alone in which direction the balance of payments will move.

The Exchange-Rate–Income Link

Now we will turn our attention to the link between the exchange rate and income. Let us assume that all other effects are absent; that is, that we are operating in the constant cost region, that investment and government ex-

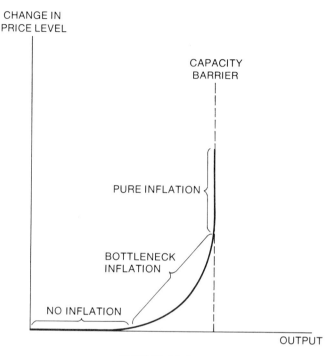

FIGURE 12-1

Full Capacity and Inflation

penditures are determined autonomously, and that trade is initially balanced. In the absence of income stabilization policies, we will observe that a devaluation improves the trade balance, provided the conditions outlined in Chapter 6 are fulfilled. The improvement in the trade balance, however, means that the country exports more than before. The increased exports will lead to a multiple expansion of national income. But as the national income expands, imports will expand as well, and the balance of payments will deteriorate.

Two countervailing forces are at work again: the devaluation will tend to improve the international balance, and the national income expansion that is induced by the balance-of-payments improvement will lead to a deterioration of the balance of payments. The balance-of-payments effects of a devaluation were discussed in detail in Chapter 6, and the income and balance-of-payments multipliers of an autonomous disturbance were dealt with in Chapter 8. Here we will briefly show the main trends of the arguments.

We start with the national income equation:

$$Y = C + I + G + EX - IM \tag{12.1}$$

Writing A for $C + I + G$, we obtain:

$$Y = A + EX - IM \tag{12.2}$$

or

$$EX - IM = Y - A \tag{12.3}$$

Domestic absorption A can be divided into autonomous A° and induced components aY:

$$EX - IM = Y - aY - A^\circ \tag{12.4}$$

Collecting terms and considering changes we can write:

$$dEX - dIM = (1 - a)dY - dA^\circ \tag{12.5}$$

That is, the balance of trade will remain unchanged ($dEX - dIM = 0$) if $a = 1$ and $dA^\circ = 0$. Autonomous changes in C, I, or G are not considered here. Hence, we are left with the conclusion that the balance of trade will remain unchanged if the sum of the domestic marginal propensities to absorb is equal to unity: $c + i + g = a = 1$. If this condition is fulfilled, we know that no new funds are going into hoarding, and the multiplier process will come to an end only when the new external leakages are equal to the external injections: $dIM = dEX$. That is, the balance of payments will not change at all.

However, if $a < 1$ and positive hoarding does take place, we find that part of the new funds will leak into hoards. Hence, the income expansion process will not continue until $dIM = dEX$, but will stop before. The induced import increase will be smaller than the export change and a balance-of-payments surplus will remain. The surplus will be larger, the greater the difference between a and 1. We may conclude that a devaluation will improve the balance of payments more if income changes are minimized.

This result could also have been obtained by simply combining the effects of a devaluation as outlined in Chapter 6 and those of the induced income changes analyzed in Chapter 8.

The effect of an exchange-rate change on the balance of payments is given by

$$\frac{dB_1}{dr} = -\left[EX_0 \frac{\delta_{EX}(\sigma_{EX} + 1)}{\delta_{EX} + \sigma_{EX}} + IM_0 \frac{\sigma_{IM}(\delta_{IM} - 1)}{\delta_{IM} + \sigma_{IM}} \right] \tag{6.11 restated}$$

The effect of this change in dB_1 on the balance of payments in a model incorporating foreign repercussions is analyzed in equation 8A.16. Substituting $dB_1 = dIM_2^0 - dIM_1^0$, we obtain the final effect of a devaluation incorporating both exchange-rate and income changes on the balance of payments as:

$$\frac{dB_1}{dr} = -\frac{s_1 s_2}{s_1 m_2 + s_2 m_1 + s_1 s_2}\left[EX_0\,\frac{\delta_{EX}(\sigma_{EX}+1)}{\delta_{EX}+\sigma_{EX}} + IM_0\,\frac{\sigma_{IM}(\delta_{IM}-1)}{\delta_{IM}+\sigma_{IM}}\right]$$

$$(12.6)$$

Appropriate simplifications as presented in Chapters 6 and 8 may be made to reduce this equation to manageable proportions. It is clear, however, that $s_1 s_2/(s_1 m_2 + s_2 m_1 + s_1 s_2)$ becomes larger as the marginal propensities to import decrease in size. A policy of holding down new imports (small m) will maximize the balance-of-payments improvement to be gained from devaluation. Of course, this result rests on the probably unjustified assumption that the price level remains unchanged.

The Exchange-Rate–Price-Level Link

Let us turn to a third pair of variables: the exchange-rate–price-level link. We will assume that full-employment conditions prevail and that therefore real income levels remain unchanged. If the balance of payments reacts normally to a devaluation, exports increase and imports decrease in value. But exports can increase only if resources are set free to produce the export goods. Consequently, prices will be bid up.

Under competitive conditions prices will increase until enough resources are set free to produce the export goods. As prices at home increase, exports will fall off and imports will rise as consumers adjust to new relative prices. The price effects will exactly counterbalance the exchange-rate effects if linear production functions prevail. Real incomes will remain unchanged due to our assumption of full employment.

There are various possibilities under which the balance of payments may nevertheless improve subsequent to a devaluation. In each case the condition is that somehow real absorption is reduced to free the resources required to improve the balance of trade without causing a corresponding price increase.

Money Illusion. Money illusion refers to the phenomenon that individual economic units make their spending decisions according to the money income they receive rather than their real income. As money incomes increase due to the price rise, people will reduce the proportion of money spent if the marginal propensity to consume is smaller than the average propensity to consume. Hence, real absorption falls, thereby freeing the resources for balance-of-payments improvements.

Real Balance Effect. An increase in prices will result in decreased purchasing power of money. As people attempt to restore the familiar relationship between wealth and cash balances, they will spend less. As absorption falls, the road is open for balance-of-payments improvement.

Interest-Rate Effects. Closely related to the real balance effect is the interest-rate effect. If the money supply remains constant, cash becomes scarcer and interest rates increase. At the same time, the inflation that is under way will also induce people to offer higher interest rates. Hence, the proportion of income saved may increase and reduce real absorption. Of course, we are assuming that people will not loose confidence in money as a store of value—as in hyperinflations—and try to hedge against the inflation by purchasing real assets.

Distribution Effects. If the devaluation results in higher profits for the export industry, and the marginal propensity to spend out of profits is smaller than the marginal propensity to spend out of wage income, it follows that absorption will decrease. The balance of payments might improve. However, this tendency might be counterbalanced by lower profits in the import-competing industry.

Investment Effects. As the export industry realizes increased profits, new investments may be undertaken. This, of course, represents an increase in absorption and the balance of payments will deteriorate.

Which one of these—and other possible—effects dominates is an open question.

The Capital-Movements–Output Link

We will discuss the linkage between capital movements and output levels under flexible and fixed exchange rate systems. It turns out that the difference between fiscal and monetary policy actions is crucial for the purpose of this analysis.

Flexible Exchange Rates. In Figure 12-2 we show the familiar Hicks-Hansen *IS-LM* diagram. The interest rate is depicted along the vertical and the level of output on the horizontal axis. Let us assume that we engage in an expansionary *fiscal* policy. The *IS* curve will then shift to the right. Output levels and interest rates increase. As the domestic interest rate rises, foreign capital is attracted. But under a system of flexible exchange rates, the balance of payments is always in balance. Hence, the capital inflow must be matched by a deterioration of the trade balance, causing the *IS* schedule to shift leftward. If the country is small in world capital markets, the capital inflows will continue until equilibrium is restored at the old interest rate. The output level and interest rate will return to their original values.

On the other hand, an expansionary *monetary* policy will shift the *LM* curve to the right, lowering the interest rate (Figure 12-3). This will lead to an outflow of capital and—following the previous chain of reasoning—an improvement in the trade balance. As the trade balance improves, the *IS* curve will shift to the right until the old interest rate is reestablished and capital flows will consequently cease. In the process, output has expanded.

That is, under flexible exchange rates fiscal policy actions will not suc-

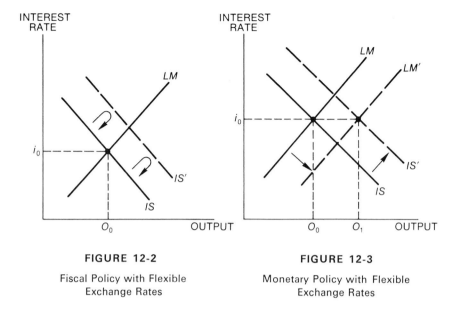

FIGURE 12-2

Fiscal Policy with Flexible
Exchange Rates

FIGURE 12-3

Monetary Policy with Flexible
Exchange Rates

ceed in changing the output level, but monetary policy actions will do so more successfully than in the absence of international capital movements.

Fixed Exchange Rates. The same framework may be used for the analysis of fiscal and monetary policy actions under fixed exchange rates. An expansionary fiscal policy that shifts the *IS* curve from *IS* to *IS'* in Figure 12-4 will result initially in higher interest rates and an expanded output. Unless prices change (due to the output-price link discussed previously), the trade balance will remain unchanged while capital flows in. The capital inflow will increase the money supply (unless it is neutralized by the authorities), and consequently the *LM* curve will shift to the right. Interest rates will return to their original level and output will expand further.

Under expansionary *monetary* policy actions, the *LM* curve (Figure 12-5) will shift to the right, causing a fall in interest rates. Capital will flow out of the country, causing the money supply to drop (again in the absence of sterilization policies by the authorities). The drop in the money supply will shift the *LM* curve leftward to its original position—again under the proviso that foreign interest rates remain unchanged.

Under fixed exchange rates, fiscal policy is effective in changing output levels, but monetary policy is not.

These four examples may suffice to illustrate possible links between capital movements, output levels, and exchange-rate changes. Similar observations may be made with respect to price changes and their relationship to the other variables discussed.

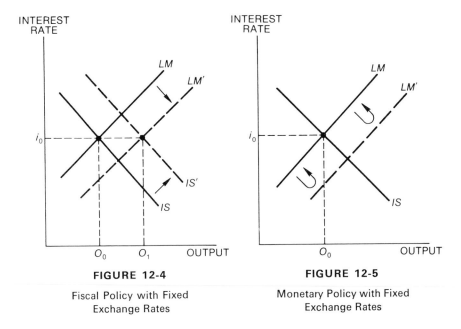

FIGURE 12-4

Fiscal Policy with Fixed
Exchange Rates

FIGURE 12-5

Monetary Policy with Fixed
Exchange Rates

THE EFFECT
ON INTERNATIONAL RESERVES

The effect of financing a balance-of-payments disequilibrium on a country's international reserves is rather direct. Whenever there is a balance-of-payments surplus, the country's reserve holdings will increase, and when there is a balance-of-payments deficit its reserves will decrease. There is only one caveat to be added to this straightforward linear relationship: in case the country's liabilities are held abroad as part of other countries' international monetary reserves—as in the case of the key currencies—a numerical increase in the country's holdings of reserves may take the place of a decrease in other countries' holdings of the key currency. Similarly, instead of experiencing a fall in its own reserves, the key-currency country may experience an increase in its liabilities to foreign monetary authorities.

Under most circumstances, an increase in a country's monetary reserves will be accompanied by an increase in its own money supply. The reason for this linkage is just as obvious: a country that runs a balance-of-payments surplus finds that there is an excess demand for its own currency. If the monetary authorities want to prevent the currency from appreciating in international markets, it sells its own currency against gold or foreign exchange that is added to its international reserves. But the sale of the country's own currency increases the money supply in the hands of the public. The reasoning is reversed in cases of balance-of-payments deficit. Of course, the monetary authorities may change reserve requirements for commercial banks, engage in open-market operations, or take other actions designed to neutralize the change in the domestic money supply.

THE OPTIMAL POLICY RESPONSE

A country that encounters a new instability in its external accounts is confronted with a whole spectrum of possible policy responses. The question is which one of these possible responses is optimal from the country's point of view. If the policy makers want to maximize the welfare of the country's residents, they will have to identify the policy response that inflicts the least cost upon the country or conveys the largest possible benefits.

A thorny problem arises if an adjustment policy adopted by one country imposes higher costs on other countries. The familiar "beggar my neighbor" argument associated with devaluation in times of unemployment illustrates only one of the possible manifestations of this problem. We will return to this problem later.

Proponents of *automatic* adjustment mechanisms often argue that the adoption of flexible exchange rates or a pure gold standard would relieve the authorities from all worry about external adjustment problems. They also often argue that the system proposed is efficient because it will actually eliminate all external disequilibrium situations. They do not, however, show that the particular system suggested is *efficient* in the sense that it offers the least-cost (or maximum benefit) solution in all external adjustment situations. For instance, in situations of full employment and inflationary pressures it may be less costly to the country to appreciate its currency than to let the specie flow mechanism dictate an even further increase in the price level. Similarly, in a situation of general unemployment and external surplus the rules of the flexible exchange rate system call for an appreciation of the currency. This appreciation would in all likelihood further aggravate the unemployment problem. Again, it is questionable whether the exchange-rate adjustment should be permitted to impose this additional cost on the economy or whether fiscal and monetary policy measures designed to increase the level of economic activity would lead to a less-costly reduction of the external surplus. The latter policy might well represent a more efficient alternative.

Which policy or policy mix represents the most efficient external adjustment alternative will depend on the general economic conditions prevailing at the particular time. In Figure 12-6 we depict a hypothetical set of curves showing the marginal costs of adjustment associated with the elimination of an external imbalance, say a deficit, by the use of exchange-rate changes MC_r and income changes MC_y. We argued before that the costs associated with the various adjustment policies will depend on the particular economic situation encountered at that time. Also, the shape of the adjustment cost curves need not be as shown, though it seems reasonable to assume that the marginal costs associated with the use of one policy will increase as further use is made of that policy.

If the marginal adjustment curves are as drawn in Figure 12-6, exchange-rate adjustment is the most efficient policy for all imbalances shown. On the other hand, if the marginal adjustment cost curves resemble those of Figure 12-7 and the country is confronted with an external disturbance of

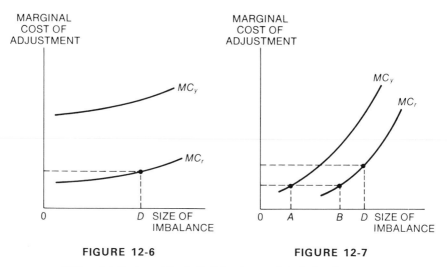

FIGURE 12-6   **FIGURE 12-7**

Different Adjustment Costs Call For Appropriate Policy Responses

size OD, the exclusive use of exchange-rate adjustment would result in marginal adjustment costs equal to MC_D. It will be less costly, and hence more efficient, to use a *mix* of both adjustment policies. That is, the rational policy maker will use each policy until the marginal costs associated with it are equal to those of the other policies:

$$MC_r = MC_y.$$

Consequently, it would be advantageous to use income adjustment to remedy OA of the imbalance and exchange-rate adjustment for OB. We note that $OA + OB = OD$.

Let us emphasize again that the optimal policy mix may include other instruments in addition to those referred to and will also change with varying economic circumstances. Among the most important variables that influence the size of the adjustment costs are: (1) the unemployment rate; (2) the rate of inflation; (3) obstacles to mobility of factors of production; and (4) the length of the time horizon over which adjustment is to be accomplished.

OPTIMAL CURRENCY AREAS

The argument just presented has direct relevance to the optimal currency area problem. An *optimal currency area* is defined as a territory within which only one monetary unit circulates or within which the value of all monetary units in relation to each other is permanently fixed. Towards the outside adjustment is to be accomplished via exchange-rate changes. If all relevant parameters bearing on the costs and benefits of adjustment remain constant, we are able to define an *optimal currency area* as a region that minimizes the total adjustment cost via exchange-rate changes on the one hand and other adjustments on the other hand.

In Figure 12-8 we show hypothetical marginal income and exchange-rate adjustment costs as a function of the size of a region. Clearly, we have to establish first that income and exchange-rate adjustment costs are related to the size of a region. This is an empirical question. It can be safely argued that

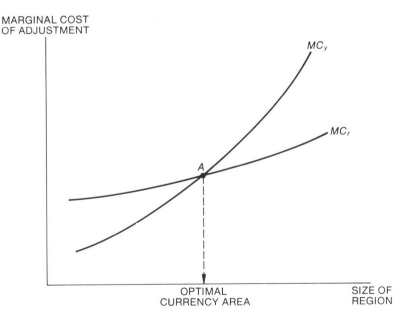

FIGURE 12-8

Optimal Currency Areas

income adjustment costs to a given external imbalance increase with the size
of the region. Small regions have a high marginal propensity to import from
the outside, and large regions have a low marginal propensity. Earlier (Chapter 8) we have shown that the income adjustment costs are inversely related
to the marginal propensity to import. Hence, the marginal income adjustment
costs MC_y will increase with the size of the region. Regarding the relationship
between regional size and exchange-rate adjustment costs, much less can be
said. Presumably we will find that for a large region the elasticity of supply of
export goods is larger than the elasticity of supply for a smaller region. The
demand curve for its export goods will probably become less elastic as a larger
market share is controlled by the region. On the import side, the supply curve
faced by the region will become less elastic as a larger market share is attained.
The demand curve will probably become more elastic as the region's size
increases and import substitution becomes more and more likely. Furthermore, if the time horizon under consideration increases, both supply and
demand elasticities are likely to become larger. No clear pattern emerges if
this information is inserted into equation 6.23, which shows the marginal
cost of exchange-rate adjustment. We might therefore argue that the income
adjustment costs are likely to become eventually larger than the exchange-rate
adjustment costs. In Figure 12-8 the crossover occurs at point A, which
therewith defines the optimal currency area.

With the help of empirical estimates derived earlier (Tables 6-2 and 8-2)
we can calculate the exchange-rate and income adjustment costs for several
countries (Table 12-1). If the income adjustment costs are lower than the
exchange-rate adjustment costs, this may be taken as evidence that under the
circumstances the country in question might find it advisable to join in a
larger currency area with other countries. The reverse holds true if $MC_y >$

TABLE 12-1

EXCHANGE-RATE AND INCOME ADJUSTMENT COSTS

Country	MC_r		MC_y
Canada	0.95	<	5.21
Denmark	0.82	<	2.65
Germany	2.04	<	6.49
Italy	4.00	>	2.90
Japan	1.92	<	7.58
South Africa	0.52	<	6.54
Sweden	3.85	>	2.65
Switzerland	2.38	>	1.79
United Kingdom	2.22	<	3.13
United States	0.64	<	22.22

Source: Tables 6-2 and 8-2.

MC_r, in which case the country might find exchange rate changes less costly than income changes. According to the estimates of Table 12-1, only Italy, Sweden, and Switzerland would find it advantageous to join in a larger currency area.

However, we should not forget that these calculations (1) refer to a model that assumes the existence of capacity underutilization making income adjustment possible, and (2) that the elasticities are calculated from yearly data over the period 1951–66. As pointed out previously, the state of the national economy, the degree of factor mobility, and the time horizon under consideration are of prime importance in determining the adjustment costs. The optimal currency area argument has validity only for a *static* situation. The true test for a currency union, such as the one envisioned by the European Economic Community by the end of the seventies, will come when there exists a conflict of interest between the member nations as to the most desirable common external exchange rate.

THE OPTIMAL INTERNATIONAL MONETARY SYSTEM

There remains the question whether it is possible to devise an institutional framework that will minimize the costs associated with international adjustment and thereby help to maximize the benefits to be derived from international transactions. Such an optimal international monetary system would consist of a set of institutions or rules that would bring about speedy adjustment at minimum cost. To devise such a system is no mean task, and history has shown that the various systems tried did not survive severe crisis situations.

The pre-World War I gold standard broke down when the stresses imposed by wartime inflation could not be overcome by adjustment triggered by specie flows. The flexible exchange-rate system tried during the interwar period fell victim to the nationalistic policies instituted by countries attempting to overcome the Great Depression. The IMF-Dollar system of the post-World War II period is being subjected to severe strains as a result of the deterioration of the dollar's preeminent position on the world scene.

Whether it is possible to devise a system that would have weathered all these crisis situations and still have provided smooth, efficient adjustment is highly questionable. Any system that is to be used effectively in the future must assure that a mix of various adjustment methods can be used to rectify international disequilibrium situations. The precise method to be used in any given set of circumstances will vary depending on the state of the economy of the countries affected. *Flexibility* to pursue optimal national economic policies tempered by the constraint that these policies should not impose any greater costs on other countries is one of the basic requirements for any such system. Devaluation to remedy domestic unemployment problems—to mention only one frequently cited example—should not be allowed if this merely shifts the unemployment to other countries. Yet, the same policy may be mutually advantageous if the devaluating country's trading partners experience full employment and excess-demand inflation.

Fully automatic adjustment mechanisms are unlikely to resolve every adjustment problem in an optimal fashion. Nationalistic policy making is likely to result in competitive attempts to shift problems to other nations. The most promising avenue of progress seems to lie in increased international and multinational policy coordination. A necessary first step consists of the exchange of medium-term economic policy plans. International bodies, such as the Organization for Economic Cooperation and Development (OECD) and the International Monetary Fund (IMF) may act—as they have already done on a small scale—as a coordinating body for economic policy making. The publication and analysis of the various national policy proposals may help to identify possible policy conflict situations, and more congruent policy alternatives may be explored. By this method of avoiding situations that could create new disequilibriums, the policy makers will be able to cope much more readily with the remaining unplanned imbalances.

Increased freedom to use a variety of policy instruments might well go a long way towards minimizing the costs associated with international adjustment to external disturbances. Unless it can be demonstrated conclusively that reliance on one adjustment mechanism will minimize the cost of adjustment under all circumstances, an international adjustment system relying on one automatic mechanism will not be efficient. Although reliance on one automatic adjustment mechanism may assure the maintenance of external equilibrium, this may be achieved at very high costs that the countries may not be willing to bear.

In recent years it has been proposed to widen the margins within which exchange rates are free to fluctuate. This is a step in the right direction. While there is no magic about a band of permissible fluctuations of 1 percent versus 2.25 percent or 5 percent, it shows that under different circumstances the optimal width of the band may change.

Similarly, countries are often willing to let the rate of inflation or unemployment increase by 1 or 2 percent if this will help to achieve external equilibrium. However, there is a strong reluctance against permitting high rates of inflation or unemployment for external reasons alone. This may well be an indication of official concern about the increased marginal costs of adjustment associated with the various adjustment methods. Flexible use of a variety of adjustment methods tailored to the specific circumstances under which they are used may help to reduce the burden of adjustment to international monetary disturbances and therewith contribute to an improvement in the welfare of the citizens of all countries.

SUGGESTED FURTHER READINGS

CORDEN, W. M., "Monetary Integration," *Essays in International Finance No. 93.* Princeton, N.J.: Princeton University Press, 1972.

GRUBEL, HERBERT G., *The International Monetary System.* Baltimore: Penguin Books, 1969.

KREININ, MORDECHAI E., and H. ROBERT HELLER, "Adjustment Costs, Currency Areas, and Reserves," in W. SELLEKAERTS, ed., *Essays in Honor of Ian Tinbergen.* New York: The Macmillan Company, 1972.

McKINNON, RONALD I., "Optimum Currency Areas," *American Economic Review* (September 1963).

MUNDELL, ROBERT A., *International Economics.* New York: The Macmillan Company, 1968.

———, and ALEXANDER K. SWOBODA, eds., *Monetary Problems of the International Economy.* Chicago: University of Chicago Press, 1969.

SPITALLER, ERICH, "Prices and Unemployment in Selected Industrial Countries" *IMF Staff Papers,* (November 1971).

TAKAYAMA, AKIRA, "The Effects of Fiscal and Monetary Policies Under Flexible and Fixed Exchange Rates," *Canadian Journal of Economics* (May 1969).

WHITMAN, MARINA VON NEUMANN, "Policies for Internal and External Balance," *Special Papers in International Economics, No. 9.* Princeton, N.J.: Princeton University Press, 1970.

APPENDIX

The Theory
of Economic Policy

Specialization and exchange lie at the heart of any modern economy. Specialization results in increased productivity and output of commodities. Exchange opens up the possibility of mutual gain from the specialization process. Specialization without exchange would be an idle exercise that would result in the baker eating only bread and the butcher only meat. But by exchanging the commodities produced, the attainment of higher welfare levels for all participants in the exchange process is possible.

In the absence of a common monetary unit, economic exchange involves barter of one commodity for another. The introduction of a monetary unit not only provides a common unit of account but also a medium of exchange. In addition the monetary unit may serve as a store of value. In most countries the central government has control over the money supply and uses this control as a means of regulating the rate of economic activity within the country. The territory within which a particular currency circulates freely is called a currency area. In the modern nation-state the currency area frequently coincides with the boundaries of the state. Because currency areas often coincide with national boundaries, we also speak of international monetary problems. But strictly speaking there is no need for national borders and currency areas to coincide. Several small countries use the currency of their larger neighbors, and movements are under way to unite the countries of the European Economic Community into one currency area by 1980. Economic transactions involving economic units that belong to different currency areas create special problems because they not only involve simple economic exchange but also have an effect on the currencies of the nations in which the two economic units are located. These special international monetary problems are the center of our attention in this book.

A multitude of economic units are engaged in international trade and finance. They include the individual who purchases a radio or camera manufactured abroad, the multinational corporation that is engaged in business ventures in various countries, the governmental and monetary authorities of individual countries, as well as international organizations like the International Monetary Fund and the World Bank.

We may differentiate two broad groups among all actors on the international monetary scene: individual economic units and monetary authorities. Individual economic units, be they consumption or production units, buyers or sellers, large or small, public or private, engage in international monetary transactions because they are attempting to maximize their own welfare. An individual might purchase a foreign automobile because it is cheaper or offers higher quality than a domestically produced car that is equally expensive. An electronics firm may sell abroad because it finds customers there; a refinery might import crude oil from a cheaper foreign source; consumers might purchase imported beer or a foreign automobile. In all these transactions the basic motivation is to obtain a commodity at a lower price or sell it at a higher price than is possible at home. Both partners in the exchange stand to reap some of the gains of specialization and exchange.[1]

We will assume that the monetary authorities of a country have a basically different motivation that guides their policy actions. We assume that they do not attempt to maximize their own personal welfare or the "profits" of the central bank, but that they pursue policies designed to achieve the overall goals of the economy. What these goals are and how the policy makers may attempt to achieve them is the topic of this appendix.

COUNTRIES AS ECONOMIC UNITS

Basically, the difference between an individual economic unit and the monetary authorities is that the individual is concerned only with his own economic actions. He sells goods abroad not to be able to import an equivalent amount but because he is able to obtain a higher price abroad than at home. Later on he might or might not purchase foreign or domestic goods. The monetary authorities, on the other hand, are not engaged in direct international trade or investment. They are concerned with the effect of the transactions of all *other* economic units on the currency that is under their control.

How governmental authorities make the decisions they do make is the subject of the theory of economic policy. We will discuss three widely used frameworks for the economic-policy making: (1) the fixed-target approach; (2) the least-squares social welfare function; and (3) the cost-benefit approach.

THE FIXED-TARGET APPROACH

The fixed-target approach to economic policy is based on the assumption that the country's decision makers attempt to maximize the collective welfare of the country's residents. It is furthermore assumed that the preferences of the residents can be expressed in the form of an aggregate economic welfare function. The economic welfare function relates the collective welfare of the residents to certain variables. The numerical values of the variables that will bring about a maximization of the economic welfare of the country's residents are referred to as *targets* or policy *objectives*.

[1]For a detailed exposition of the determinants of trade volume and direction, see H. R. Heller, *International Trade: Theory and Empirical Evidence*, 2nd ed., (Englewood Cliffs, N. J.: Prentice-Hall, Inc., 1972), Chaps. 3–5. For the gains from trade see Chap. 11.

For instance, we may argue that the welfare of the residents depends upon the level of unemployment and the rate of change in the cost of living or a similar price index. In this simple example, the level of unemployment (U) and the rate of change of the price level (ΔP) are the variables upon which the level of social welfare (W) depends:

$$W = f(\Delta P, U) \tag{A.1}$$

The specific values of ΔP and U that will maximize the welfare W are the targets or policy objectives.

It is by no means clear that a zero rate of change in the price index is the most desirable state of affairs. For instance, it has been argued that in developing countries it may be advantageous to maintain a certain rate of inflation, as this will foster an income and wealth redistribution from the traditional and presumably rich landholders to other economic sectors where the resources will be used more effectively. Neither is it obvious that a zero rate of unemployment is the appropriate target. Some people may quit their job voluntarily and spend a few weeks searching for a more lucrative job, and they may be able to do this more effectively if they first quit their old job. This job search may involve a cross-country move to a more prosperous area. Also, employers may find it advantageous to be able to hire new workers quickly as the need arises.

But let us assume for the time being that we have established a zero rate of price-level change and a zero level of unemployment as the most desirable targets. In Figure A-1 we measure the change in the price level along the vertical axis and the unemployment rate along the horizontal axis. Our target is point T at which we have a stable price level and no unemployment.

Next, the policy maker has to choose an appropriate *policy* instrument

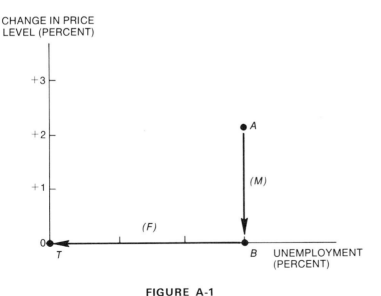

FIGURE A-1

A Two-Targets-Two Instruments Model

(policy instruments are those variables that are under the control of the policy maker). For instance, taxes and expenditures are the principal fiscal policy instruments of the government. Reserve requirements for commercial banks, open-market operations, and discount-rate changes are examples of monetary policy tools. Tariffs and quotas are policy instruments that are often used in the international sector. As a general rule, the policy instrument that has the relatively greatest influence on a given objective is assigned to this target. The policy maker then chooses a numerical value of the policy instrument such that the target will be reached.

If the system is to work effectively, it is necessary that the number of policy instruments is at least as great as the number of targets in order to assure the attainment of all targets. If this condition is not fulfilled, some targets may not be reached, thereby making the maximization of social welfare impossible. Another implicit assumption is that all policy instruments are independently variable and that they exercise a differential effect on the target variables. That is, no two policy instruments are supposed to have an identical impact on the same target variables. If this latter condition is not met in each case, the relationship between each policy tool and each target variable will not be unique. Consequently, not all targets may be attained even if the number of policy instruments is equal to the number of targets.

Let us return to the example of Figure A-1 to illustrate. The two policy tools at our disposal are assumed to be fiscal policy (F) and monetary policy (M). The direction of the vectors shows the influence that a change in the policy variables has on the rate of change of the price level and the level of unemployment. In our simplified example monetary policy influences only the rate of change of the price level, and fiscal policy affects only the unemployment level. In this case, monetary policy will be assigned to the price-level target and fiscal policy to the unemployment target. If the economy is initially in a state characterized by point A, the two vectors shown will move the economy to the target point T.

Specifically, the following five-step sequence is involved in policy making: (1) the social welfare function is defined; (2) the policy objectives, or targets, are quantified; (3) policy instruments are assigned to the various targets; (4) the functional relationship between instruments and targets is quantified; and (5) the optimal policy is determined.

Largely due to its great simplicity, the fixed-target approach enjoys a considerable degree of popularity both among economists and policy makers. However, it is associated with several shortcomings, which should be pointed out.

1. The social welfare function is rarely specified in practice. Instead, the targets are directly specified by the policy maker—without showing explicitly the relationship between the targets and social welfare.

2. Due to the fact that the targets are to be specified as finite numerical values, the fixed-target approach cannot take adequate account of targets that have optimal values equal to infinity. For instance, *ceteris paribus*, it is more desirable to have a higher growth rate than a lower one, and there is nothing to prevent us from wishing that the growth rate should approach infinity. The true constraint on the achievement of a target are the alternatives that have to be sacrificed in order to attain the first target.

3. An important problem with the fixed-target approach arises if the number of available policy instruments is smaller than the number of targets selected. In this case the policy maker would have to drop targets from the

list until the equality of instruments and targets is again assured. Yet, no rational *a priori* criterion suggests itself that could be used to eliminate one target in favor of another one.

4. Another problem concerns the partial attainment of a given target. How large a deviation from a target calls for corrective action and the use of policy instruments? Only in rare cases will it be possible to attain a target exactly. One way out is the substitution of target zones for target points, but then a problem arises as to the proper specification of the target zones, and the theory gives no guide as to how wide the target zones should be.

5. A further criticism is that there is no specification of the trade-offs between targets. It is assumed that essentially all targets are attainable, as long as the number of policy instruments is equal to or larger than the number of targets. In reality, however, there may be a trade-off between the achievement of various policy targets. Interdependence between various policy objectives do exist, and the attainment of one target may be costly in terms of the alternative targets that have to be sacrificed. The most prominent example of this kind of interdependence is provided by the Phillips curve, which attempts to specify the trade-off between unemployment and inflation.

6. A related point is that there may be a cost to carrying out the policy action itself: information has to be collected and analyzed, policy decisions have to be made, directives must be issued, and finally the economy has to adjust to the new policy. This process utilizes economic resources and thereby is costly in itself. Especially if a target is almost—though not completely—attained, it may not be optimal to incur the additional costs of policy making and execution if the expected gains from attaining the target completely are relatively small.

7. The policy instruments may influence several target variables at the same time. We may illustrate with our previous two-targets, two-policy-tools example. In Figure A-2 a given monetary or fiscal policy is assumed to exercise some influence on both the level of unemployment and the rate of change of the price level. Thus, the policy vectors (M) and (F) are no longer horizontal and vertical lines. As before, if the initial situation is characterized by point A', a combination of fiscal and monetary policy will bring the country to the desired target T'. But even if one target is already attained, like in the situation shown by point P', it is necessary to employ both fiscal and monetary policy to attain the simultaneous targets indicated by point T'. One policy instrument alone is not enough to attain one target if the other target is already attained and the policy instruments have an effect on both targets simultaneously.

8. It may also be necessary to "overshoot" one or both targets by a considerable margin in order to put the economy into a position such that the second target can be attained. Figure A-2 illustrates this case, too. Starting at point A', monetary policy (M) may help us to attain the price target P', but an overshooting to point B' is required to bring the target T' into alignment with the fiscal policy vector (F). The required overshooting of one target to make it possible to attain the second one may be associated with considerable adjustments costs.

Obviously, there is no difference between the policy vectors leading from A

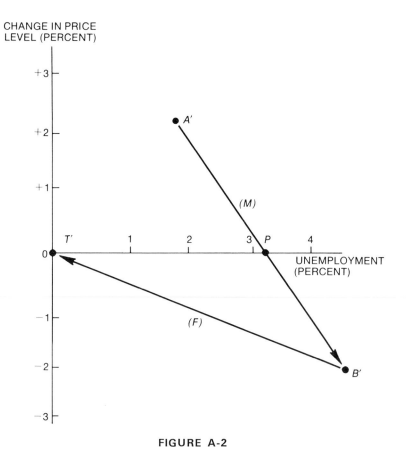

FIGURE A-2

A Two-Targets-Two Instruments Model with Interdependence

to T in Figure A-1 and the ones going from A' to T' in Figure A-2 in terms of comparative statics of the initial and final equilibrium values. However, if certain costs are associated with the use of the policy instruments themselves, policies ABT and $A'B'T'$ are not equivalent. Dynamic effects should be considered, too. The adjustment of the economy from A' to T' is not instantaneous, and the path followed in getting from A' to T' is important. It is entirely possible that undesirable secondary effects are associated with wide swings in price and employment levels, and that therefore a policy that minimizes these swings would be preferable to one characterized by relatively large swings.

Much attention has been devoted to the case of two targets and two policy instruments in the context of an *open* economy. The two targets are generally taken to be the achievement of external and internal balance. *External balance* is defined as equilibrium in the balance of payments; *internal balance* is defined as attainment of full resource-utilization without inflation. The policy instruments may be any pair of policy tools that conform to the requirement that they exercise a differential effect on the two targets. The size of the governmental budget, the rate of interest, the exchange rate, and similar variables are generally considered. We will return at a later point to a more complete discussion of the two-target, two-instrument model in an open economy.

We may conclude that although the fixed-target approach offers a useful first step, we should recognize the difficulties and problems hidden behind its simple framework and realize that it should be used with caution in the formulation of economic policy.

THE LEAST-SQUARES WELFARE FUNCTION APPROACH

Some of the problems of the fixed-target approach can be avoided by the use of the *least-squares welfare function*. This approach assumes that the policy makers attempt to maximize a social welfare function whose arguments consist of the squared differences between the targets and the actual values of the various policy objectives, which are then weighted in an appropriate way. While this specific formulation probably was adopted because of its convenient mathematical properties, it also avoids some—but not all—of the pitfalls of the fixed-target approach. The main advantages of the least-squares welfare function as compared to the fixed-target approach are threefold: (1) the trade-offs between different policy targets are specified explicitly; (2) smaller and smaller welfare gains are associated with successive marginal movements towards the target values; and (3) the number of policy instruments no longer has to be equal to the number of targets.

1. Consider the following least-squares social welfare function:

$$W = -[\alpha(\Delta P_T - \Delta P_A)^2 + \beta(U_T - U_A)^2]$$

where W indicates social welfare, ΔP the change in the price-level index, U an unemployment-level index, and the subscripts $_T$ and $_A$ refer to target levels and actually observed levels of the variables. α and β are the weights attached to the different targets.

The trade-off between the targets is specified by the ratio of the parameters α and β, which are the relative weights assigned to the two targets. A larger weight indicates that the target is relatively more important. Of course, the weighting procedure may still involve arbitrary decisions on behalf of the policy maker, who may not know the true social welfare function. But the specification of the weights at least makes explicit the opportunity costs in terms of the other target.

2. The least-squares social welfare function attributes relatively small welfare gains to improvements in variables that are already close to their targets, and large welfare gains to improvements of a similar absolute magnitude in a variable that is currently far removed from its target. For instance, let us consider the relative welfare gains to be realized by reducing the rate of inflation from 3 percent to 2 percent on one hand (an improvement of 1 percentage point), and a reduction in the inflation rate from 10 percent to 9 percent on the other hand. The price target is assumed to be a constant price level ($\Delta P_T = 0$). The calculation follows:

TABLE A-1

Price Target ΔP_T	Actual Price Change ΔP_A	Welfare Index $-(\Delta P_T - \Delta P_A)^2$	Improvement in Welfare Index Due to Decrease in Inflation by One Percentage Point
Situation 1			
0	+3	−9	+5
0	+2	−4	
Situation 2			
0	+10	−100	+19
0	+9	−81	

That is, the least-squares social welfare function attaches a welfare improvement of five points to a reduction in the rate of inflation from 3 to 2 percent and a weight of 19 points to a reduction in the inflation rate from 10 to 9 percent. Are these weights really justified? Someone might argue that the reduction from 3 to 2 percent represents a 33.3 percent decrease in the inflation rate and the decrease from 10 to 9 percent only a 10 percent reduction. Yet, a much larger welfare improvement is indicated in the latter case. This example brings out clearly that the choice of quadratic weights is by no means noncontroversial.

Due to the fact that the *squares* of the deviations of the actual from the target levels enter the social welfare function, there is a bias towards a reduction of the widest deviations from the specified target levels. But it should be remembered that this specification was adopted mainly for mathematical' convenience. Nothing prevents us from replacing the squares by alternative weights that would more accurately reflect the welfare significance of the deviations of actual from target values. If greater deviations are considered more (less) undesirable, the power of the exponents may be increased (decreased) to reflect this.

3. The third advantage of the least-squares approach as compared to the fixed-target approach is that the stringent requirement of a one-to-one relationship between policy targets and instruments is abandoned. Even if the number of policy instruments is smaller than the number of arguments in the social welfare function, a meaningful maximization procedure is possible. One instrument may have an effect on several targets, thus influencing a whole set of deviations of actual levels from target levels. The desirability of altering the value of the instrument variable may be judged on the basis of its expected net effect on all relevant target variables. Thus, it is entirely possible that under the least-squares welfare function approach none of the targets are fully attained. Instead, a certain balance may be struck between the attainment of the various policy targets and a true second-best solution obtained. Any proposed changes in the value of a policy instrument may be judged by their total effect on all targets. And this, in turn, may be related to the change in social welfare. A desirable policy change, naturally, always involves an improvement in social welfare, even if this implies moving away from some targets—provided other targets are thereby attained more fully.

Difficulties do remain with the least-squares welfare approach. For one, no criterion exists according to which the proper weights to be assigned to various targets can be determined. This remains a matter of judgment for the policy maker. Some economists have devised empirical methods[2] by which the implicit trade-offs actually used by the authorities can be estimated *ex post*. But clearly much work remains to be done on this topic.

Second, the question of infinite target values is not resolved in a satisfactory manner. The deviation between an actual finite growth rate and an infinite target is still infinity, and a social welfare function cannot properly be specified under these circumstances.

Third, costs associated with the specification and execution of policy actions are not considered. One possibility would be to include appropriate cost estimates for the use of policy variables in the social welfare function, but this is generally not done. In short, although the least-squares social welfare function offers some important improvement on the fixed-target approach, serious shortcomings remain.

THE COST-BENEFIT APPROACH

In recent years, cost-benefit analysis has been found useful in dealing with problems of applied welfare economics. In particular, cost-benefit analysis has been used to evaluate the welfare changes associated with specific economic investment or development decisions. The range of possible applications is wide and includes such diverse projects as highway and waterway construction, defense economics, and forest management. Most of the applications of cost-benefit analysis have a decidedly microeconomic flavor, in spite of the fact that some of the projects considered—like dams, nationwide irrigation systems, and highway networks—definitely affect the entire economy. Much of the cost-benefit analysis actually undertaken is of the partial-equilibrium variety and therewith neglects general-equilibrium repercussions. However, there is no reason why general-equilibrium considerations may not be taken into account both on a theoretical and empirical level.[3]

The cost-benefit approach reduces all economic policy choices to the attainment of a single goal: the maximization of the difference between benefits and costs, or the maximization of net wealth. It replaces the array of decision criteria of the fixed-target approach and the least-squares welfare function approach by a single criterion. However, it is obvious that wealth maximization is a narrower concept than maximization of social welfare. It is acceptable as the sole goal of economic policy only to the extent that there is a direct relationship between the two concepts, in which case wealth maximization might perhaps be considered a reasonable approximation to the maximization of social welfare. Whether such a relationship in fact exists remains an open question that we cannot even attempt to answer here. The problem belongs to the field of welfare theory. We will simply assume that there is such a positive relationship.

[2]G. L. Reuber, "The Objectives of Canadian Monetary Policy, 1949–61," *Journal of Political Economy*, April 1964; and W. G. Dewald and H. G. Johnson, "An Objective Analysis of the Objective American Monetary Policy 1952–61," in D. Carson, ed., *Banking and Monetary Studies* (Homewood, Illinois: Richard D. Irwin, Inc., 1963), pp. 171–89.

[3]A comprehensive treatment of the methods of cost-benefit analysis is given by E. J. Mishan, *Cost-Benefit Analysis* (London: Unwin University Books, 1970). A cogent defense of the method is provided by A. C. Harberger, "Three Basic Postulates for Applied Welfare Economics," *Journal of Economic Literature*, September 1971, pp. 785–97.

As a first exercise, it may be useful to compare the cost-benefit approach to the fixed-target approach in terms of the criticisms 1 through 8 that we levied against the fixed-target approach (see pages 218–19).

1. The relationship between social welfare and wealth maximization is explicitly stated. Anything that increases social benefits or decreases social costs (both properly discounted) will also increase social welfare. Two important criticisms remain: (1) the problem of income-distribution changes, and (2) the decreasing marginal utility of wealth (or income). We will ignore problems of income-distribution here. A separate branch of economic theory deals with these problems.[4] But let us mention that also traditional national income accounting ignores income-distribution problems. Many economists would not argue with the proposition that a higher national income is preferable to a smaller one. Or, if one prefers, that a higher per capita national income is superior to a smaller one.[5] Income distribution is generally ignored as a problem when using national income accounting data.

   Regarding the second point—the constancy of the marginal utility of wealth (or income)—we may apply to a similar argument. Incremental increases in national income are not generally discounted on the basis that they are worth less than previous increases due to perceived decreases in the marginal utility of additional income. The basic principle of additivity is used worldwide as a basis for national income accounting, and few economists have strong objections to the practice. The cost-benfit approach utilizes the same principle.

2. Infinite target values do not pose any special problems as the procedure simply calls for a comparison between benefits and costs. For instance, the present discounted benefits of a higher growth rate (in the form of future higher income streams) will have to be compared to the costs (such as foregoing present consumption).

3. In the cost-benefit framework, there is no requirement that the number of targets should not exceed the number of policy instruments available. The effect of each policy instrument on all targets may be assessed, and the net benefits (or costs) resulting from the policy change calculated. In that manner, we may identify an optimal policy even if only one policy instrument is available.

4. In case of partial attainment of a target, the costs and benefits associated with this partial attainment may be evaluated in the customary fashion. But the cost-benefit approach allows us to assess the changes in wealth associated with any policy change.

5. Trade-offs between targets are explicitly specified by the dollar value of the costs and benefits associated with the attainment of each target. There is no further need for subjective evaluations of targets in terms of their contribution to economic welfare. Instead, trade-offs may be measured in an objective way.

6. The costs of policy making may be explicitly recognized in the cost-benefit

---

[4]For a comprehensive treatment of the subject see: Martin Bronfenbrenner, *Income Distribution Theory* (Chicago: Aldine, 1971).

[5]On this point see also E. Denison, "Welfare Measurement and the GNP," *Survey of Current Business*, January 1971, pp. 13–16.

framework. If there are large costs associated with the decision-making process or the adjustment from one equilibrium to another, we may take these costs into consideration in assessing the relative merits of policy alternatives.

7. and 8. In the cost-benefit framework, there exists no assignment problem as to which targets should be matched with what instruments. Dynamic effects are difficult to consider, but this difficulty stems mainly from our ignorance of relevant empirical magnitudes. Once the adjustment patterns are known, the cost-benefit framework is ideally suited to take the costs and benefits arising in different time periods into account by applying proper discounting procedures.

Most of these improvements come about because a single objective criterion is placed between the individual targets and the final subjective goal of social welfare maximization. Because the objective goal of wealth maximization is placed between the targets and the subjective goal of social welfare maximization, the calculation of objective trade-offs between various targets becomes possible.

Table A-2 offers a schematic comparison between the various approaches discussed.

TABLE A-2

1. Fixed-Target and Least-Squares Welfare Function Approach

Subjective Goal		Objective Targets
Maximize	subjective	Attain
social	relationship	policy
welfare	⟵——————⟶	targets

2. Cost-Benefit Approach

Subjective Goal		Objective Goal		Objective Targets
Maximize	subjective	Maximize	objective	Attain
social	relationship	wealth	relationship	policy
welfare	⟵—————⟶		⟵—————⟶	targets

To illustrate, let us look at the traditional main policy targets of full employment of resources, a stable price level, and a high growth rate. All may be related to the goal of wealth maximization. In order to achieve the goal of wealth maximization, it is necessary that resources be fully utilized. If resources are perpetually unemployed, wealth cannot be at its maximum value because the income stream derived in any time period is not maximized. Second, fluctuations of the general price level will be accompanied by information costs about changing market conditions, resource misallocation due to the substitution of real assets for *fiat* money, and increased costs associated with the revision of production and consumption plans. A higher growth rate, *ceteris paribus*, implies a higher future income stream, which—using appropriate discounting procedure—implies higher wealth. There is nothing contradictory between a theory that relies upon cost-benefit analysis on one hand and the traditional targets of full employment, stable prices, and a high growth rate on the other.

Cost-benefit analysis can be used as the basis of much of the analysis of alternative international financial systems. It is hoped that an explicit cost-benefit approach can provide a more precise framework for the analysis of international financial problems than is customary. But by making such a strong simplifying assumption about the goal of national economic policy, one is bound to neglect and leave aside the perhaps important influence of other variables. We do not negate this possibility. All that is attempted here is the construction of a consistent framework for analysis, within which international monetary problems may be analyzed.

SUGGESTED FURTHER READINGS

CORDEN, W. MAX, "The Geometric Representation of Policies to Attain Internal and External Balance," *Review of Economic Studies* (October 1960).

DENISON, EDWARD, "Welfare Measurement and the GNP," *Survey of Current Business* (January 1971).

FLEMING, J. MARCUS, "Targets and Instruments," *IMF Staff Papers* (November 1968).

HARBERGER, ARNOLD, "Three Basic Postulates for Applied Welfare Economics," *Journal of Economic Literature* (September 1971).

MUNDELL, ROBERT, "The Appropriate Use of Monetary and Fiscal Policy for Internal and External Stability," *IMF Staff Papers* (March 1962), pp. 70–77. Reprinted as Chap. 16 in MUNDELL, *International Economics*. New York: The Macmillan Company.

———, "The Nature of Policy Choices," Chap. 14 in *International Economics* pp. 201–16. New York: The Macmillan Company, 1968..

SMITH, WARREN, "Are There Enough Policy Tools?" *American Economic Review* (May 1965).

THEIL, HENRY, "Economic Models and Welfare Maximization," *Weltwirtschaftliches Archiv* (1954), pp. 60–81.

TINBERGEN, IAN, *On the Theory of Economic Policy*, Amsterdam: North Holland Publishing, 1952.

———, *Economic Policy: Principles and Design*, Amsterdam: North Holland Publishing, 1952.

Index